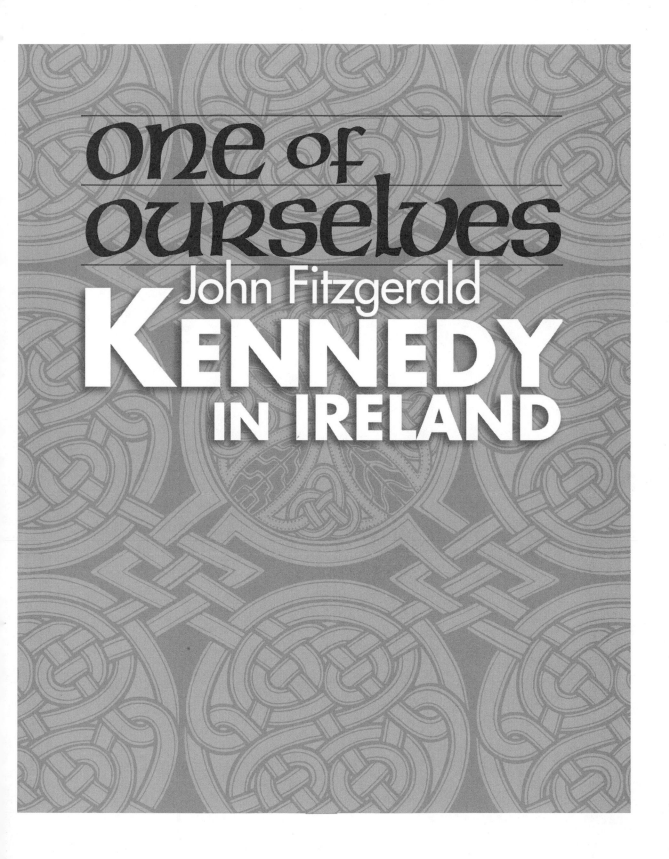

one of ourselves

John Fitzgerald
KENNEDY
IN IRELAND

Coming down Williamsgate Street in Galway, Kennedy enjoys his last morning among his fellow Irishmen. Note the backs of the heads of the photographers and cameramen, who rode ahead of Kennedy on the back of a truck.

one of
ourselves

John Fitzgerald
KENNEDY
IN IRELAND

By James Robert Carroll

Images from the Past

Bennington, Vermont

2003

1 2 3 4 5 6 7 8 9 10 XXX 10 09 08 07 06 05 04 03

Library of Congress Cataloging-in-Publication Data

Carroll, James Robert, 1951-
    One of Ourselves : John Fitzgerald Kennedy in Ireland /
    by James Robert Carroll.—— First edition
        p.   cm.
    Includes bibliographical references and index.
    ISBN 1-884592-40-6
    1. Kennedy, John F. (John Fitzgerald), 1917-1963--Travel--Ireland.
    2. Visits of state — Ireland. 3. Kennedy, John F. (John Fitzgerald),
    1917-1963 — Pictorial works. 4. Ireland — Description and travel.
    5. Ireland — Pictorial works. 6. Kennedy family. 7. Fitzgerald family.
    I. Title.

    E842.47.C37 2003
    973.922'092—dc22

                                                    2003015607

©2003 James Robert Carroll

Published by Images from the Past, Inc.
P.O. Box 137, Bennington, VT 05201
Tordis Ilg Isselhardt, Publisher

www.imagesfromthepast.com

Printed in the USA
Design and Production: Ron Toelke Associates, Chatham, NY
Map of Ireland by Ron Toelke

Printer: RAAND Print Specialties, Albany, NY

For my father

Joseph Robert Carroll,

who loved Ireland and

admired John F. Kennedy

Contents

Acknowledgments

A word about the man to whom this book is dedicated, because this is also a form of acknowledgment. My father, Joseph Robert Carroll, would have been delighted beyond words to know that I have written a book on Ireland. He would have been doubly pleased to learn that his extensive personal library on Irish history was a tremendous aid in the writing of this work. He traveled to Ireland several times, stopping in bookshops in Dublin, Limerick, and elsewhere to add to his collection. On my first trip to Ireland in 1982 with my youngest brother, Sean, we walked in our father's footsteps, visiting many of the same establishments, picking up more finds for him as well as for us. I am certain the seed of this book in some way was planted by my father many, many years ago during our frequent talks about Ireland, its history and our family's history, Irish culture and, my father's field, music. His intense interest was a gift he gave to me. This book is a humble effort to return a gift in kind.

This work has relied on the talents, resources, and support of almost as many people as President John F. Kennedy must have counted on to put together his visit to Ireland — indeed, in some cases, this work has relied on the very same people who put together Kennedy's visit. I'm not sure I could fill a couple of airplanes, as he did, but I'd be close.

The John F. Kennedy Library and Museum in Boston was essential in the creation of this book. As imposing as its massive collection is, its mysteries were revealed, thanks to Stephen Plotkin, reference archivist, who was a walking reference himself and even, as the closing hours hovered, pitched in on photocopying. Also much thanks to Sharon Ann Kelly and Michael Desmond, archives technicians, for helping to keep my requests straight and running smoothly. In the audio-visual archives, Allan B. Goodrich, supervisory archivist, was generous with his time, expertise, and the considerable photographic and film resources of the library. I am grateful to him. I would also like to thank James B. Hill in the audio-visual archives. On my second visit when Allan was incapacitated due to a fall on the ice, it was James who helped me locate images, and he later located the image of nuns, as well as handling both ordering processes to perfection. Additional thanks to Jennifer Quan, assistant controller at the John F. Kennedy Library Foundation.

The Library of Congress in Washington is, of course, an indispensable repository, and its people in the newspaper research room in the James Madison Building were always helpful, particularly G. Travis Westly, who kick-started my travels through 1963 in the newspapers of the United States, Ireland, and England. Also deserving of credit are Tracey Barton, Charles W. Bean, Thomas Bigley, Jerome Brooks, Norman C. Chase, Christopher Damrosch,

Elizabeth Faison, Georgia Higley, Thomas P. Jabine, James King, Anne Lewis, Rodney Marshall, Bernard Michael, Kiyoyo Pipher, Robin Shields, Sara J. Striner, Mark Sweeney, Thelma Todd, Norma Toro, Chrystal Tyree, Karen Walfall, Pamela Watkins, and Basil Wilson. A special thanks to Betty Turner, reference librarian in the John Adams Building.

At the National Library of Ireland, a formidable force kept newspaper microfilms flowing. My appreciation for guidance, friendliness, and speed to Francis Carroll, Bernard Devaney, Mark Hardy, Sandra McDermott, Thomas Desmond, James Harte, Anita Joyce, Francis Lowe, John O'Sullivan, Patrick Sweeney, Noel Brady, Lucy DeCourcy, Glen Dunne, Paul Jones, John Browne, Jennifer Byrne, Teresa Callan, Niamh Coleman, Helen Collins, Martin Horan, John Lakes, Joseph McCarthy, Barry McCormack, Karl McDonnell, Michael McHugh, Siobhan Malone, Tony Merrifield, Keith Murphy, Aran O'Reilly, Maeve Sullivan, and Ciaran McEniry.

At the National Archives of Ireland in Dublin, Christy Allen, John Brazil, Paul Carolan, and John Delaney have my appreciation for going the extra distance to ensure that I saw what I needed. All were extremely knowledgeable and cheerful.

At Leinster House in Dublin, home of Ireland's Parliament, the author and his family were given special treatment and interesting stories by Noel Kelly and Liam Rogers, and we are much obliged.

Carol Coleman and Hilary Roberson of the Washington bureau of Radio Telefis Eireann (RTE) came through when I needed aid, as did Yuien Chin at NBC News in New York.

Warmest gratitude must be expressed to Gay and Randa Murphy, of Inch in County Clare, for lending books, their memories, and wonderful hospitality.

Forty years have, as might be expected, claimed many of those who played large and small parts in this story. But some participants and observers are doing quite well and were more than willing to share their memories with the author.

First and foremost I wish to thank President Kennedy's sisters, Eunice Kennedy Shriver and Ambassador Jean Kennedy Smith, who had privileged perspectives from which to witness the events in Ireland and an understanding of what the days there meant to their brother that could be had only by his own flesh and blood. Ambassador Smith, of course, wrote a new chapter in the Kennedy family's relationship with Ireland when she served her nation in Dublin, arriving precisely on the thirtieth anniversary of the president's visit. She revealed to me that the timing of her Senate confirmation set the coincidence in motion, that she didn't plan the date of her arrival for such symbolism. "It was all by accident," she said. But nevertheless, perfect.

Equally generous was Sen. Edward Kennedy, the president's brother, whose abiding devotion to Ireland and unswerving determination in the search for lasting peace in Northern Ireland are unquestioned on both sides of the Atlantic. The senator offered some warm memories, great stories, valuable insights, and historical background that this writer could not have found from a hundred other sources.

Sen. Kennedy's press secretary, James Manley, and, most especially, deputy press secretary Melody Miller, also must take a bow for assisting me in making contacts that no amount of thanks can repay. Without the latter's patient and diligent assistance, this book would have lacked essential pieces.

Those who willingly subjected themselves to countless questions and, in some cases, several follow-up telephone calls, have my unending thanks. Theodore C. Sorensen helpfully provided the view from the president's inner circle; Pierre Salinger was gracious and kind; the late Malcolm Kilduff was overflowing with stories, and it's a shame he never wrote his own account of the Kennedy years; Lenny Donnelly and her husband, Raymond Donnelly, shared recollections, mementos, and a wonderful rainy Sunday afternoon; Dr. Patrick Hillery, former president of Ireland and his country's minister of education at the time of Kennedy's visit, was ready with stories, new details, and useful analyses; John Hume, Nobel Peace Prize laureate and former leader of the Social Democratic and Labor party in Northern Ireland, consented to be interviewed just after a return from the hospital; Jerald F. ter-Horst had some very helpful observations about the press coverage; Jean Price Lewis has a terrific memory for names and an address book to go with it; Pauline Fluet reminisced about Eire and agonized with the author over the fate of the New England Patriots; and Dorothy Tubridy was a font of terrific information about Irish history, the Kennedys, and her conversations with President Kennedy; Eoin Minihan spoke at length about his late father, Andrew Minihan; Tom Wicker shared his memories and impressions; Oscar Johnson's account of the preparations for Kennedy's appearances and his own involvement in them was lively and quite helpful; Richard Finnegan provided some important historical and social perspective; and former Irish Sen. Maurice Manning generously provided a text of his remarks on the significance of Kennedy's visit.

Special aid, too, came from Patrick Kelly, press secretary for the Embassy of Ireland in Washington. He had invaluable suggestions for people and sources that enriched this book. He also aided in a couple of translations. I cannot thank him enough.

Steven Thomma, political writer for Knight-Ridder Newspapers in Washington, was thoughtful and patient in reviewing this manuscript and suggested improvements the author gratefully accepted. He is a dear friend.

Thomas Farragher at the *Boston Globe* was lightning-fast in getting his hands on some research and also read the manuscript. He is also a valued pal.

Fredreka Shouten, a reporter with the Gannett News Service in Washington, generously shared some information she spotted in her readings. She is a generous and good friend and colleague.

Much thanks, too, to Gannett photographer Heather Martin Morrissey, who handled a critical assignment with speed and care.

Sonya Bernhardt, publisher of the *Georgetowner* in Washington, was of considerable assistance in my detective work.

Robert L. White, who held one of the largest private collections of John F. Kennedy's more personal effects until donating it to the Florida International Museum in St. Petersburg, was extremely generous in making available the Irish travel guide used by Kennedy in his 1947 trip. I also am indebted to Clare Murray, marketing director for the Florida International Museum.

Tom Kenny and Beth Goodwin at Kennys Bookshop and Art Gallery in Galway watched the book traffic like hawks for my requests, and were ready with alternative suggestions when their exhaustive searching didn't always pan out. Many thanks to them. Also, a thanks to David Cunningham at Cathach Books in Dublin, who turned up a hard-to-find volume for me, right on his shelves, at the beginning of this research, as well as another book, right near the end.

And that prompts a blanket thanks to all the bookshops in the United States and Ireland, stocking old and new, that helped to fill the gaps of this author's knowledge like great, auxiliary libraries. Please patronize them.

I also wish to express my gratitude to Arlene Aaronson and Alica Kolar, assistants to Theodore C. Sorensen; William Cobert, director of the American Irish Historical Society; Margaret Blade at Galway's *Connacht Tribune*; Annette Beausang at the *Irish Times* in Dublin; Sean Reidy, chief executive officer, John F. Kennedy Trust, New Ross, Ireland; Jean Brennan, Department of Politics, University College Dublin; and Evan M. Duncan, Office of the Historian, Bureau of Public Affairs, the Department of State in Washington.

I also extend thanks to colleagues at the *Louisville Courier-Journal,* including Edward E. Manassah, Bennie L. Ivory, Arthur B. Post, Jr., Andrew Alderette, John A. Mura, Keith L. Runyon, Kristin Wilkison, Joe Taylor, Gideon Gil, Deborah Yetter, Al Cross, Joseph Gerth, Tom Loftus, and James Malone.

There are not enough proper words, in English or Irish, to express my debt to my publisher, Tordis Ilg Isselhardt, who was excited about this project from the mention of the idea and who backed me every step of the way. She showed endurance and admirable patience as the manuscript slowly took shape and deadlines slid. She was always ready with great suggestions. Her experience and good judgment improved this work immeasurably, and her artist's eye was critical in the selection of the illustrations. Without Tordis, this book could not have been born. With Tordis, this book became much better than I could have dreamed.

Tordis also assembled a top-notch team to make the magic that created this book: Ron Toelke and Barbara Kempler-Toelke, designers, gave this work its handsome look inside and out; Glenn Novak, editor, made sure the author didn't embarrass himself or mangle the language or history; Diane Brenner beautifully indexed the plethora of names and subjects; Beryl Frank ensured we found the right printer to bring all the magic together; Steve Carlson at Upper Access Book Publicity applied his know-how to the never-more-important marketing end; Jill Hays was our in-house expert on the Irish language; and Peggy Burns was wise counsel and hands-on helper throughout.

I am fortunate to have two wonderful brothers, the above-mentioned Sean, and our middle frère, Peter. They share our father's love for Ireland and they gave me valuable feedback and a constant stream of proper Irish humor on this project. Peter contributed to shaving off my research time by pitching in himself during a trip to Dublin. My brothers and I also are blessed with a terrific sister, Nancy, who embraced the concept of this project at the mention of the word "Ireland" and took on a chore in the Boston Public Library. She is so immersed in Irish culture that she is taking on a couple of projects of her own. And, with her actress's ear for language, she can so well camouflage herself in the Irish dialect that she is taken as an exile from County Clare.

My mother, Joan Hebert Carroll, remains this author's greatest fan. She shares my deep interest in presidential history and Boston lore, and has a phenomenal memory for events she has lived through. Her mother and father, the late Dorothy and Placide Hebert, intersected the Kennedy story briefly many years ago: one of the altar boys in their wedding at St. Aidan's Church in Brookline was, my grandmother was quite sure, young John F. Kennedy.

My family deserves extreme gratitude for putting up with the herky-jerky schedules I sometimes had to keep, abandoning them at the beach for side trips into Boston, being absent on many Saturdays and on many evenings for endless stops at the Library of Congress, for perpetual tip-tapping on the computer after Sunday breakfast, before parties, and far into the night and early morning, especially when I was on a roll, or at least thought I was. And they braved Ireland in November, which turned out not to be much of a sacrifice, so I could camp out in government reading rooms. We did our bit to help keep the Celtic Tiger purring while we were in Dublin and walking in President Kennedy's footsteps through Ireland.

My daughters, Fiona and Brenna, in love with Ireland, listened attentively to their father's stories of his discoveries, and tagged along from time to time on research, helpful with the copying chores. They are not awed by archives and research rooms. They are wonderful companions.

My wife, Carol, is the epitome of understanding and encouragement. She bore too much of the family schedule, but always was ready with a loving word and, in truth, a motivating directive: "I'll take care of this. You go and work on your book." She is also a great editor. I am a lucky fellow.

James Robert Carroll
April 19, 2003
Alexandria, Virginia

Introduction

John Fitzgerald Kennedy was not one for introspection in public nor, by most accounts, in private, except what could be reflected through his flashes of self-deprecating humor, a very Irish trait. But his usual reserve appeared to dissolve during his trip to Ireland in June 1963. To understand why and how that happened, some context would be helpful.

Overshadowed to a considerable degree by his impassioned speech in sight of the Berlin Wall only hours before, the visit of the president of the United States to the land of his forebears was no less electric and, for Ireland and those of Irish ancestry in the United States, no less momentous.

The trip to what was then West Germany and its divided capital was a Cold Warrior's mission, an appearance gauged to confront the Soviet Union on the world stage over the Berlin Wall, the physical embodiment of the Communists' corrupted and failed policies. "Freedom has many difficulties and democracy is not perfect, but we have never had to put up a wall to keep our people in, to prevent them from leaving us," Kennedy said. And, too, the German visit was a clarion call to the free world to stand with Berlin, as he was doing. "Ich bin ein Berliner," the president declared, to the thunderous roar of tens of thousands.

Berlin was at its essence an exercise in realpolitik, and it was bracing and eloquent. In short, Germany was about the head.

Ireland, on the other hand, was a pilgrimage to a different and deeper place, outside the usual boundaries of global politics.

"This is the part that he really looks forward to. The rest of the trip is political. Ireland is pure heart," journalist Benjamin C. Bradlee, then a reporter for *Newsweek,* later managing editor and finally executive editor of the *Washington Post*, recorded in May 1963 as Kennedy spoke excitedly about his then-upcoming trip to Ireland.

For Ireland and the man it instantly embraced as an adopted son, four days in June forty years ago changed everything. Kennedy embodied all the Irish had achieved and won in the New World, and he bestowed solid stature on the new Ireland in the Old World. Kennedy and Ireland understood this intellectually. But with nearly every honor Ireland could bestow ringing in his ears, sprinkled on his head, pressed into his hands, and laid at his feet, Kennedy was left breathless in a delirious celebration of history and heredity, the centuries of ceaseless agonies and sacrifice redeemed.

It was this emotion, which seems to have come upon him as a surprise, and a pleasant one, that Kennedy uncharacteristically revealed in a letter to President Eamon de Valera on departing Ireland.

"I want to thank you," Kennedy wrote, "for a visit that has been one of the most moving experiences of my life.

"Your gracious wife," he continued, "taught me the Irish word for welcome, *'fáilte.'* I did not know *'fáilte'* could mean as much as you and the Irish people have made it mean for me during the past four days. I will have the memory of this wonderful Irish welcome in my heart always."

Likewise, in a letter to Prime Minister Sean F. Lemass, Kennedy went beyond the official thank you.

"I would like through you, Mr. Lemass, to thank all of the Irish people who have made my visit such a memorable one," the president wrote. "The wonderful hospitality I have been showered with has indeed made me feel that I had 'come home.'

"Meeting so many of the Irish people and their leaders was particularly enjoyable and I have been gratified by their sympathetic understanding of the problems which we in the West face," Kennedy went on.

Then, after thanking Lemass for their own talks, Kennedy closed with this: "From the bottom of my heart, God bless Ireland."

This book is about Kennedy's journey home, a journey that inaugurated a new relationship between Ireland and the United States that has endured for four decades.

It may seem hard to imagine now, but for the United States in 1960, Kennedy's election to the presidency was a turning point in American politics. After a century of at times virulent bias against Catholics and Irish in America, the nation elevated an Irish-Catholic to its highest office. Kennedy had embraced his heritage. And he was determined to acknowledge his debt to the millions who had come to America's shores on crowded ships and had changed their new country in so many ways. Already, the United States, with its then-25 million Irish-Americans, and Ireland were bound by ties of family. Kennedy's return to Ireland, though, was a moment of profound weight and great poignancy, an event that melded statesmanship with kinship in a way that no American president had achieved in any foreign nation before, and unlike any president has done since.

"We Irish are the greatest wandering people in the world. We feel totally linked to people of Irish descent across the world," explained John Hume, Nobel Peace Prize laureate and founder and former leader of the Social Democratic and Labor party in Northern Ireland. "So the emergence of John F. Kennedy as president created great pride throughout the Irish community."

"Here was one who personified dramatically the cycle of history," said the *Tipperary Star.*

"Mr. Kennedy has returned to Ireland as the living symbol of the Irish triumph over the trials and tribulations of history," the *Evening Herald* in Dublin stated.

"The great-grandson of the famine emigrant who left in misery and sorrow comes to his point of origin honored like a king. We welcome him for himself and in memory of many generations," the *Irish Independent* wrote on the day Kennedy landed.

Patrick O'Donovan of the *London Observer* found the Kennedy tour "an almost sacramental" event.

"Occasionally in the history of a country, a thing happens that means more than can be put quite into words," he wrote. "The visit of President John Kennedy to Ireland was one of those things. It was not merely a state visit; it was not a spit in the eye for England. It was simply history coming round in a calm, just and majestic circle, back to the point where it should have begun."

Kennedy and Ireland were, the *Cork Examiner* said, "a union of hearts."

The American president was hailed by the newspaper as "the outstanding representative of our race in that other Ireland across the Atlantic. . . . The magnitude of his gesture is without precedent in the historical connection between the two countries."

For Ireland, in 1963 an independent state only forty-one years old, engagement in world politics beyond its prickly relations with Great Britain was a still-evolving process. Incredibly, no significant head of state had visited Ireland until Kennedy. And while Ireland had contributed troops to the United Nations' peacekeeping effort in Congo, the Irish had yet to win admission to what was then known as the European Common Market. Ireland itself was evolving, casting off vestiges of an agrarian colony of a global power and striving to create a modern industrial state. As might be expected, change came most slowly to the rural areas, where mail still arrived by bicycle and milk went to the dairy in a donkey cart. Yet the staggering poverty of earlier days was receding. Photographers covering Kennedy's visit had to stage pictures, for want of the real thing, of young Irish lads not wearing shoes. Even so, many trappings of the Space Age came late to Ireland: the Irish television service had been born less than two years before, on December 31, 1961. And Dublin's O'Connell Street, its central boulevard, was still unmarred by a single traffic light when Kennedy's motorcade sailed its length.

Kennedy's ascent to the White House suddenly vaulted Ireland to a special and unique status. For, while four decades earlier Ireland had, in the words of nineteenth century patriot Robert Emmet, taken her place among the nations of the earth, Eire had become the mother country not only to a sizable portion of people in the most powerful among those nations, but also to its top leader. With his visit in June 1963, the Irish-American president paid homage to that relationship.

The visit served to erase any vestiges of bad feeling among Irish-Americans about Ireland's neutrality in World War II, and Kennedy's tour underscored a sea change in Irish international relations under Prime Minister Sean Lemass and External Affairs Minister Frank Aiken, an accelerating shift — first signaled by United Nations membership and the commitment of troops to Congo — away from isolationism to greater global engagement.

Less apparent at first but clearly more deliberate in following months was Kennedy's interest in aiding the Irish economy. After his return to Washington, Kennedy set about arranging a U.S. tour for Lemass so that the Irish leader could make pitches for more American investment in Ireland and increasing trade with his nation. In short order, Lemass's efforts proved fruitful. Kennedy, meanwhile, proposed steps to assist Ireland's fishing industry.

On the last day of the presidential trip, Kennedy and de Valera announced that they would be co-chairmen — symbolic leaders, really — of a newly created American Irish Foundation, a group set up in New York to promote educational and cultural exchanges between Ireland and the United States. The foundation was the precursor to follow-on organizations that would become The Ireland Funds and would, by 2002, foster philanthropic projects and cultural exchanges in Ireland and Northern Ireland involving some twelve hundred non-profit organizations.

And, just as Kennedy's example was an inspiration for countless American young people to enter public service, including a young man from Arkansas named William Jefferson Clinton, so too was his trip to Ireland an inducement to Irish youth to serve in government. Ireland's former president, Mary Robinson, has often spoken of Kennedy as an influence. John Hume, one of the pivotal figures in the peace accords in Northern Ireland, had two pictures on his wall at home: those of Martin Luther King, Jr., and John Fitzgerald Kennedy.

Indeed, although it could not have been known at the time, Kennedy's 1963 visit was, it can be argued, the prerequisite to future U.S. involvement in the peace process in Northern Ireland. Kennedy told the Irish, the Americans, and the world that the United States had a stake in Ireland's future, just as Ireland had had a stake in building America. The president's brother, Sen. Edward Kennedy of Massachusetts, became a central player in Northern Ireland peace efforts from 1969 onward. The president's sister, Jean Kennedy Smith, served as U.S. ambassador to Ireland during critical years of those peace efforts that led to the Good Friday Agreement.

But underlying all the analysis about historical turning points, global status, economics, and policy was a simple, obvious fact: John Fitzgerald Kennedy touched a nation, and it touched him, in June 1963.

We see a president slowly reveal more of his private self, the self usually reserved for the domestic domain of the upstairs of the White House on those nights when, over drinks with family and friends, he sang to Irish records and talked of the history of his ancestors. In Ireland, Kennedy kissed a cousin in public, sang in public, directed children in song and joined in — all far removed from the casual cool he projected at home. And at one point, after a prayer, the president crossed himself — something that veteran White House correspondents could not recall ever having seen during a public appearance.

"I imagine," wrote Arthur Schlesinger, Jr., Kennedy's in-house historian, "that he was never easier, happier, more involved and detached, more complexly himself," than in the days of his Ireland visit.

Eunice Kennedy Shriver, Kennedy's sister and hostess in Ireland, isn't sure her brother was able to entirely shed the weight of the presidency during his visit, but, she said, "He was very happy there. He was laughing all the time."

His brother's days in Ireland, Sen. Edward Kennedy said, were "his happiest moments as president."

Kennedy in Ireland was in a different time and place from our own. It was neither simpler nor more naïve than our time, but perhaps more open to possibility. It is unavoidable, then, that a faithful account of this journey and its impact is rather upbeat, positive, perhaps a bit uplifting. So be it.

Criticism, as shall be detailed, there was — at least initially, from inside the Kennedy White House and from a perplexed and dismissive American press that came to settle upon a shorthand explanation for the trip to Ireland as a "sentimental journey to the Auld Sod."

But brickbats were few. And in Ireland, the only things thrown were flowers, confetti, and, perhaps in the cooler shade of decades of reflection, some overblown but nonetheless excusable praise. The *Kerryman* complained of "just one irritation persisting throughout — the poor standard of public speaking on our side," addresses it likened to "funeral orations," though the reader will judge whether that seems somewhat harsh. It is the intent of this book to capture as much as humanly possible the taste and feel of those summer days four decades gone.

The Irish and John F. Kennedy, it will quickly be apparent, were aswirl in a tide of their own making.

Once underway, Kennedy's trip in Ireland generated such a spontaneous upswelling of emotion, such impassioned expressions of adoration — and that is the word — for the American president that for a writer to depict the events of June 1963 in any other way would fog reality.

In truth, Kennedy was much admired abroad — indeed, perhaps less critically than at home during his lifetime — and nowhere was this admiration more universally shared than in Ireland.

"It was the first time that all Irishmen agreed on the same thing at the same time," journalist Donald S. Connery observed.

It has become a cliché to note that on the walls of many Irish homes are portraits of the pope (current or, for the older generation, Pope John XXIII) and John Kennedy. It is certainly no less true that Kennedy's portrait hangs in many American homes with those of — religions and recreational proclivities depending — religious leaders or sports heroes.

To be sure, the euphoria over Kennedy's time in Ireland was not universal. Nor, one might venture to say, understood. Among the most condescending assessments came one from the *National Observer,* an American weekly newspaper (now defunct) owned by Dow Jones & Co., proprietors of the *Wall Street Journal.* "Germany," the *Observer* observed, "seemed unreal in a deep-throated Wagnerian sense. But, in Ireland, it was as if the President had fired

Ted Sorensen and hired an itinerant leprechaun to write the script. Ireland was aged-in-the-keg Blarney; the Irish, recognizing this kind of drama instinctively, gave it everything they had. The President gave it right back. Everyone (with the possible exception of a few blue-nosed Britishers across the Irish Sea) enjoyed it. On the stage of history, it meant nothing, but it was first-class comic relief, and who can say that maybe that's not necessary, too."

The stereotype overload was one approach.

Even in Ireland, not all who glance backward see magic or import.

"The aftermath of such intoxicated expressions of desire is usually self-contempt," Fintan O'Toole, columnist and chief drama critic for the *Irish Times*, wrote recently of Kennedy's trip. He was five at the time of the visit. "I sometimes think that much of the public life of my country since 1963 has been an attempt to fill the hole in our self-image that Kennedy's visit had exposed. We were supposed to be a deeply spiritual people, concerned with God, the land and the nation. The ecstasy evoked by the appearance among us of the first citizen of the great republic of the West revealed to us how utterly bedazzled we were by all the things we were not meant to want: his cool, sexy glamour, his impregnable aura of wealth and his ability to embody the fridges and TVs, the porches and pools that our American cousins conjured up in those family photographs. We were embarrassed by our sudden, naked impulse to worship the golden calf. . . . We had disgraced ourselves by being so gormlessly awestruck in our adoration of America."

One shudders for the actors on the Abbey stage who have been similarly dispatched. But, as the saying goes, that's one man's opinion.

That a depth of feeling for Kennedy persists on both sides of the Atlantic cannot be disputed. For the Irish, it was, and is, about more than fridges and pools.

It was about kinship. Between a nation and a man. And between two nations.

Crosby S. Noyes, foreign correspondent for the *Washington Evening Star,* witnessed this firsthand, and eloquently grasped its meaning, during Kennedy's visit to County Wexford.

In the space of twenty-four hours, Kennedy had experienced the "two sorts of rare days in the lives of American presidents," Noyes wrote.

The day before, in Berlin, had been of "the big and earthshaking sort."

"The other kind of rare day occurred yesterday at New Ross, Dunganstown and Wexford. It could hardly have been more different from Berlin if it had been another planet. But it was no less moving and no less successful for that.

"What happened to Mr. Kennedy in these small Irish towns was rare in terms of history," Noyes continued. "It was like seeing an American president in a setting that was probably common enough in Lincoln's day. But it amounted to an experience that few American presidents have enjoyed since.

"For those involved it was certainly a very important occasion, and yet there was an intimacy about it that gave it the quality of a family affair.

"There was a genuineness about it that has been all but lost in more progressive nations. There was friendliness and curiosity," Noyes concluded, "together with a total lack of the sort of frenzy that automatically attaches itself to the person of the president in other lands."

"He and the crowds understood each other," Garret FitzGerald wrote of Kennedy's "immediate rapport" with the Irish, years before FitzGerald became prime minister. "It was a relationship that no one who is not Irish can ever fully understand. The Irish, contrary to popular belief, are not a sentimental people, and they have no time at all for those third- and fourth-generation Irish-Americans who return to Ireland believing it to be full of leprechauns. John Kennedy was unsentimental too. He was tough, loved a laugh, and treated us as we really are. That's why he was different, and that's why we worship the Kennedy family."

Kennedy's visit was nothing short of "the social and psychological highpoint of the 1960s" in Ireland, according to historian Sean McMahon.

In July of 1999, when the world was shocked by the sudden death of John F. Kennedy, Jr., his wife, Carolyn, and her sister Lauren Bessette in an airplane accident, the *Limerick Leader* was moved to write an editorial about "a sense of personal loss" in Ireland. And that loss was felt all the more intensely, the newspaper said, because of the joys of earlier days, including "President Kennedy's spectacular and moving appearance in 1963 at happy Greenpark, surely one of the greatest moments in the whole history of Limerick."

The connection has never broken. In 2001, the *Sunday Mirror* in Dublin asked readers who were the top one hundred men and women of Irish descent who had had "the greatest influence on the way we live today?" The rankings: 1. St. Patrick, 2. Eamon de Valera, 3. Michael Collins, and, 4. John Fitzgerald Kennedy.

On the night of November 22, 1963, with the globe shaken by President Kennedy's assassination that day in Dallas, Texas, the darkness in Eire seemed to have descended with all the tragedies of the island's history returned for a night. The inky black never seemed more threatening, more impenetrable, more devoid of hope amidst the pieces of an era suddenly shattered and gone.

De Valera spoke on Irish television "to give public expression of our common sorrow."

"During his recent visit here," the Irish leader said, "we came to regard the president as one of ourselves, though always aware that he was head of the greatest nation in the world today. We were proud of him as being one of our race and we were convinced that through his fearless leadership the United States could continue to increase its stature amongst the nations of the world and its power to maintain world peace."

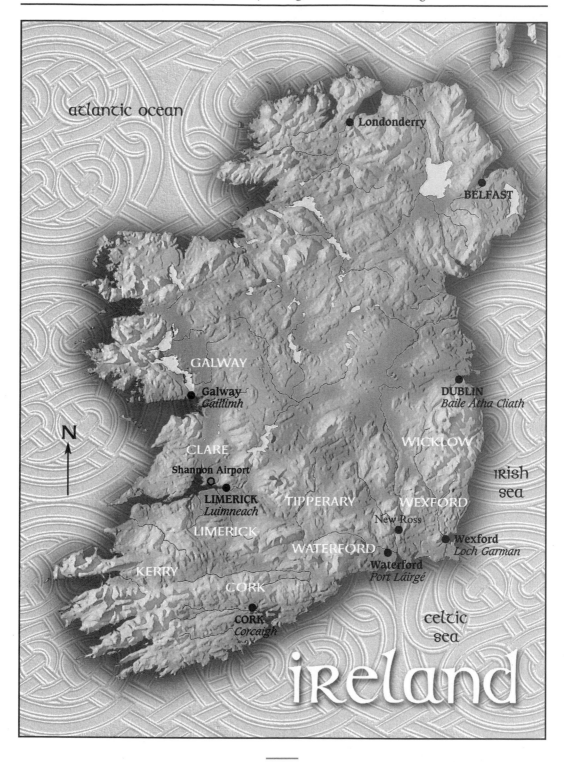

atlantic ocean

● Londonderry

BELFAST ●

GALWAY

● Galway
Gaillimh

DUBLIN ●
Baile Átha Cliath

N

WICKLOW

CLARE

irish
sea

Shannon Airport ○

● LIMERICK
Luimneach

TIPPERARY

WEXFORD

New Ross ●

LIMERICK

WATERFORD

Wexford ●
Loch Garman

KERRY

Waterford ●
Port Láirgé

CORK

CORK
Corcaigh

celtic
sea

ireland

one

June 26, 1963:
Dublin Airport and Dublin

"I am of Ireland,
  And the Holy Land of Ireland,
And time runs on," said she.
"Come out of charity,
  Come dance with me in Ireland."

William Butler Yeats
adapted from a fourteenth century poem (1933)

Portentous. Even for the ever-changeable weather of Ireland, this day had been portentous. Rain, lightning, and then hail assaulted the green landscape of the country and the spired and domed, gray and red-brick sweep of Dublin, as if to ensure that history had been washed and beaten clean for this turn in time. For that is how the day, and the JFK visit, was embraced then and later.

After all, Patrick Kennedy had gone out from Ireland 115 years before, seeking hope and fortune, bound for the New World in a creaking vessel on a roiling sea, one of thousands among thousands, and whose fate and name would have passed into assured obscurity. But for John. Johnny. Sean.

Here, in an ancient land where history is current and fresh, came the great-grandson, back from the New World, the leader of it and all the free world, aboard a majestic Boeing 707 jet, whose dignified and distinctive blue, white, and buffed aluminum design he had had a hand in, just as his ancestors had crafted heraldic emblems of old.

Back he had come, from a new land where Americans of Irish descent still could recall the "Irish need not apply" signs in factories and stores and clubs, yet had persevered and, ultimately, prevailed in 1960, with the election of an Irish Catholic to the presidency of the United States of America.

Now, in this forty-six-year-old, auburn-haired, suntanned man named John Fitzgerald Kennedy lived the embodiment of the pasts of two nations and the promise of more closely entwined futures.

On this Wednesday evening, June 26, 1963, was a golden moment. And, almost impossibly, except for Ireland, where such a thing is commonplace, it was framed with a rainbow.

"WELCOME HOME" was the three-inch-high banner in the *Evening Herald* in Dublin, which was appropriated as an impromptu sign waved by thousands who hadn't thought to bring their own.

Under a sky of clouds battling with the late evening sun, Air Force One punched through a crosswind and touched down at Dublin Airport at 7:55 p.m. Air Force Col. James Swindel eased the aircraft to a stop before the welcoming party.

With a summer gloaming that makes golf possible almost to the change of a new day, Telefis Eireann, Ireland's government-run television network, had plenty of natural light to broadcast the president's arrival to the nation live. And out from Ireland went the black-and-white images, to twenty-five million television sets across the rest of Western Europe, and up to space to the Telstar satellite, then down to the United States in time for editing into fifteen-minute and half-hour reports in the evening on the major networks. Nearly every public moment of President Kennedy's visit would be broadcast. The Irish government had made sure of it, constructing about a dozen television relay towers around the nation to ensure the president's every move would be captured.

After the cacophonous welcome of Germany, Kennedy's first moments in Ireland were rather startling.

"There's silence. . . . it's totally quiet," Theodore C. Sorensen, the president's speechwriter, recalled.

"Maybe we got our schedules mixed up here," Kennedy joked.

The long distance from the plane to the airport balcony where about ten thousand onlookers crowded might have made it hard to see what was happening. And some of the silence, the Irish leaders later explained to Sorensen, was awe.

"President Kennedy had achieved mythic proportions in Ireland," Sorensen said. "You don't clap and cheer when a member of the deity appears."

Kennedy, wearing a blue suit, walked down the stairs at the rear of his plane, setting foot on Ireland's soil for the sixth time in his life. He carried a gray hat called a Trilby in his right hand, a hat he would put on only once and very briefly. He swung that hat at his side, like some strange ceremonial totem.

Kennedy was greeted at the bottom of the steps of the Aer Lingus gangway at his plane by longtime Kennedy family friend and Ireland's president, Eamon de Valera. American-born of a Spanish father and County Limerick mother, he came to Ireland at age three when his father died. He became a teacher, then joined the Easter Rising of 1916 against the British, surviving a firing squad only because of his American origins. After independence, he was the colossus of Irish political life for nearly forty years.

Next to shake hands with Kennedy was the prime minister, the *Taoiseach* (tee-schyock), Sean F. Lemass, a man who, though he shared much of the same political history as de Valera (and lost a brother in the struggle for independence), was a young sixty-three, and more modern. The mustachioed, pipe-smoking leader would be considered the architect of Ireland's economic recovery in the late 1950s and the 1960s, exemplifying, as one observer put it, "the transition from freedom fighter to administrator and pragmatic politician."

After Lemass came Sean MacEntee, the only man topped for the day in a bowler. He served both as the minister for health and the *Tánaiste (tawn-aw-shteh)*, who is the deputy prime minister, or, literally in Irish, "heir apparent," which, time would show, he was not.

The real deputy prime minister was Frank Aiken, who greeted the president next. Aiken's portfolio was what was then called external affairs. He was the foreign minister and, as another veteran of politics since independence, the other corner of the troika with de Valera and Lemass. The seventy-four-year-old Aiken, a key figure in holding Ireland to neutrality during World War II, then surprised many by serving as "the main agent for bringing Ireland to the fore in world affairs after the war," as journalist and author Tim Pat Coogan described him. Aiken was so guarded he could be hard to read. A journalist once complained to a government information officer that Aiken had not answered a question. "He wouldn't answer that at a government meeting," retorted the information officer. Aiken would be by Kennedy's side during most of the president's time in Ireland.

Then came the U.S. ambassador to Ireland, white-maned Matthew McCloskey, who likewise would be a fixture in the presidential party, along with his counterpart, Irish ambassador Thomas J. Kiernan. These men were not cut from the same cloth. McCloskey was ambassador by virtue of his fundraising abilities for the Democratic party. Just the night before the visit, when a vote on a new tax narrowly passed, thus barely preserving Lemass's government for Kennedy's arrival, McCloskey had jumped up and applauded from the

Back to "this green and misty island": President Kennedy, with Ireland's president, Eamon de Valera, at his side, arrives in Dublin on June 26, 1963. Eunice Kennedy Shriver is just behind de Valera, standing with Angier Biddle Duke, head of protocol for the White House. Princess Lee Radziwell, Jacqueline Kennedy's sister, is in the long coat. Coming down the stairs from Air Force One, in a hat, is Kennedy's special assistant, David F. Powers.

gallery above the Dail. "That was a terrible sin for a diplomat, for anyone, to clap in the Parliament," Dr. Patrick Hillery, Lemass's education minister, recalled. Kiernan, by contrast, was the epitome of Irish diplomatic professionalism: appropriately circumspect, learned, and polished. He had just authored a book retelling Irish folktales, with his own commentary.

Kennedy's sister Jean Kennedy Smith had flown in directly from the United States the day before. The president gave her a kiss. Kennedy's entourage, trying to stay inconspicuous, hovered in the shadow of Air Force One in a small crowd. Other White House staffers had taken a backup Air Force One direct from Andrews Air Force Base outside Washington (when the plane left, its fuselage was decorated with tissue-paper shamrocks) and arrived ahead of the boss.

"He was very excited at this trip," the president's sister Jean remembered. "During the [1960 presidential] campaign, there had been a lot of talk about being Catholic, being Irish, and that was very much on his mind. He knew very well this was going to be a great trip."

Kennedy stood at attention as the Army Number One Band played "The Star-Spangled Banner." He carried the hat again as he walked past the band, cheerily thundering through "Stars and Stripes Forever," and down two columns of 107 soldiers, clad in forest green uniforms and berets, during the traditional inspection of the troops. At Kennedy's side was Gen. Sean McKeown, who had served in Congo and had become the Irish military's chief of staff. Twenty-one guns roared their salute, at five-second intervals, their clumps of smoke disintegrating in the wind.

Beyond the lines of security, Irish men, women, and children watched and, finally, cheered Kennedy's every move. Some had waited four hours.

Kennedy family friend Dorothy Tubridy thought the president seemed very tired and "in a very thoughtful mood," obviously greatly affected by his German appearances earlier in the day. But in the hours to come, Kennedy's weariness and remoteness would dissipate, giving way to his obvious joy at being again in Ireland, and Eire's joy in his being on Irish soil — as far as Ireland was concerned, for the first time, because this visit, at this time, really counted.

"The more fuss they made over him, the more he beamed," remembered Evelyn Lincoln, Kennedy's personal secretary, who accompanied her boss on the trip and gathered with the rest of the official presidential party.

The airport reception, while quite respectable and enthusiastic, gave only a hint of the tumultuous reception Kennedy was to receive during his time in Ireland.

In truth, the arrival ceremony could have been bigger. That was the Irish government's fault. Officials had restricted public access to the airport, keeping down the crowd to about ten thousand, mostly confined to the balconies of the terminal building.

De Valera, eighty and nearly blind but still standing as straight and tall as a telephone pole, clutched an umbrella as he welcomed Kennedy. Some might have thought it simply a prudent precaution, given the day, but in truth de Valera frequently carried the umbrella as a kind of walking cane to guard against mishaps from his fading eyesight.

The two leaders stepped toward the microphones. The welcome carpet turned out to be neither red nor green, but a diplomatic blue.

De Valera opened in Irish: *"A Uachtaráin Uasail. In ainm mhuintir na hÉireann uile agus thar a gceann cuirim céad míle fáilte romhat. Cuireann do theacht go hÉirinn aoibhneas ar chroí gach duine againn agus táimid búioch díot."* ("Mr. President, I welcome you in the name of all the people of Ireland. Your visit to Ireland gladdens the heart of every one of us and we are thankful to you.")

Kennedy, his eyes fixed on de Valera, appeared puzzled at first by this Irish greeting. Then, in English, de Valera continued: "Mr. President, I have thought it fitting that my first words of welcome to you should be in our native language, the language that was spoken throughout Ireland at the time of your ancestors, the language that was spoken by the great O'Kenedy clan

"Our welcome to you is universal and heartfelt": Kennedy, holding a hat he put on once and very briefly in the rain, reviews Irish troops at Dublin's airport after his arrival. The president's first moments in Ireland struck some U.S. and Irish officials as somewhat subdued.

of the *Dal gCais*, when nine and a half centuries ago, and almost on the spot on which we are now standing, under their mighty King Brian, they smashed the invader and broke decisively the power of the Norseman; that language, Mr. President, which has never ceased to be spoken, will, please God, one day soon again become the everyday language of our people.

"Mr. President, our welcome to you is universal and heartfelt. We welcome you in the first place as the head, the chief executive and first citizen of the Great Republic of the West, on whose enlightened, wise and firm leadership now hangs the hope of the world.

"We welcome you in the second place, Mr. President, as the representative of that great country in which our people sought refuge when the misery of tyrant laws drove them from the motherland, and found a home in which they and their descendants prospered, won distinction and gave devoted service in return.

"Finally, we welcome you for yourself as the distinguished scion of our race who has won first place amongst his fellow countrymen, first in a nation of one hundred and eighty millions. We are proud of you, Mr. President. We admire the leadership you are giving. We hope that your return here to the ancient motherland will give you not merely pleasure, but renewed bodily strength and an ever more determined will in the pursuit of the safety and happiness of mankind. We pray God's inspiration and blessing upon you and upon your work."

De Valera then closed with Irish: *"Fad saoil duit. Bail ó Dhia ort féin, ar do churam agus ar do chuid oibre."* ("Long life to you and may God's blessing be on you, on your family, and on your work.")

President Kennedy then spoke.

"Mr. President," he began, "there are many reasons why I was anxious to accept your generous invitation, and to come to this country. As you said, eight of my grandparents left these shores in the space, almost, of months, and came to the United States. No country in the world, in the history of the world, has endured the hemorrhage which this island endured over a period of a few years for so many of her sons and daughters. These sons and daughters are scattered throughout the world, and they give this small island a family of millions upon millions who are scattered all over the globe, who have been among the best and most loyal citizens of the countries that they have gone to, but have also kept a special place in their memories, in many cases their ancestral memory, of this green and misty island. So, in a sense, all of them who visit Ireland come home.

"In addition, Mr. President, I am proud to visit here" — at this, Kennedy's voice almost broke — "because of you — an old and valued friend of my father — who has served his country with so much distinction, spreading over the period of a half-century; who has expressed in his own life and in the things that he stood for the very best of Western thought and, equally important, Western action.

"And then I am glad to be here because this island still fulfills a historic assignment.

There are Irishmen buried many thousands of miles from here who went on missions of peace, either as soldiers or as churchmen, who traveled throughout the world, carrying the gospel as so many Irish have done for so many hundreds of years.

"So, Mr. President, with the special pride that I feel in my own country, which has been so generous to so many immigrants from so many different countries, I want to say that I am happy to be here tonight."

He bowed his head briefly as he said the last words. Then broke into a grin.

The Irish army band could not be heard above the roar of well-wishers.

Lemass led Kennedy to the terminal building for more introductions and handshakes.

Here were the powers of church and state in Ireland, from the Catholic archbishop of Dublin, Most Rev. Dr. John C. McQuaid, to the members of Lemass's cabinet and local officials. Dr. Hillery, Lemass's education minister and a future president of Ireland, remembered Kennedy's first words to the assembled government officials: "Are these the guys that kept you in office last night?"

Lemass flashed his broad smile and nodded his head, amid roars of laughter.

When Kennedy got to the lord mayor of Dublin, Sean Moore, 40, a clerical supervisor with the Dublin gas company, Lemass introduced him as "our lord mayor of two days' standing." He had been elected just two days before.

"What happened to the other man?" Kennedy asked, referring to Alderman J.J. O'Keeffe, who had visited the White House not long before.

"We have had an election since and Alderman O'Keeffe did not go forward," Moore explained to the president.

"Oh, that is what happened!" Kennedy said with a laugh. "I will see you on Friday," he added, referring to the ceremony in which he would be made a freeman of Dublin.

♣ ♣ ♣ ♣

People would speak about this day for years after as a pivotal event, an occasion that would, to borrow a phrase from Yeats, "sweeten Ireland's wrong."

Kennedy's visit was a further boost to the growing confidence of Ireland in its future, many said. And his presence lent new prestige to Ireland and its place in the world.

". . . We felt he was Irish, and he had been so successful against all odds," said Dorothy Tubridy. "He had fought so hard as a Catholic . . . to get there. I think this gave the Irish people a feeling, 'Well, we can do it, too.'"

The JFK visit, said one observer, "probably did more than any other single factor to boost Irish morale and destroy the last vestige of national self-consciousness."

And, to be sure, religious self-consciousness.

An Irish aristocrat told Irish poet and critic W.R. Rodgers what he thought Kennedy's appearance in Ireland meant: "Well, it means this, once for all, I'm an Irishman and a

Catholic. Now I know that I am not a second-class citizen."

The bond between Kennedy and the Irish was instant.

British journalist Mark Bence-Jones recalled that Americans in the welcoming crowds thanked the Irish "for this welcome to our man."

"But the Irish," Bence-Jones wrote, "were regarding him very much as *their* man."

Truly. ". . . While his first and last loyalty must be to the country of great-grandfather Pat's death, not to that of his birth," Owen Dudley Edwards wrote in the *Irish Times,* "he will not grudge Irish suggestions that here he is considered an Irishman as well as an American."

Kennedy, the *Irish Independent* in Dublin editorialized, "is the symbol of the closing of a chapter in our history."

"After three generations," the newspaper said, "a young man of fully Irish stocks has reached the last point of integration into American life — the chief executive post of the nation."

"In the ceremonial confrontation of two presidents," said the *Irish Press,* referring to de Valera and Kennedy, "a whole relationship stretching across the broad expanse of the Atlantic for centuries reaches a new climax. Those hands across the sea reaching out so often in symbolic and real appeal and assistance will meet in a firm handclasp on Irish soil. What could more appropriately signal this long and fruitful partnership? . . . In these two men, surely, all the cross-currents of shared purpose, passionate concern and long-standing friendship that have united our two peoples meet. Generations of migration and effort, of movement and hope, are symbolized in this happy encounter."

Another commentator quoted JFK in explaining the significance of the visit.

"We live in an age," Kennedy once observed, "when the conduct of foreign affairs consists of more than 'open covenants openly arrived at.'"

"For him," the commentator said, "his Irish visit will not necessitate the signing of any covenants: they have all been signed before this in ties of blood and friendship and understanding. Now it is a matter of cementing them even closer. This, one ventures to suggest, is the true meaning of his Irish visit."

What was then just becoming apparent was that Kennedy had arrived in Ireland at a moment of great change, which Ireland itself had set in motion only four years earlier.

Under the leadership of Lemass, Ireland in 1959 took new steps to dramatically expand its economy, promoting development, the establishment of new industries, more foreign investment, and additional trade.

Ireland's second most important source of foreign trade was tourism, already accounting for about $130 million in revenue annually in 1962 — up fifty percent in five years. The number of hotel rooms had jumped twenty percent since 1959, getting a big boost on the eve of Kennedy's trip with the opening on May 22 of the Irish Intercontinental Hotel in Dublin, and the debut two days later of a second Intercontinental in Cork. The Kennedy visit itself was viewed as an economic boon: millions of Americans, as well as millions of Continental Europeans, would get to know Ireland "in a manner that would not be achieved by any other comparable event," wrote economics commentator and future prime minister Garret FitzGerald.

Irish International Airlines, or Aer Lingus as it was getting to be known, tapped into the American tourist trade at New York, flying daily, nonstop flights on its Boeing 707s between New York and Shannon and Dublin, sometimes adding Boston stops. Ireland was a gateway to England and cities in Europe, and, trying to get people to stop on their way through, the Irish offered a loss leader to pump up interest in the West of the island. For a mere fifteen dollars, a bus would take visitors on a whirlwind, twenty-four-hour stopover tour around County Clare, a ramble that included a visit to an ancient abbey, an Irish dancing demonstration, tea before a peat fire in a thatched cottage, a medieval banquet at five-hundred-year-old Bunratty Castle, a tour of Dromoland Castle (recently bought by an American), and overnight lodging. For this, the government gambled that most people would cancel out the bargain by spending a lot of money at the duty-free shop in Shannon Free Airport, where 2 3/4 ounces of Shalimar perfume was tagged at twenty-one dollars, compared to fifty dollars in New York, and Waterford crystal wineglasses were $2.80 a piece, about a third of Manhattan prices. An economy-class, Dublin-New York round-trip ticket on Aer Lingus ran $458 in 1963 — not even a deal today, and a considerable sum forty years ago. First class cost $864. (Consider these facts: people in Rochester, N.Y., could buy a 1962 Ford Galaxie for about $2,400, or a new Pontiac Grand Prix for about $3,500; in Dublin, a 1963 Ford Cortina ran 585 pounds, or $1,638; a bookkeeper in Miami made about $4,000 a year; a doctor in Galway, 875 pounds per year, or $2,450; a Rochester split-level ranch house cost about $20,000; a three-bedroom house in the Dublin area, about 3,550 pounds, or $9,940. The median annual income of U.S. families in 1962 was $6,000, though one in five Americans made less than $3,000.)

Indeed, Ireland was selling itself to America as a place for sports and relaxation at extremely reasonable prices compared to elsewhere in Europe: a five-course meal in a nice Dublin restaurant would set a couple back $4.62, plus a half-bottle of Bordeaux for 77 cents; an overnight stay in elegant Ashford Castle near Cong, where "The Quiet Man" was filmed, cost $13.30 — including three and a half meals; and greens fees for golf averaged 70 cents per round.

By 1961, the gross national product of Ireland totaled nearly $2 billion, and Ireland and its 2,815,000 people were moving to become more closely tied to the European community. When England was rejected for membership in what was then called the Common Market, it torpedoed Ireland's own effort to join — but the Irish viewed this as a temporary setback only. Anticipating eventual membership, Ireland had begun slashing tariffs on European goods in early 1963.

The Irish economy had come to life. Between 1958 and 1962, national output, or gross national product, jumped by twenty percent. Foreign investment was increasing, and the economy's reliance on agriculture, while still significant, was lessening. Since 1956, some 150 new factories had been built in Ireland. At Shannon Airport, a plan to aid the ailing economy of the country's West had produced a dozen new industrial facilities so far, including three owned by American firms: General Electric, Raytheon Manufacturing, and Standard Pressed Steel. Exports — three-quarters of which went to England and its 50 million people, and most of that free of customs duties — shot up eighty-six percent between 1958 and 1961. In 1962, Irish exports totaled close to $500 million.

Remarkably, the Irish consumed more calories — about 3,500 per day in the late 1950s, compared to about 3,100 in the United States — than did any other nation of the world, according to the United Nations. The Irish actually owned more private cars per thousand people — 81 — than they did telephones — 60.

Unemployment was higher in Ireland than in most of the rest of Western Europe, but it about matched the rate in the United States then: 5.7 percent.

And — a sign many inside and outside Ireland watched as a bellwether — emigration was slowing markedly. Until 1961, some forty-three thousand Irish, on average, left the island every year. In 1962, the exodus had slowed to twenty thousand.

After World War II, the United States had helped Ireland, like many other European nations, under the Marshall Plan. Ireland borrowed $128.2 million from the United States between 1949 and 1952, and was given an additional $18.2 million in grants. Some American money helped to build three scientific laboratories at Dublin's Institute for Industrial Research and Standards. One of the structures was named after William Barton Rogers, a Wexford emigrant of the nineteenth century who, in his new country, founded the Massachusetts Institute of Technology.

Trade between the United States and Ireland was a bit lopsided. While Americans bought $22 million in Irish goods in 1962 — primarily frozen beef — the Irish bought $58 million in American products. A third of U.S. exports to Ireland was tobacco. Other major categories were fruit, wheat, and machinery.

The Irish punt, or pound, was tied to the British pound (and English money was accepted in Ireland, even though the reverse was not true) and in 1963 was worth about $2.80 to the U.S. dollar.

A secret background paper prepared for Kennedy for his trip concluded that "the Irish economy is characterized by a mood of modernization and optimism."

♣ ♣ ♣ ♣

There were brief greetings inside the airport building as the American president was introduced to more Irish government officials and dignitaries. Kennedy spotted his friend

Dorothy Tubridy in the gathering and walked over to greet her.

Kennedy stepped into his open Lincoln, a vintage model from the Eisenhower era flown in from Berlin earlier in the day, for the ten-mile ride by motorcade into Dublin. Three-foot-by-three-foot Irish and American flags were mounted on the front bumper of the car. De Valera sat beside Kennedy. If Kennedy had been a typical traveler arriving in Ireland's capital city outside the rush hours, the trip to the city center would have taken about eighteen minutes. On this day, the twenty-three-car motorcade would consume an hour.

At Larkhill on the airport road, the procession passed through drapes erected for one hundred yards, with red, white, and blue on one side, and green, white, and orange on the other; past a banner bearing the three castles of Dublin's coat of arms, and another with the words "*céad míle fáilte*" — "a hundred thousand welcomes."

At first, in the stark industrial area beyond the airport, the crowds were thin. There were picnickers who had staked out ground here and there, but hardly mobs on Collinstown and Swords roads. Some people waved their Irish and American flags from the gate of a thatched-roof cottage, the quintessential Irish house. Ambassador Kiernan recalled being "a little bit disappointed myself . . . that everything was so quiet and having been perhaps too much official" at the airport. But then, as the motorcade wound onto Drumcondra Road and into the leafy neighborhoods on the edge of Dublin, with houses and shops on both sides of the road decorated in streamers and flags, the crowds grew and grew — in some places twenty people deep. Down Dorset Street the procession went, then North Frederick Street. Some people had climbed into the trees. Kids hung from light poles. Some people perched on stepladders, while others leaned over the edges of their roofs. Others stood on dirt piles from suspended roadwork. Iron and steel mogul Fred Kennedy had erected a huge sign in front of his business: "A Kennedy Salutes a Kennedy."

Kennedy and de Valera saw countless people carrying placards. "Welcome Home, John Kennedy," several said. Some dispensed with the president's Anglicized first name, changing it to the Irish, Sean. Still others, for full effect, dispensed with Kennedy, too. He was *Seán Ó Cinnéide* (shawn oh kyinnaydyeh).

There was a touch of politics, too. "No partition for the Congo, why Ireland?" one sign asked. Said another: "Undivided Ireland welcomes President Kennedy."

Shop windows displayed large pictures of the American president. Many of the souvenirs being hawked seemed aimed at Americans rather than the Irish, who normally weren't much for kitsch like papier-mâché green derbies and shamrocks. In record stores, "Thank God for John F. Kennedy" was the latest novelty. Padraic O'Rourke's words set to Joseph Gornley's music trumpeted Kennedy's role in the Cuban missile crisis of the previous October: "Then here is to John Kennedy of Irish race and name / The ruler of America, we glory in his fame. / When war clouds loomed above us, his bravery won the day. / Thank God for John F. Kennedy and the gallant U.S.A."

Movie theaters took down their usual billings, replacing them with "Welcome President Kennedy."

On O'Connell Street in the center of Dublin, O'Beirne and Fitzgibbon, a men's clothing store, went to the trouble of erecting a special display pointing out that a dozen signers of the Declaration of Independence were native Irishmen, including John Hancock and Charles Carroll, and that another was of Irish descent. In the American war for independence, the store quoted George Washington's stepson Custis as saying, Ireland could boast of a hundred men for every soldier represented by any other country.

The motorcade crossed Dublin in a constant roar from the throngs. Administrative assistants Pauline Fluet and Lenore "Lenny" Donnelly were among the White House staffers riding a bus near the tail end of the parade. People were trying to shake their hands through the partly opened bus windows. "It was unbelievable how thundering it was," Donnelly recalled.

"You would have thought that everybody in that bus was a Kennedy," Fluet said. "There we were, just a bunch of nobodies in this bus, and they were cheering us. They were

No longer subdued, vast crowds greet Kennedy (standing in second car) after he leaves Dublin Airport on his way into Ireland's capital.

so fascinated by him being there, they were just overwhelmed."

At one point, Kennedy was tempted to take a break, and he sat down in the car and mopped his face. But the sea of cheering and waving Irish pulled him back to his feet, and he stood all the rest of the way through Dublin.

The women yelled to Kennedy: "Welcome, Jack!" Girls bellowed to him: "Stay with us, Jack!" Others hollered, "Have a good time here!" Along with the Irish and American flags (the latter had been sold out across Ireland for days), people waved John F. Kennedy flags. The Irish followed American politics closely — even more so now that Kennedy was in the White House. The president's brother Robert F. Kennedy was referred to in Irish newspaper headlines as "the attorney general," as if he were a member of the Lemass government. In Dublin pubs, heated discussions about the president's prospects for a second term were regular fare. On this day, along the motorcade route, many Irish sported Kennedy campaign buttons.

Ireland had detailed sixty-five hundred members of the Garda Siochana, the Irish national police, and soldiers to provide security; along the motorcade route an officer or soldier stood every five yards, much closer still every mile nearer to the middle of the capital. All leave was canceled for the eighteen thousand members of Ireland's army.

"I bet," a red-haired officer said, "this makes the English jealous."

There were folks from Northern Ireland along the route. In fact, officials had been reporting a flood across the border: two hundred cars an hour had been crossing into the Republic before Kennedy's arrival, a greater rate than during the holidays.

"Isn't he just wonderful?" gushed Sheila Walsh, a typist from Belfast who had run down to Dublin for the day. "It was really worth the trip to see him."

Kennedy's motorcade slowly moved into the central city, to Parnell Square East, and finally sloping down to famed O'Connell Street, where Kennedy had walked anonymously on earlier trips. The divided boulevard is Ireland's main street, at that time anchored at the northern end by one of the city's most famous landmarks, albeit a remnant of British colonialism, Lord Nelson's pillar (it would be blown up before decade's end by IRA sympathizers). The top of the great pillar, which offered one of the best views in the city, was closed by police, partly out of fear that spectators might fall, and partly for security concerns. Kennedy looked back and up at the pillar as the motorcade slid along the east side of O'Connell, following what would be the normal traffic pattern south, toward the statue of the man for whom the great commercial street was named: Daniel O'Connell. Seated, O'Connell the Liberator appeared to be contemplating the River Liffey before him, where swans paddled in water so brown one writer likened it to "a Guinness leakage."

Before the American president was an astounding sight. All the way down the boulevard, every light pole and rooftop flew the Irish tricolor and the American Stars and Stripes. Dubliners stood dozens deep along the sidewalks on the west side of O'Connell, and at least ten deep on the east side. Many hugged the sides of Nelson's column. From nearly every balcony and window in the stone, low-rise buildings, people cheered. Others clung to straining branches. They cheered Kennedy, they cheered people they didn't recognize in following cars, they even cheered the president's security detail.

A jeweler's carillon played "Home, Home on the Range." A messenger cycled through the crowd, the red, white, and blue on the front of his bike. The souvenir hawkers made their last pitches: "Flags, only six pence each! Flags and badges!" they yelled.

Riding through the packed streets, Kennedy persisted in standing, while de Valera remained seated. The thought occurred to the Irish president, he remembered a few years later, "what an easy target he would have been." Kennedy's security detail was concerned about the exposure, but de Valera took comfort in the tremendous outpouring the Irish were giving Kennedy. "I knew there was no danger about it at all," the Irish leader said.

Here and there, packs of boys on bicycles pedaled furiously in a vain attempt to catch the passing presidential limousine.

Partway along O'Connell, the procession passed Ireland's holiest of holies in its fight for freedom: the General Post Office, where de Valera's fellow patriots had fought a pitched battle with British troops in 1916. (De Valera himself was guarding a different site, Boland's Flour Mills at Mount Street Bridge, some distance from the GPO. The Irish president would have liked to show Kennedy his place of triumph, but "there was no time," de Valera said.) Pits from bullets and explosions remained on the imposing columns. It was just before reaching the Post Office, near the Parnell Monument, that Kennedy was showered with paper and ticker tape — the latter the first such precipitation in Irish history. What he did not see, back at the end of the motorcade, was the crowd closing together in a swarm, surging down O'Connell Street behind him. Marching at a respectful distance beyond, led by a brass band, was a group of men, some from the Belfast Republican Prisoners' Committee, carrying banners, one of which read, "Irishmen are in British Jails." By the time the group reached the center of the city, they were swallowed in the humanity.

The official estimate put the turnout in Dublin at a quarter of a million. That would be about half the city's population. Every hotel within five miles of the city had been booked. For those who still wanted to get home, extra trains were being run out of Dublin in the evening to Athlone, Waterford, Wexford, and Dundalk.

Onto Westmoreland Street the motorcade crept, then College Green, Dame Street, Parliament Street, Grattan Bridge, North Quays, Parkgate Street, Main Road, and then up to Phoenix Park. Tens of thousands pressed as close as they dared to the procession, while the motorcycle escorts, police, and the U.S. Secret Service pushed them back. A few intrepid souls somehow had climbed to the roof of Trinity College and walked gingerly on the fragile tile. An old woman left her fruit stand to wait to see Kennedy pass by. She saw him and was pleased. "I'm glad we gave him such a welcome," she said. "He's a credit to our country."

A seventeen-year-old young lady was smitten. "Now that I've really seen the president in person," she declared, "I think he is one of the most handsome men in the world."

A County Mayo policeman doing Dublin duty was one of the few who were under-whelmed. "I will not be sorry when the Kennedy visit is over," he snapped. "There is noth-ing so hateful as having to stand here doing nothing." It had been a long day for the man.

Almost at the end of the journey, Kennedy and de Valera were washed in a sudden show-er. Kennedy, abandoning his aversion to headgear, put on his hat and a raincoat during the downpour. As soon as it abated, he quickly took the hat off. Entering the grounds of Aras an Uachtarain, the Irish president's house, Kennedy took off the raincoat. As he stepped from the limousine, he threw the coat back into the car, stepped into the house, took out a comb, and ran it through his hair.

Above Aras an Uachtarain, the Irish and American flags waved from the rooftop, along with the Irish president's flag, a harp on a field of blue. The stop was for a brief hello to the president's wife, Sinead Bean de Valera, then a formal parting after a little refreshment. Some said it was sherry, though that's not what Ireland is best known for.

Ambassador Kiernan greeted Mrs. de Valera.

"What did you think of the procession?" he asked her.

"Don't ever tell this to anybody: I didn't see it," she revealed. She had been caught up in her reading, she told the envoy. She had never had enough time to read while raising her children, and then playing with her grandchildren.

"Now, since I came out here for the first time I can read and I have a cubbbyhole down below with books around," Mrs. de Valera explained. "And I just immerse myself in read-ing. And would you believe it? I forgot altogether the procession was on. I was reading."

Just ten minutes after he arrived, Kennedy left the president's house. He was besieged by waiting thousands as his car tried to negotiate across an open area. U.S. Secret Service agents and Irish police hurriedly formed a wedge to make a narrow path to the iron gates at the entrance to the American embassy. But at last the presidential car could proceed no farther. So the guest of honor stepped out and walked through the gates. On the other side, he hitched a ride in the gatekeeper's car for the last quarter mile to the American ambassador's residence.

"What do you think of it?" Kennedy asked aide and friend Dave Powers about what they had just experienced.

"If you ran over here," Powers said, "you'd beat de Valera in his own precinct."

De Valera later called Kennedy's entrance into Dublin "a triumphal procession," a reception unlike any that had ever been accorded a foreign visitor.

Protocol figures into everything in matters of state. And with the American president, so did international security concerns. So it was that Kennedy did not stay at the president's house with the de Valeras, much to the Irish leader's keen disappointment, but rather made his base at the American ambassador's residence a short distance away.

Kennedy stayed in Dublin during his four-day visit to Ireland, and his motorcades from place to place through the city were a sensation. Despite his back trouble, the president would often stand to let people see him better. Here he is with the *Taoiseach*, Sean Lemass, who is sitting down behind the bubbletop, on June 27.

De Valera was told that everywhere Kennedy went, he needed to be able to stay in immediate contact with Washington. The Irish leader couldn't have missed that at the airport, where, on a closed runway, a Stratocruiser called Talking Bird sat, radios and eighteen crewmembers at the ready, just in case all other communications broke down. In this era of Cold War tensions, Kennedy was never more than two minutes from talking to the White House. That required a lot of equipment — mainly telephones that could use secure or scrambled lines. But even for the lunch and garden party at de Valera's residence, special Washington lines were installed. Forgetting about all the new gadgetry, de Valera at one point absent-mindedly picked up a phone on his desk, only to discover he was talking to Washington.

Press arrangements for Kennedy's visit were considered only slightly less exotic. Of the 150 members of the media covering the trip, about 100 were regular American correspondents from the White House. They were headquartered for the duration of Kennedy's stay at the elegant Gresham Hotel, where no fewer than fifty new telephone lines were installed — a job that necessitated the tearing up of Thomas Lane outside the hotel. The Irish government made sure that besides extra phones, there were a couple of dozen sound-proof telephone booths on one hotel balcony, and a bank of telex and teleprinter machines linking the Irish capital with Washington on another. The Gresham's main ballroom was the press center, and reporters were offered all they could possibly want to know about the host country from Aer Lingus, Bord Failte (the Irish Tourist Board), CIE (Ireland's bus and railroad network), Ireland's Department of External Affairs, and the United States Embassy. There were some souvenirs, too, like the forest-green plastic valises emblazoned with a gold Irish harp and "Visit of President Kennedy."

As a swamped official in the Irish foreign office handed out press credentials to a crushing mob, a BBC reporter asked which previous visitor to Ireland had caused such an uproar. "Cromwell," the official snapped.

Establishing reliable communications was a matter of national honor, according to Michael Hilliard, Ireland's minister for posts and telegraphs. "This is a most serious challenge," he told the Post Office Workers' Union annual conference in Killarney, where workers filed complaints about lack of heat in some branches, "and it is vital from both a national and international viewpoint that we should emerge with colors flying."

Government officials had worried for some time how telephone equipment stressed by the already heavy summer call traffic would hold up under the load of a presidential visit. They had warned only days before Hilliard's speech that "disruption will have to be expected."

But Kennedy's visit had speeded up expansion plans for the Irish telephone system. Additional lines were being put in all across Dublin and in the other cities and towns where the president was being hosted. Trunk lines from Dublin to Waterford, for example, were increased from 79 to 103, and a new cable between New Ross and Waterford doubled capacity between those communities.

At the ambassador's residence, Kennedy was exhilarated by his arrival. It had been a crowded day, starting in Germany, and then this bedlam in Dublin. The adrenaline was still pumping. He was not quite ready to retire. And here he sat in a place of supreme irony. In the days of the Famine, the house had belonged to the chief secretary, England's representative in Dublin, whose harsh policies contributed to the mass exodus that included Kennedys and Fitzgeralds.

Now, President John Fitzgerald Kennedy sat in the grand house and munched on a chicken sandwich and chatted with his family and inner circle, including sisters Eunice and Jean, sister-in-law Lee Radziwell, and old pals LeMoyne Billings and Dave Powers. The president had taken off his jacket, loosened his tie, and kicked off his shoes. His welcome, he told them, had been "fantastic." He was taken by the faces in the Dublin crowd. They could have been from Boston, all agreed. Jean was exhilarated. "The reception was totally overwhelming," she said. When she would come back thirty years later as U.S. ambassador to Ireland, the Irish would constantly talk of "the most wonderful days" of June 1963, she recalled. "And that was true. You could just feel it in the air."

The president was moved by impulse to stand up and sing. Powers, with a memory for Irish songs, joined in. The song was "The Wearing of the Green," the writer lost to time.

Oh, Paddy, dear, an' did ye hear the news that's goin' round?
The shamrock is by law forbid to grow on Irish ground.
No more St. Patrick's day we'll keep, his colour can't be seen,
For there's a cruel law agin the wearin' of the green!

I met wid Napper Tandy and he took me by the hand,
And he said "How's poor ould Ireland, and how does she stand?"
She's the most distressful country that iver yet was seen,
For they're hangin' men and women there for wearin' o' the green.

If he could have gotten away with it, without causing a riot, Kennedy, it seems certain, would have ended his evening somewhere off Grafton Street, sitting at a bar well-polished by decades of elbows, his pint of Smithwick's at the ready for the dry pauses between songs.

The *Irish Times*, Thursday, June 27, 1963

U.S. HEAD OF STATE WELCOMED LIKE HOMECOMING HERO

Today's programme for U.S. President

Through the heart of the city

The procession crossing O'Connell Bridge with, immediately behind the Presidential car, Mr. Kennedy's bodyguard and behind them a motor-cycle

two

I want to go to Ireland

I am troubled, I'm dissatisfied, I'm Irish.

Marianne Moore
Spencer's Ireland *(1941)*

John Fitzgerald Kennedy had been contemplating a trip back to Ireland from his first days as president. And the Irish government certainly was eager to see him. But Irish officials in Dublin and Washington were careful not to be presumptuous, and did not press for advantage with the new president just because of his ancestry. ". . . Possibly we bent backwards to avoid any kind of what I would regard as intrusion," said Ireland's ambassador, Thomas J. Kiernan.

That is not to say the Irish weren't absolutely delighted with Kennedy's election to the presidency in 1960. That event, recalled Dr. Patrick Hillery, who had become Lemass's education minister the previous year, "created great excitement" in Ireland. Lemass told Hillery: "The Irish people everywhere are walking taller today because an Irishman has been elected president of the United States."

Early on in his administration, Kennedy told Kiernan he felt the Congress would hold him to account for his trips, that he would need a good reason to put Ireland on his official travels.

And Ireland hadn't figured at all in past presidential itineraries.

In early 1962, Kennedy's first ambassador to Dublin, Edward G. Stockdale, passed the news to Irish Minister of External Affairs Aiken that Kennedy intended to put Ireland on a European itinerary should one come to pass over the next months. Aiken, as might be expected, was pleased and assured Stockdale that Kennedy would be "heartily welcome" any time. All the Irish needed, Aiken said, was a particular date from the White House and "all arrangements would at once be made" for an official invitation to be issued by de Valera.

At a June 9, 1962, dinner in Washington's Mayflower Hotel for the new U.S. ambassador to Ireland, Matthew McCloskey, Kennedy told the story of a 1945 visit to Dublin, where he stayed with U.S. envoy David Gray. The American diplomat had had a recent meeting on some matter with the Irish. "Let me just say one thing to you," Kennedy quoted Gray telling him. "Don't ever send an Irishman to Ireland as ambassador. They will play 'Danny Boy,' 'Wearing of the Green,' take him to High Mass, and he is all through."

With McCloskey, "we figured we might as well take a chance," the president joked. "So I want us all to stand and drink a toast to the man who we are going to all visit in the next year or so."

In July 1962, McCloskey, a Philadelphia contractor who had served as chief political fundraiser for Kennedy in the 1960 presidential campaign, set down in Dublin with a presidential promise: Kennedy would visit before leaving the White House. Perhaps, McCloskey suggested, the trip might come when the new U.S. Embassy, then under construction in the Ballsbridge section of Dublin, was opened.

That U.S.-Irish relations were warming after some difficult years during the Eisenhower administration was clear.

During the Cuban missile crisis in October 1962, Ireland had played a role in the United Nations in defusing opposition among neutral countries to Kennedy's blockade of Cuba. The Irish were on the Security Council at the time, and Aiken helped persuade the other neutral nations that a blockade was better than allowing Russia to carry out further deliveries of nuclear missiles onto Cuban soil, which seemed certain to bring nuclear war with the United States. A resolution demanding an end to the blockade was thwarted.

The promise of a presidential visit to Ireland obviously helped, too.

When Secretary of State Dean Rusk stopped over briefly in Dublin on December 16, 1962, curious reporters wondered whether his talks with government leaders encompassed arrangements for a presidential visit.

"There was no discussion of an actual visit here on my present trip," Rusk told the journalists. "I don't think I even have to ask President Kennedy the question though. He will always enjoy a trip to Ireland."

On the last day of 1962, McCloskey raised the matter of a visit to Ireland in the coming year directly with Rusk in a meeting in Washington. Rusk assured him he would try to set up a day or two in Ireland on a European tour that seemed to be in the offing. McCloskey passed that on to Irish leaders.

But the right moment didn't come until the spring of 1963.

The impetus for the visit came from Kennedy himself — and apparently against the advice of his Department of State, which saw no diplomatic advantage in such an excursion, and of his close advisors known as the "Irish Mafia," David F. Powers and Kenneth P. O'Donnell. Powers was special assistant to the president, sort of the official greeter at the White House, a job suited to the man's memory for names and his sunny disposition. O'Donnell, as reserved as Powers was extroverted, was Kennedy's appointments secretary. In truth, they were far more than their job descriptions. The two men were Kennedy's long-time friends, confidants, sometimes even his foils.

The June European trip started out as a state visit to West Germany, intended to help strengthen that nation's commitment to the North Atlantic Treaty Organization, the military alliance between Western Europe and the United States against the then-Soviet Union and the Eastern European states it held in its grip. Then, Italy was added to the itinerary after some concerns were expressed by that nation that it was feeling underappreciated. The State Department, ever alert to British sensitivities and watchful for chances to reinforce the close relationship between the United Kingdom and the United States, later successfully urged Kennedy to at least make a brief stop with Prime Minister Harold Macmillan. It was a late add to the trip and, despite Macmillan's political troubles, was not a hard sell. Kennedy and Macmillan were friends, and Macmillan years before had been a father figure to Kennedy's late sister, Kathleen. The two leaders had met every four or five months during Kennedy's presidency.

One day, as O'Donnell was going over details of the European tour, Kennedy announced he wanted one more expansion of the schedule.

"I've decided that I want to go to Ireland, too," the president said.

"Ireland?" O'Donnell replied. "Mr. President, may I say something?"

O'Donnell was known for being frank with Kennedy and getting away with it. Kennedy, indeed, counted on such candor.

"There's no reason for you to go to Ireland," O'Donnell said. "It would be a waste of time. It wouldn't do you much good politically. You've got all the Irish votes in this country that you'll ever get. If you go to Ireland, people will say it's just a pleasure trip."

"That's exactly what I want: a pleasure trip to Ireland," Kennedy insisted.

At first, O'Donnell didn't think the president would press the matter. McGeorge Bundy, Kennedy's special assistant for foreign affairs and national security, agreed with O'Donnell that Ireland was an unnecessary addition that would simply stretch the trip without any tangible gain.

Back with Kennedy the following day, O'Donnell passed on Bundy's opinion. The president, reading a newspaper at the time, had had enough counsel on the matter.

"Kenny," his boss snapped, "let me remind you of something. I am the president of the United States, not you. When I say I want to go to Ireland, it means that I'm going to Ireland. Make the arrangements."

There certainly was no pressing international matter to dictate an Irish stop, speechwriter Sorensen later said. "The trip had a more personal, sentimental value to the president, and that's why it was added."

England's Lord Longford, a somewhat eccentric fellow who early on befriended Eamon de Valera and was in Ireland for Kennedy's visit, wrote that "the story brings out revealingly the utter absorption of Kennedy's aides in his interests *as they saw them*; some aspects of the real man eluded them." (Longford's emphasis)

On March 15, Ireland's ambassador presented Kennedy with the traditional St. Patrick's Day gift of shamrocks. (Kennedy spent March 17, St. Patrick's Day, with his father, Joseph P. Kennedy, Sr., in Massachusetts.)

The president, Kiernan, and the U.S. chief of protocol, Angier Biddle Duke, went through the public presentation before reporters. Then, back in the White House Oval Office, Kennedy invited the ambassador out into the garden, leaving Duke behind.

"I'm glad to say that I can go to Ireland and I'd like you to find out if that's agreeable to your government," Kiernan remembered the president telling him. Kennedy continued: "I told you before about the difficulty. Ireland is not a nuisance in international affairs or is not one way or the other in the picture very much, so that there's no justification to Congress to go. For that reason I'll have to make the visit in association with another visit."

That would be with the Germany-Italy trip, Kennedy said.

Kiernan jumped at the news.

"Well, the dates, you may take it straightaway without referring to the government, will be agreeable, and you can come and have a comfortable rest," the ambassador said.

"I don't want to rest in Ireland," the president corrected, to the surprise of the envoy. "I want to go around and meet people. I want to meet plenty of people. I don't want to stay in Dublin. I don't want too many official receptions. I don't want any of the stuffed-shirt arrangement, if you can avoid it. Just to meet people. But, it certainly won't be a rest. The more I can cover, the better it will be. That's what I call a rest."

Kiernan cabled Dublin that Kennedy "wanted a proper official visit." The envoy urged his government to carefully plan what Kennedy should do in Ireland, "as he is the first Irish president of the United States and as he is now ruling out anything in the nature of a casual stop-down visit as the tail-end to more important visits."

President de Valera wasted no time sending the official invitation.

"I have the honour . . . to extend to you and Mrs. Kennedy, on my own behalf and on behalf of the Government and the people of Ireland, a most cordial invitation to be our guests and to pass with us such time as is available to you on a State visit to our country," the Irish leader wrote Kennedy on March 27. "It will be a source of joy and pleasure to me to learn that you will be able to accept this invitation, and I hasten to assure you, Mr. President, that the warmest of welcomes will await you and Mrs. Kennedy from my wife and myself and from the Government and the people of Ireland."

President Kennedy replied: "I am delighted to have your letter of March twenty-seventh and to accept your warm and generous invitation for a visit to Dublin during our forthcoming trip to Europe. I fear that my schedule will not allow a very long stop in Ireland, but there is no country and no city I would rather visit."

Kennedy told de Valera that the schedule hadn't been set yet, but he was thinking of arriving either on June 27 or June 28. "If these dates are in any way inconvenient for you, I hope you will let me know," Kennedy closed.

Word of an Irish visit began leaking out in early April, while the White House quietly was still trying to pull together details of the trip. The *Boston Sunday Globe* published on April 7 a North American Newspaper Alliance story about a projected trip. In Dublin the same day, the *Sunday Review* likewise had good sources: the Kennedys themselves. Reporter Eoin O'Mahony, doing double duty for the *Review* and for Radio Eireann, interviewed

Attorney General Robert Kennedy and Massachusetts Sen. Edward Kennedy, as well as unnamed sisters of the president, who predicted a presidential visit was upcoming. All that remained was the official announcement from the Irish government, O'Mahony wrote.

By Monday, April 16, the White House press corps was pressuring White House press secretary Pierre Salinger for confirmation. After all, Ireland's Ambassador Kiernan had been seen at the White House the previous Thursday, and that was well past St. Patrick's Day.

"I have no information on it at this time," Salinger told the press.

"This made Salinger about the only person who didn't seem to know," chortled a United Press International dispatch.

Indeed, in Dublin that morning, the *Irish Times* had confirmed through its Washington sources that Kennedy would include Ireland in his upcoming European tour. Ambassador McCloskey would admit only that a trip had been under discussion for some time and that Kennedy was giving the idea serious attention. The envoy added, however, that he did not think there would be such an early decision as the *Times* had uncovered. "I just hope that it is correct," McCloskey said of the newspaper's information.

One piece of information Salinger did share was that Mrs. Kennedy was expecting the couple's third child. Given her history of difficult pregnancies, the thirty-three-year-old first lady was ordered by her doctors to cancel her activities and take it easy. That meant that a trip to Europe for her was out of the question. President Kennedy had a substitute: his sister Eunice Kennedy Shriver. Her husband, Sargent Shriver, was director of Kennedy's Peace Corps.

"He called up," Mrs. Shriver recalled, "from the White House, and said, 'How would you like to come and be hostess on the trip?' I said I thought that would be great."

She had been to Ireland previously and had friends there.

It was some time during the early days of planning that Kennedy let family friend Dorothy Tubridy in on the secret. She had encouraged him "madly" to make the trip since he had become president. She had promised to "persecute" Kennedy until he scheduled a visit.

One of eleven children, Tubridy grew up in a household where Ireland and its history were constant subjects. She and her husband, Michael, a captain in the Irish army and one of the finest horsemen in the world, had traveled internationally for horse-jumping competitions, representing Ireland. Nothing made her prouder than watching the tricolor rise up a foreign flagpole after her husband had won. Then, in 1954, his horse stepped into a rabbit hole while walking across a field. He fell from the saddle and was killed. With a young daughter, the widow went to work, and became a public relations executive for Waterford Crystal. Dorothy Tubridy became not only a representative of Waterford, particularly in America, but also a saleswoman for Ireland. "All my life, I've been bragging about Ireland," she admitted. Tubridy had been close to the Kennedys since the early 1950s. During her regular visits to Washington, she always stayed with Robert and Ethel Kennedy, whom she had met before Jack and Jacqueline. When Jack became president, she had a Waterford bowl engraved with the Kennedy crest. She left it for him in his office with a note: "To remind you where it all began." Kennedy kept the bowl on his desk throughout his presidency.

Tubridy knew how closely the Irish followed American politics, and John Kennedy's presidency in particular. They consumed everything they could read about Kennedy and his family. And she knew of the president's great love of Ireland; so it just seemed to her that the man and the country should be together.

". . . I tried to explain this to him, you know, that I knew if he came to Ireland, he would feel how much they really loved him," Tubridy later related. "I knew he would identify with the Irish and they with him. I knew he'd feel that. You can't tell a person. It's just something you have to experience, which he did."

Then she was called to the White House one day for an unofficial visit.

"I want you to be the first to know I'm coming to Ireland," the president told her.

Tubridy had Kennedy's ear on Ireland, what to do, where to go, what was appropriate. When he first talked about going to Ireland, he was inclined to visit Dublin only, mainly because at that time it appeared his schedule would be extremely tight and his stay short. Tubridy pressed him to do more.

"I felt that he should see more of the country and spread himself, so to speak, more, so that the people in other parts of the country would be so delighted to have him, too," she recalled.

"Yes, yes. Perhaps I should. I'd better think about that," Kennedy told her. "What do you think the people in Ireland would like me to do?"

Well, she answered Kennedy, it was clear that not all of Eire could come to see him in Dublin. He should go to the South and the West. Tubridy particularly pushed for Galway. That was certainly doable by helicopter, it was agreed. And so the trip grew. That explained why, by the time Kennedy met with the Irish ambassador, the president wanted to go everywhere in Ireland.

On Saturday, April 20, the official word finally came: Kennedy would add Ireland to his previously announced itinerary of West Germany and Italy (Great Britain had not yet officially been included). Details were to be filled in during the coming weeks.

In Ireland, de Valera's office released the announcement at the same time as the White House: "The president of the United States of America has accepted a cordial invitation from the president [de Valera] to visit Ireland, following his visit to Italy and Germany in June.

"Details of the visit are being arranged by the ambassadors of both countries and will be announced at a later date."

Dublin was for sure, and New Ross in County Wexford was likely. At this point, the presidential visit was to be two days in duration.

No matter. No more speculation, no more rumors. In joy and excitement, Ireland contemplated what it had dared not dream of. "Welcome, J.F.K.!" yelled the front page of Dublin's *Sunday Independent*.

"Jack in June," exulted the *Sunday Review*. An Irish government official called the enthusiasm about the trip "amazing."

"It goes far beyond our wildest expectations," the official said.

Kennedy's visit also would mark a new chapter in Irish relations with the rest of the world for, as the *Irish Times* pointed out, "this will be, in effect, the first visit of the head of an important state to this country and may lead to the visit of other political personalities."

That was the global perspective. There was the local one, too, in County Wexford.

"You can be sure President Kennedy will get the greatest reception of his life," promised James Kennedy, a third cousin of the president residing in Dunganstown, near New Ross.

Mary Ryan, James Kennedy's sister and resident of the farm from which President Kennedy's great-grandfather had left for America, called word of the president's plans "the greatest news we have ever had."

"We've been waiting and hoping for weeks, ever since all those rumors of the visit began," Mrs. Ryan said. "He is a great man to think of visiting us now with all that he has on his mind."

In New Ross, the practical reared its head.

"There are no public funds in New Ross to meet the cost of preparations and arrangements which must be made to greet the president," said Andrew Minihan, the bearded chairman of the Urban District Council who was known for wearing a derby on important days. "But he can be assured of one of the most genuine welcomes of his life."

Tubridy, back in Dublin, received a quick note from Kennedy. The trip was getting a little longer. The plans now were calling for a presidential arrival on Wednesday, June 26, with a stay until "at least late Friday," the president said.

"I hope it can be made as pleasant as possible and not a lot of heavy activities," Kennedy wrote, apparently forgetting for a moment that he was the president of the United States, and the first Irish-American president with roots directly back to the Republic of Ireland.

On May 2, Dublin's lord mayor, Alderman James J. O'Keeffe, accompanied by Ambassador Kiernan, visited the White House for a thirty-minute chat with Kennedy. O'Keeffe was in the United States with a delegation of members of the Retail Grocery, Dairy, and Allied Trades Association. The mayor and the president talked about the possibility that the American leader could squeeze in watching the Irish Derby on June 29.

O'Keeffe also let it be known that he might not actually be the lord mayor on the day of Kennedy's visit. The office is for a one-year term, he explained, and no Dublin lord mayor had been given a consecutive term since 1945.

"We don't trust them for more than a year!" quipped Kiernan, to general laughter. (And, indeed, O'Keeffe was replaced, on June 24, by Sean Moore.)

O'Keeffe was impressed that the American leader was well-versed on Ireland.

"Mr. Kennedy's knowledge of Ireland is really complete," the lord mayor approved.

As a measure of the Irish esteem for Kennedy and what he symbolized for the nation, Ireland's leaders began exploring the idea of making the American president an honorary citizen of Eire. This honor would be truly remarkable, given the fact that such citizenship had never been granted to anyone. There was unanimous support for the idea — all it would take was a bill in the Parliament and the signature of de Valera.

"It's gone to my brother," Kennedy told Ambassador Kiernan of the citizenship idea. "He's the main fellow and he may turn me down. I'd love it, but we'll see what he says."

As the White House and Attorney General Robert F. Kennedy's staffs researched the matter, the legal questions and complications grew. It was likely there had to be some congressional approval. There was an issue about precedent. It became so murky and complicated that McGeorge Bundy called Kiernan in April and said that it would be best if the citizenship proposal were dropped.

Salinger and O'Donnell headed up a twenty-four-person White House advance team to Dublin on May 6 to plan how to fill Kennedy's time in Ireland. Also in the party were Gerald Behn, head of the Secret Service's White House detail; presidential aide Brig. Gen. Godfrey McHugh; protocol chief Angier Biddle Duke; White House social secretary Letitia Baldridge; and assistant White House press secretary Malcolm Kilduff. They took the jet that served as Air Force One, giving the pilot an opportunity to familiarize himself with Dublin airport.

Kennedy's trip to Ireland was generating more interest among American reporters at the White House than any other trip since he took office, Salinger told the Irish press just minutes after he landed. And the boss was excited, too, of course.

"I had a long talk with him before I left Washington," Salinger said, "and I can tell you he is looking forward to his Irish visit with the keenest possible interest."

The advance party met with Ambassador McCloskey at his residence, and later O'Donnell, Salinger, and McCloskey met with Lemass to go over plans. By the end of the day, Salinger was able to tell a packed press conference in the Gresham Hotel that Wexford and New Ross were, indeed, going to be presidential stops.

"It is the president's desire to go to these two places," Salinger told Irish reporters, "and we have confirmed it today in talks with officials of your government."

Salinger, with U.S. Secret Service agents, White House communications specialists, and McCloskey in tow, drove the next day to Wexford and New Ross to give local leaders the official word that the president would, indeed, come to their towns. He would visit the John Barry memorial in Wexford and speak from the quay from which Kennedy's great-grandfather had sailed more than a century before.

"This will be the greatest day in the history of the town," declared William Stafford, a member of the New Ross Urban District Council and the New Ross Harbour Commissioners.

In Wexford, U.S. Army Maj. James Maschmann, the president's helicopter pilot, viewed a proposed landing site in front of the railway station. He shook his head, "No." Behn, of the Secret Service, looked at the buildings around the edge of the proposed landing site. He, too, shook his head. After a study of the maps over a champagne breakfast at the Talbot Hotel, the Gaelic football field was settled on as a landing site.

The reconnaissance was repeated in New Ross. Then, White House officials unofficially let it be known that Dunganstown, indeed, was being considered. Salinger and O'Donnell drove down the winding road to the farm.

"I hope when he comes, he will come in and have a cup of tea," Mary Ryan told reporters. She gave her official guests a tour of the house and farm. Major Maschmann walked around the fields near the house to ensure their suitability as a landing zone.

It began to appear that most of the estimated eighteen thousand Kennedys living in Ireland were going to claim direct connection to the president and demand an audience.

Mrs. Ryan was vexed by the sudden influx of supposed kin.

O'Donnell witnessed a blow-up on the day he and Salinger visited.

"You haven't shown your face at this door in twenty years," Mrs. Ryan scolded one man, wagging her finger at him, "and now you're horning in here because President Kennedy is coming!"

O'Donnell asked the target's name. "John Kennedy," the man replied.

Salinger went out of his way to reassure his Irish hosts that all was coming together nicely.

"The Irish leg of the journey is the highlight of the president's visit to Europe this year," he said. "The Irish government is making every effort to ensure that things go smoothly and easily. It is a joy to work with your officials. . . . It all has to be approved by Washington, of course."

All this feel-good press agentry went down poorly with some. "The visit by the president of the United States is reaching the limit in sickening idolatry," Pat Murphy of Dublin wrote to the *Sunday Review.*

When Salinger and the others left, Kilduff stayed behind. He was put up in the Gresham Hotel, a White House telephone was installed in his room, and he was watched over by the hotel manager, Paddy O'Sullivan, who was, inexplicably, Hungarian. "Macduff," as Kennedy called Kilduff, had been hired the previous summer out of the State Department, where he had won high praise for his advance work for Secretary of State Rusk. Kennedy, who had known Kilduff for the briefing books he prepared for the president before his well-known press conferences in the State Department auditorium, had personally asked him to join the team in the West Wing.

Kilduff's first discovery in Dublin: the Irish "had no idea what was involved in a presidential visit," he said. "Of course, they had never had a presidential visit."

When Kilduff suggested something, his Irish hosts often would react through the experience of the only fairly recent visitor who caused a stir.

"They would say, 'When Princess Grace was here . . .' That's all they likened it to," Kilduff despaired.

On May 18, the outline of the official itinerary was released in Dublin, revealing that the president would be staying a day longer in Ireland than first thought, from the evening of June 26 to the afternoon of June 29.

Dublin, where Kennedy would stay every night of his visit, set to work on how it would honor its guest well before he set foot in the country. On May 27, the Dublin City Council voted by acclamation that it would make the president the forty-eighth freeman of Dublin during his visit.

Galway was now on the itinerary. So was Cork, where, unlike Galway, it was decided to go ahead with elections on June 25, three days before President Kennedy would visit. Cork and Galway were obvious stops once it was known how long Kennedy would stay in Ireland. They were the next largest cities in Ireland, and to skip them would have meant "tremendous political difficulty" for Irish leaders, according to Ambassador Kiernan.

Some Cork residents hoped the president would agree to kiss the Blarney Stone. One Dublin wag opined that the stone "would help solve some of his 1964 election problems."

But Salinger later would demur on behalf of his boss. Kissing the stone, as everyone knows, involves bending backwards, with the help of handrails, almost to the point of being upside down. The president, Salinger reminded reporters, avoided strenuous activities that might aggravate his chronic back troubles, including a strain he suffered while planting a ceremonial tree in Ottawa in 1961.

As the schedule was built, it became clear there would be a lot of Dublin in the itinerary.

"They're hijacking the president," rose the complaint from New Ross, put down for a forty-five-minute presidential stop. New Ross was sure Kennedy would prefer to stay with his relatives rather than flit from party to party in the capital.

Initially, Limerick was not put on the list of presidential stops. That generated a minor furor in the city at the mouth of the Shannon River. After all, hadn't John F. "Honey Fitz" Fitzgerald, the one-time mayor of Boston, maternal grandfather of the president, come to Limerick because he believed his family had its roots in the area?

Limerick would not be denied. Lord Mayor Frances Condell let it be known Kennedy was expected. By the end of May, city officials were saying it was "virtually certain" the president would be in the city. But they waited. By June 13, Limerick Corporation officials still had no definite word.

Skibbereen did not make the cut, despite considerable research by retired U.S. Navy Lt. J.J. Cadogan. Born in Cork and a resident of San Francisco, Cadogan had found Fitzgeralds on a farm near Skibbereen, a town some distance from Cork. President Kennedy's pastor in the family's winter home in Palm Beach, Florida, Msgr. J. O'Mahony, a Cork man, urged a Skibbereen stop. But the town was not to be as lucky as Limerick. It was not added.

Waterford got a look, but also couldn't be accommodated.

♣ ♣ ♣ ♣

And then, amidst all the meticulous planning, the elephant in the room in U.S.-British relations, Northern Ireland, stood up and trumpeted.

The White House received an invitation from the government in Belfast, through Macmillan, for Kennedy to visit the Giant's Causeway, a dramatic area of strange, polygonal formations of rock columns along the County Antrim coast.

Some London political observers saw the invitation as a camouflaged effort by Macmillan to improve his standing before the next national elections. It was believed Macmillan would have wanted to meet with Kennedy in Northern Ireland.

"There is no question of politics," insisted a Northern Ireland government spokesman. "This is purely a cultural affair."

In truth, politics could not be divorced from an invitation for an American president to visit a territory whose status and future were in perpetual dispute.

There were legitimate ties to the United States beyond all those Irish-Americans whose ancestors came from the six counties. American commercial interests had a toe-hold in the North, operating some twenty U.S.-owned factories where a decade before there had been one.

But this was not the president of the U.S. Chamber of Commerce who was being invited to Northern Ireland, and no amount of business connections could offset the political problems a stop by Kennedy would create.

Harry Diamond, a Republican Labour member of the House of Commons in Northern Ireland, said that the prime minister for Northern Ireland, Capt. Terence O'Neill, should take the hint that he was not going to win the kind of recognition he was seeking "for this transitional state." Diamond derided the invitation as an effort to win American endorsement of a policy of unfair discrimination against the Nationalists in the North.

"I would not like to see him coming," he said of Kennedy. "It would be treating the Republic and its Six Counties equally and endorsing the status quo here."

The United Ireland Association in London sent a telegram to the American ambassador there, protesting the invitation to Kennedy from the North, saying it "is designed to endeavor to create a situation in which he could be represented as endorsing partition."

The Association of Old I.R.A. and *Cumann na mBan* in London blistered Macmillan for interfering "in the internal affairs of Ireland, and [we] repudiate his right to invite the president of the United States to any part of the 32 counties in Ireland."

The president also had received some protests from among the Republicans in Northern Ireland, urging him not to visit Ulster. For example, the Very Rev. Thomas Canon Maguire, of Newtownbutler in County Fermanagh, telegrammed the president to urge him to refuse any invitation to the North as long as the island remained divided, and to take advantage of his good relations with Macmillan to end partition.

The *Irish Times* in Dublin called Macmillan's invitation "uninspiring reading."

O'Neill's prestige was lessened by not handling his own invitations, the newspaper editorialized, but it added "it is no less to be deplored that ancestral voices (of which the Old I.R.A. is one) should immediately prophesy war."

"Surely President Kennedy is in a position to judge the weight of invitations; surely it is his own affair where he goes. If he wants to go to Antrim it is no business of anyone on this side of the border. One thing is quite certain: President Kennedy does not require to be coached on the status of Northern Ireland or our partition problem, and — despite any enthusiasm he may feel for the place where his roots are — it is most unlikely that he wants to involve himself in this problem. He has his own, and over here he will be on holiday. Moreover, as a naval man, the president may have grateful feelings for the use of the ports in Northern Ireland in the last World War. In any event, it is bad manners to complicate his visit by disputes which, as an American citizen, are no concern of his. It shows a sad lack of maturity if we cannot allow a visit to retain the quality of a visit. No guest is put at ease by family quarrels. Our critics say that we as a nation display a humourless lack of proportion to demonstrate our grievances. The Donneybrook Fair ghost should have been laid long since. Let us not raise it for the president. It is unlikely to appeal to a man of his experience."

Unbeknownst to Kennedy, some Nationalist members of Parliament in Northern Ireland wanted to raise partition with the president during his visit. They pressured Ireland's Department of External Affairs for a face-to-face meeting with Kennedy, as well as with Aiken, but they were rebuffed.

Kennedy was tactful in his answer to Northern Ireland.

"Thank you very much for your warm invitation to participate in the opening ceremony at the Giants' Causeway this June," the president wrote on May 5 to Captain O'Neill. "I appreciate your thought in this invitation and I regret to have to answer that the time available for my visit to Europe does not permit this additional stop."

A spokesman for O'Neill sought to put as much polish on the rejection as overstatement would allow: "The president obviously sent this very pleasant message directly to Mr. O'Neill so that he would receive it before he himself [the president] sent a reply via the British prime minister [through whom the six-county invitation was forwarded] or issued it through the State Department. President Kennedy's journey to Europe is obviously a rush trip, and no one, for example, seems to know how long he will be able to stay in Eire after his visit to Germany and Italy. We hope that he will, at some time in the future, be able to visit Northern Ireland, where he will receive a warm welcome."

This was a clear snub, said Cahir Healy, a Nationalist member of the British Parliament.

"I think the prime minister was foolish to send out the invitation in the first place," Healy added. "I think he did it on the spur of the moment without full consideration of the implications." In fact, O'Neill was 0-2 on official invitations to Northern Ireland. Canada's prime minister, Lester Pearson, also had declined politely.

The *Belfast Telegraph* shrugged that the invitation simply had been issued too late. No snub intended, the newspaper insisted, noting that Northern Ireland, as part of the United Kingdom, was allied with the United States in NATO.

Dublin politicians and newspapers took heart. Kennedy, as they saw it, was sending a strong signal that U.S. support for uniting Northern Ireland and the Irish Republic would get new impetus. Kennedy, the press pointed out, had made public statements opposing the partition of Ireland while he was in the Congress. And there was domestic politics to consider back home, Dublin's *Sunday Independent* was sure.

"For President Kennedy to go to the partitioned part of Ireland would be an act of political suicide so far as the great Irish-American vote in the United States is concerned," the paper opined.

"JFK Declines Invite to North," the *Irish Press* rejoiced across its front page.

From Stormont Castle in Belfast, O'Neill didn't seem to take offense.

In a chatty letter on May 6 to Kennedy, O'Neill told how Northern Ireland was working to save the ancestral homes of earlier presidents. They had located Chester A. Arthur's roots in Cullybackey, County Antrim, and Woodrow Wilson's in Strabane, County Tyrone. He said he hoped to send Mrs. Kennedy photographs of the restoration efforts.

Indeed, much was made then and later of Northern Ireland's ties to the White House. Arthur's father, William, indeed had left for America from Dreen, Cullybackey, in 1816; and Wilson's grandfather, James Wilson, had emigrated. Northern Ireland tracked down the tentacles to nine other presidents. Andrew Jackson's parents left Boneybefore, Carrickfergus, in County Antrim in 1765. James K. Polk's roots went back to his great-great-great grandfather who emigrated around 1680 from Coleraine, County Londonderry. James Buchanan's father left Deroran in County Tyrone. Andrew Johnson's grandfather was from Mounthill, Larne, County Antrim. Ulysses S. Grant's great-grandfather's home was in Dergina, County Tyrone; he had sailed to the United States around 1760. Grover Cleveland's maternal grandfather emigrated from County Antrim. Benjamin Harrison laid claim to two great-grandfathers from Ulster. William McKinley's great-great-grandfather departed for America about 1743 from Conagher in County Antrim. And Theodore Roosevelt's maternal ancestors were traced to Gleno, Larne, County Antrim.

O'Neill concluded his missive to Kennedy with a story from a visit he had made to Philadelphia three years earlier, when an elderly gentleman told him: "The Scotch-Irish own

America and the Southern Irish run it!" "I would point out," O'Neill quickly added, "that this was previous to your inauguration!"

Kennedy did not leave O'Neill's letter unanswered, as he might have. His reply thanked O'Neill for "the personal warmth" of the invitation to the North. The president said he was quite interested in the restoration of the ancestral homes of presidents.

"I hardly dare to comment on your amusing story about the relationship between the Scotch-Irish and the Southern Irish in the United States because it would seem unwise to transfer arguments about the ownership of Ireland to the larger area of this country, but I will say that we take pride in all the good Americans that have come out of all parts of Ireland and are grateful to you for your interest in this relationship," the president wrote.

Kennedy ended the letter with an intriguing invitation: "The next time you come to Washington, I hope you will let me know so that we can meet and have a talk."

The recriminations in Belfast continued for some days after President Kennedy's polite demurrer.

Diamond, on May 15 at Stormont, suggested the whole matter had been a political stunt by O'Neill.

The Northern Ireland prime minister insisted otherwise.

Captain O'Neill said he could have asked the American president to visit the NATO communications center in Derry (or, as the Unionists call it, Londonderry).

"I tried to show some statesmanship," O'Neill defended himself. "I could have asked him to visit the American Hall of Remembrance in the War Memorial Building in Belfast. Instead I specifically chose something entirely non-political and non-religious, so as not to give offense to his hosts in the South."

"Later perhaps . . ." the *Sunday Review* in Dublin editorialized about a Kennedy visit to Northern Ireland. "But we hope Captain O'Neill will be invited down to meet our distinguished guest." He would wait in vain for the envelope in the mail. Only the "nationally-minded opposition" were invited from Belfast to Dublin.

The whole matter "did seem inept," the *Irish Times* scolded. "It was an error of judgment to ask Mr. Macmillan to send out the invitation as if the entertainment in Northern Ireland was some sort of children's party; it was unseemly to appear to want to cash in on the natural jubilation in the Republic at the first visit of an active American president to Ireland. It was probably not intended to be dog in the manger; but it had the slightly faded air that all last-minute invitations have."

The already battered Macmillan did not escape the matter unscathed.

In the House of Commons on May 21, Labour party opponents considered it open season on the Tory prime minister.

"Has the prime minister," Labour's Emanuel Shinwell inquired, "not made a recent approach to President Kennedy for a meeting in view of the president's intention to visit Eire and, in this connection, if it is not strictly confidential, is it possible to inform the country what is happening? Is the prime minister, in his approach to President Kennedy, cooking up something in preparation for the next general election?"

Shinwell's Labour compatriots cheered him on. The government side was riddled with disdainful laughter.

"I think there is some confusion," Macmillan suggested. "At the request of the prime minister of Northern Ireland I transmitted — since we are responsible for the foreign relations of Northern Ireland — to the president an invitation from the prime minister of Northern Ireland to a ceremony at the Giant's Causeway, but the president regretted that he could not fit this into his program."

Shinwell persevered: "What was the purpose of the meeting taking place at the Giant's Causeway? Were the contemplated conversations of such secrecy that it was necessary to engage the Giant's Causeway for this purpose?" The House echoed with the delighted laughter of Macmillan's inquisitors.

The prime minister smiled.

"This was not a meeting I would attend," he said. More laughter.

"This was an invitation from the government of Northern Ireland," Macmillan reiterated, "who thought it might interest the president, while he was in Eire, to attend what I understand is to be a ceremony of some importance and, indeed, of an historic character, while he was there. He said, in reply, that he regretted he was not able to do so."

Labour got that. But this was too good to resist.

Emrys Hughes, of Independent Labour, took up the cudgel.

"Can the prime minister say whether he is just acting as a postman for the prime minister of Northern Ireland?" Hughes queried. "Does he not realize that President Kennedy is going to Ireland so that he can have a couple of days' rest in a decent, intelligent, and civilized country which has no missiles and no nuclear deterrent?"

Guffaws all around.

"And," Hughes added, "does the prime minister think that President Kennedy would really want to go to Ulster to take part in an Orange walk?"

Amid the hilarity, shouts of "Hear, hear!"

"Well, sir," Macmillan soldiered on, "I hope the president will have a nice time of rest — although, when I saw some of the figures of the preliminary program, it is always very difficult, indeed, to have a full rest. . . ."

But this idea that the prime minister would like a meeting with Kennedy so near the next election — surely he had heard of it, Labour pressed.

"All I can say," Macmillan answered, "is that a lot of very silly things are said, but in this case not only was the premise false, but the inference was also false."

And, of course, a meeting with Macmillan was added to the trip.

♣ ♣ ♣ ♣

In mid-May, Kennedy conducted some of his own advance work for Ireland, from a distance.

He agreed to participate in a program on Radio Eireann called "Meet the Clans."

"Ireland and the United States," Kennedy said, "are two nations tied by bonds of memory and affection, but we are drawn together not only by sentiments of the past but also by the challenges of the future."

Reminding listeners of what by now nearly every Irish citizen knew, that his great-grandparents on the Kennedy and Fitzgerald sides had left Ireland more than a century before, the president continued: "Perhaps it is less well known that we are related to other great Irish clans — my father's mother had as her maiden name Hickey, while my maternal grandmother, who is now ninety-seven, [is] Mary Hannon. I would therefore like to send special greetings to all those in Ireland who bear the family names — Kennedy, Fitzgerald, Hickey, and Hannon."

The radio message previewed some of the themes that would be elaborated on during his June visit.

"When my forebears crossed the Atlantic a century ago, the journey took six weeks or longer and the ocean was a wide and formidable barrier. Today a jet plane crosses the distance in six hours or less. Our two countries are near neighbors in the Atlantic community. Like all good neighbors we know that isolation affords neither safety nor prosperity.

"We work together to seek wider horizons of trade; we share our system and experiences in meeting the common problems of all people, evolving new industries and new technology, achieving jobs for our young, security for the old, and dignity for all.

"Our two countries work closely together at the United Nations and at the council tables of the world on behalf of man's urgent search for peace.

"I send cordial greetings to the men of the Irish Armed Forces who have braved danger in distant countries, not under an Irish flag to protect any selfish interest of Ireland, but under the flag of the United Nations to uphold an interest of all mankind — the safeguarding of peace. During the American Revolution, George Washington spoke, and I quote: 'Patriots of Ireland, champions of liberty in all lands, be strong in hope; your cause is identical to mine.'

"Now as Ireland and the United States look forward to the challenging years ahead, we can, in Washington's words, 'be strong in hope,' for now, as then, we know our cause is identical with that of all mankind."

♣ ♣ ♣ ♣

Preparations in Ireland speeded up as the arrival date of the president approached.

The biggest change in plans was announced on May 18. There was good news and bad news: the good news was that the presidential tour was to be expanded to four days, starting with his arrival on the evening of June 26 through his departure on June 29. The bad news was for the equestrian set: a Kennedy visit to the Irish Derby at the Curragh was not in the cards.

The Irish debated amongst themselves whether the welcoming carpet should be red or green.

Cork and Wexford, meanwhile, both decided Kennedy would be given the honor of being granted the freedom of their cities. On May 27, about two-thirds of the forty-five members of the Dublin Corporation gathered to vote for a resolution conferring upon Kennedy the freedom of their city "and that he be, and is hereby, elected and admitted to be an honorary burgess of the county borough of Dublin pursuant to the provisions of the Municipal Privileges Act, Ireland, 1876."

The competition for the president in Ireland seemed unending. As one city was gently let down, another would pop up. So it was, for example, that the small city of Ennis, in County Clare, put in a hopeful bid on May 29 — coincidentally, Kennedy's birthday. But Ennis wouldn't make the cut.

The leaders of New Ross, meanwhile, were a bit peeved that Kennedy's schedule for their town was so short. They appealed for more time with the president. After all, his connections with New Ross were a major reason for his trip. And they had tried to be reasonable. But American officials were adamant that what was scheduled was scheduled, and no more would be done.

On June 12, an American government Convair bearing five technicians began checking out the approaches to Dublin Airport, as well as its navigational aids. Nothing was left to chance.

The next day, four U.S. Army Sikorski H-34 helicopters, based in Verdun, France, arrived in Ireland and began flying practice runs to the cities and towns Kennedy would visit.

Army Chief Warrant Officer Oscar Johnson was one of the pilots of the Choctaws, as the choppers were known.

This was Johnson's first visit to Ireland, so he took advantage of his slow speed of seventy to eighty knots and his low altitude of five hundred to six hundred feet to soak up the scenery.

"They say there are forty shades of green in Ireland, and I believe it," he said.

The helicopters were quite a curiosity in 1963 rural Ireland.

"In most of the places we went, people would just come and gather around," Johnson recalled. "It was kind of hard to keep them away."

The same day the helicopters arrived, Salinger flew into Shannon Airport to survey Cork and Galway for final arrangements. He celebrated his thirtieth birthday with a lunch hosted by Ambassador McCloskey at Bunratty Castle.

Limerick's lord mayor was at the ready at Shannon, and again at Bunratty, to encourage Salinger to put her city on the official itinerary.

"I am keeping my fingers crossed," Mrs. Condell said.

Salinger promised to convey her invitation to the president, but he didn't hold out much hope.

Other than Limerick's limbo, the schedule of the presidential tour in Ireland was set on June 14: Dublin the first evening, complete with a motorcade through the city; New Ross, Dunganstown, and Wexford, then back to Dublin on the second day; Cork on the morning of the third day, to be followed in the afternoon by a presidential address to the Dail and the conferring of honorary degrees by National University and Trinity College; and finally, on the last day, a swing to Galway and a departure from Shannon Airport.

How long would the visit to Cork be? reporters asked Salinger. About one and a half hours, he replied.

"Two hours," joked Alderman Sean Casey, Cork's lord mayor.

Cork was added by the president, Salinger volunteered. "He gave no reason," the press secretary added, but he pointed out the Fitzgerald wing of the family had connections to the area.

Five days after her talk with Salinger, Condell got upsetting news: Kennedy couldn't squeeze Limerick onto the schedule. The lord mayor said she was "very disappointed." On top of that, there were reports that officials in County Clare were unwilling to allow Condell to come to Shannon to confer the freedom of Limerick on Kennedy. County Clare subsequently denounced the reports as "completely untrue."

Then, three days after getting bad news, on June 21, a dramatic reversal: sweet victory, Limerick was on. It would be shoehorned between Galway and Shannon. No time for a motorcade through the city. Green Park Race Course was settled upon as the ideal presidential drop-in spot. He would swoop in by helicopter for a half-hour. The mayor ordered up the construction of a ceremonial platform at the course and set about having a proper silver box, or casket as it was called, to hold Kennedy's scroll proclaiming him a freeman of Limerick. "We are trying to put a month's work into a week," Mrs. Condell informed. But this was not a complaint.

Kilduff revealed four decades later that the Limerick stop was never in doubt. "It was always written into the schedule," he said. The White House didn't tell Condell out of fears that she would take over the president's day in western Ireland. "She wanted him to go to this school and that school," Kilduff explained. As it was, the Limerick visit was made official too late for government printers: it had to be typed on slips of paper and stapled to the official schedules handed out by the White House and the Irish government.

Back at the White House, an entourage assembled comprising nearly every staffer who could claim Irish blood. Some fifty people were to fly directly to Ireland on a government jet. "Oh, the Irish all wanted to go to Ireland," David Powers's assistant Lenny Donnelly said. The White House still had to run, but the president wanted as many Irish staffers as possible to join him, to share the experience of seeing their ancestral homeland.

On June 17, Ambassador Kiernan dropped by the White House to assure the president that the "green carpet" was being rolled out for him. Kennedy told the envoy he had great expectations for his trip.

The president had dived into his homework for the Irish leg of his European tour. Kennedy, O'Donnell and Powers remembered, "read Irish histories, traced the lineage of the Kennedys and the Fitzgeralds, studied the writings of John Boyle O'Reilly and the exploits of the Irish Brigade in the American Civil War. . . ."

"I guarantee," Salinger boasted to an Irish journalist, "that the president will surprise you guys with his knowledge of Irish history."

Another Washington official told the same writer: "Here we are, briefing this man, giving him everything we've got on Ireland, trying to forestall every query he might have, and knowing all the time he probably has ten times as much information on Ireland as we'll ever have, at his fingers' ends."

"He's getting so Irish," Powers quipped, "the next thing we know he'll be speaking with a brogue."

One day, Powers showed the president the Kennedy family tree and its roots back to the Gaelic origin of his name, Cinneide, which translates to, among other things, "helmet head."

"Let's keep that quiet," the president jokingly insisted.

In New Ross, all was being readied for Kennedy. Details of exactly what was happening when were to be filled in.

"We're adhering rigidly to the schedule," said one urban councilor, "until we know what it is."

On June 18, an American flag donated by the Troy, N.Y., division of the Ancient Order of Hibernians was handed over to Andrew Minihan, chairman of the New Ross Urban Council, by Ronnie Delany, a 1956 Olympic champion and now sales officer with Aer Lingus. The flag would fly over a local municipal building called the Tholsel during Kennedy's visit.

There was grumbling about how arrangements were coming together — that is, the president wasn't being given enough time among the people he had come to see. Surely he didn't want all this hopping about.

"I'm sure," resident Sean Doyle declared at one meeting, "the president's plans would not at all be what they will be."

Have mercy on our American guest, "Well-Wisher" from Cork pleaded in the *Irish Press*.

"If it is not too late," said the writer, "could I appeal to the government, local authorities, newspapermen and people generally to refrain from putting President Kennedy to the trouble of making more speeches than are absolutely necessary — merely for our own glorification.

The *New York Journal-American,* Friday, June 28, 1963

"The attitude of certain local councils is especially lamentable. They are obviously motivated solely by the idea of getting publicity for their own areas. The big thing is that the president will be here in Ireland — among his friends."

Tensions in the Irish government, meanwhile, were running high, and it had little to do with Kennedy's visit and a lot to do with domestic politics. Lemass was facing a critical vote on a sales tax. Many believed he would lose and be forced to step down just as Kennedy's visit unfolded.

Political opponents were bristling at the paucity of information about Kennedy's tour and, specifically, about how the Parliament would proceed in welcoming the president.

Lemass told his colleagues discussions already were underway in a parliamentary committee. Not so, protested a Labour party member. "There will be," Lemass sought to reassure him.

When supposedly secret, almost minute-by-minute details of plans for Kennedy's appearance before the Parliament suddenly appeared in the *Irish Press,* a Dublin paper friendly to the Fianna Fail party headed by Lemass (the paper, not incidentally, was founded by de Valera) and referred to by opposition leaders in Fine Gael as "the government newspaper," there was a furor in the Dail. Opponents wondered, during question time on June 18, whether there had been some kind of government leak. No, there had not, Lemass insisted. There was talk about a possible investigation of the leak, but it was mostly for effect. One member of the opposition suggested Lemass was attempting to make a political stunt of Kennedy's upcoming trip. "You were trying to make Kennedy a Fianna Fail candidate," accused another.

Two days later, tempers flared again, as critics denounced Lemass for his "audacity" in allegedly leaking the schedule. Nevertheless, by day's end, the prime minister and the opposition joined in the motion formally inviting Kennedy to address a joint session of the Houses of the *Oireachtas* (ur-yak-tass) in the Dail chamber.

Efforts to gauge the importance of Kennedy's trip to Ireland stretched the abilities of some journalists in that nation to the extremes. The *Cork Weekly Examiner,* for example, called the upcoming presidential tour the greatest visit by a public figure since St. Patrick landed.

The American press for the most part whimsically viewed Kennedy's upcoming tour in Ireland as something personal, a touching of the ancestral base, as it were.

"The Ireland leg, of course, is a sentimental one," the *Washington Sunday Star* opined.

The notion that the Irish portion of Kennedy's European tour was the least serious was encouraged by White House aides, both before and during the visit, despite the president's obvious intentions to lay down some new markers in the relationship between the United States and Ireland.

"Germany was business. But Ireland is fun," one presidential aide would say in the course of Kennedy's Irish travels.

In truth, as the date for departure approached, the entire European enterprise was viewed with skepticism in the American media and among the president's critics and political opponents. In West Germany, aging Chancellor Konrad Adenauer was merely marking time until his successor, Vice-Chancellor Ludwig Erhard, would take over in the autumn. In England, Macmillan's government was reeling with War Minister John Profumo's admission that he had shared a consort named Christine Keeler with a Soviet naval attaché. In Italy, Premier Amintore Fanfani's government, which had invited Kennedy, had fallen, replaced by yet another in the endless procession of post-World War II administrations, headed, until the next time that was sure to come soon, by Giovanni Leone. At the Vatican, where Kennedy also would visit, Pope John XXIII had only recently died, replaced by Pope Paul VI on June 21.

At home, Kennedy's administration had just unveiled its new civil rights plan aimed at addressing long-ignored needs of the nation's blacks — a plan received by a heavily skeptical Congress — while frustration erupted in clashes between police and demonstrators in Savannah, Georgia; Gadsden, Alabama; Cambridge, Maryland; and Harlem in New York City. Indeed, racial tensions were further heightened with the June 12 assassination of Medgar Evers, Mississippi field secretary of the National Association for the Advancement of Colored People. The president met at the White House on June 22 with thirty civil rights leaders, led by Dr. Martin Luther King, Jr., to discuss the plans for a civil rights march on Washington in August. (The day before, eight restaurants in Prince George's County, Maryland, outside Washington, agreed for the first time to begin serving blacks.)

"Not Necessary, But Nice," read a headline in *Time* magazine. "Off in a Cloud," was the line over the trip in rival *Newsweek*. The *National Observer* called the venture Kennedy's "planned but apparently pointless trip."

"Cancel that trip," the *New York Times* advised.

The Republicans, including Arizona's Sen. Barry Goldwater, the 1964 presidential hopeful, were quick to question Kennedy's overseas plans.

Beyond any political or policy matters was an American unease about chief executives jetting around the globe. After all, in 1963, the majority of Americans still had never set foot in an airplane.

"Americans were still a little uncertain whether the president could run the country when he was abroad," explained Jerald F. terHorst, who covered the White House for the *Detroit News* and went on the Europe trip.

It is a charming notion, that the people of one of the world's superpowers could afford to be so insular. But for a large number, life was good and the rest of the planet was extremely remote. The New York Stock Exchange was at 720.78 on the Dow Jones Industrial Average; people could buy portable televisions for $100; Kennedy's beloved Boston Red Sox were trailing their arch-rivals, the New York Yankees, by four games; Morris L. West's *Shoes of the Fisherman* was on the best-seller list; "Lassie," "The Ed Sullivan Show," and "Hawaiian Eye" were among the nightly television fare on the three commercial networks; *Lawrence of Arabia, The Birds,* and *How the West Was Won* were drawing movie theater crowds, soon to be captivated by Elizabeth Taylor and Richard Burton in *Cleopatra.* The latter spectacle would have competition with the release of a film about a World War II hero named Kennedy, called *PT 109.*

Kennedy was not discouraged about criticism of his trip and would not be deterred. He told Eamonn Andrews, the chairman of the Radio Eireann Authority who was visiting Washington, that he had no intention of changing his plans and looked forward to the Ireland leg. Andrews met with Kennedy, as well as with Salinger, on the very day the *New York Times* editorial appeared.

European problems could not be resolved by Kennedy immediately, a sympathetic analyst observed: "What he can do is to re-establish the presidency of the United States in a position of world leadership — and, in that context, even the sentimental visit to Ireland seems more appropriate, for in his visit to Ireland, the president underlines the European and insular origins of most of the people of America."

Kennedy himself was determined to deliver in person his vision of a U.S.-backed Western alliance in Europe, both vigilant against the Soviets and ready to pursue new openings to a more secure peace.

The olive branch he offered the Soviets in his American University speech on June 10, in which he stated his desire to "make the world safe for diversity," needed to be followed up and reinforced by being seen and heard in Europe, Kennedy believed. Moreover, many problems afflicting leaders in Italy and Germany were rooted in American policies towards Europe, so it was more than appropriate for him to help alleviate those leaders' concerns.

McGeorge Bundy was concerned enough about the criticism of the tour that he asked the United States Information Agency to assist in putting together "reasons for the president's trip to Europe." The somber and respected former CBS reporter Edward R. Murrow, brought into the USIA by Kennedy, dictated the key points: Kennedy could articulate U.S. policy regarding Europe more effectively there than in Washington; Kennedy's presence would provide reassurance that American interest in the region hadn't abated because of efforts to find accommodations with the Soviet Union or the ongoing frustrations with France's Charles de Gaulle; the timing of the trip with new governments actually was perfect, allowing Kennedy to have an impact before "policies [were] fixed and prejudices solidified"; touching base with Macmillan was important before the test ban talks in Moscow; Germany was to undergo its first leadership change since the end of World War II and Kennedy would have a chance to consult with Erhard before his taking office; Italy should be encouraged to continue its support of the U.S.-led Western alliance; and, Kennedy would have gone to France but "he wasn't invited."

Eire required no explanation from Murrow.

"Any reporter who doesn't know why the president is going to Ireland," he said, "should turn in his typewriter."

One reporter actually found administration officials who were trying to put some substance on the Ireland portion of the trip — whether this was an afterthought was impossible to tell — the gist of which was that trade between Ireland and the United States, as well as between those countries and the Common Market, would be an important topic.

Skeptical reporters who didn't believe Kennedy's tour would happen had delayed getting their inoculations for Europe — a requirement in those days. Now they were scrambling.

On a hot and muggy Sunday, Air Force One left Andrews Air Force Base outside Washington, winging eastward. Ahead was a ten-day, 12,250-mile journey packed with twenty-five speeches. It was Kennedy's eighth and longest foreign journey. In there somewhere was JFK's "pleasure trip" to Ireland.

three

June 27, 1963:

New Ross, Dunganstown, Wexford, and Dublin

That's Parnell himself that's passed, he said,
  when the cheering had subsided.
Ireland's greatest son.
I'd sell me hat,
  I'd sell me horse an' cab,
  I'd sell meself for him, be Jasus,
  I'd nearly sell me soul, if he beckoned me to do it.

Sean O'Casey
I Knock at the Door *(1939)*

For a supposedly sentimental visit that got passing mention in the weeks before, Kennedy's Ireland stop suddenly was front-page news back home. "JFK Wows 'Em in Eire," read the Page One banner in the *Washington Daily News* this day. Having a little fun with the president, an editorial cartoon inside showed an Irish woman holding up her child to meet Kennedy. "Say Hello to Your Cousin Jack," said the woman in the cartoon. The child was drawn as a miniature of Kennedy, with a toothy smile just like the president's. And everyone in the crowd behind wore identical Kennedy grins, teeth flashing.

The front page of the *New York Mirror,* one of the largest newspapers in the United States at the time, carried a photo of Kennedy's car working its way through Dublin. "Wild Over JFK. Tears of Joy in Eire," the paper trumpeted. "Kennedy Scores . . . In Dublin . . . In Berlin," read the bold black headline in the *Los Angeles Times*. Back in the president's hometown, the *Boston Evening Globe* would be on the streets in time to hit the newsstands outside the subway stations telling about his visit later in the day to Dunganstown. "'Sentimental Journey' Elates JFK," the *Globe* would report. *Newsday,* on New York's Long Island, would win best headline for wordplay on this day: "Kennedy Takes Breath of Eire."

The *Irish Independent* greeted Kennedy in proper Irish with a huge headline: *"Céad Míle Fáilte."*

Sybil Connolly, the Irish designer, overheard one European ambassador say: "It is the conquering Alexander returning to his people."

The president rose early and felt the exertions of the previous days in his back: the travel, long hours on his feet talking and shaking hands, the speech-making, the standing in open cars waving — all were taking a toll.

Kennedy's chronic back trouble was public lore by 1963. Yet it also was true that his back generally had been feeling better in this year than it had for a long time.

Prime Minister Lemass, arriving a half hour late, met with Kennedy at the U.S. Embassy on this morning of the Irish trip and noticed the president's obvious discomfort.

". . . As he came down the stairs, I noticed he came fairly heavily," the prime minister said, ". . . as if he had some difficulty in walking down, whereas normally he liked to give the appearance of being agile and light-footed."

The president, of course, never complained of his ailments in public. In private, with close friends, staff, and other world leaders, he sometimes would excuse himself briefly to take a break.

But there was little time for pause in Ireland.

The fifty-minute conversation between the president and the mustachioed, pipe-smoking prime minister was wide-ranging.

Kennedy started off congratulating Lemass on a recent victory enacting a general sales tax, called a turnover tax, a move the Lemass government felt was absolutely essential to improve social services.

It is not recorded whether the two men chuckled about Kennedy's joke the day before, but Lemass had barely avoided the collapse of his government on the eve of the presidential visit. The 2.5 percent sales tax proposal was a hotly debated matter in the Parliament. If Lemass hadn't prevailed, it would have amounted to a no-confidence vote and he would have been forced to step down. But when it had come time to vote, the night before Kennedy landed in Dublin, two independents joined with the seventy members of Lemass's Fianna Fail party to pass the tax, 72-71. It was the same vote by which Lemass had been chosen Taoiseach eighteen months before.

In his talks with Kennedy, the Irish leader revealed a little strategy: the outcome really had been predetermined, and the opposition was allowed to pad the negative votes only after it was clear the government would prevail by one vote for the required majority.

The discussion then turned to Ireland's economy in general. Lemass said the country wasn't doing too badly: the annual increase in production was about four percent, although agriculture accounted for better than a third of that. As important as agriculture was to Ireland, Lemass believed it played too much a central role in driving the economy. On another positive note, Ireland's population was increasing a little, the prime minister noted.

The defeat of Ireland's application in 1961 to the European Economic Community, also known as the Common Market , was a disappointment, Lemass said, because it would have given Ireland greater access to new markets, instead of relying on the English market for seventy-five percent of its total exports — primarily livestock and other agricultural products. With England and Ireland in the Common Market, Irish farmers would have better prices for their goods, Lemass maintained.

Lemass characterized relations with England as harmonious. When Kennedy asked what would happen if Ireland pressed for admission to the Common Market on its own, the Irish leader insisted that would not be desirable, indicating the British likely would rewrite trade agreements in ways that would be less favorable to Ireland. The general assumption in Dublin, Lemass said, was that Common Market membership would be a reality by 1970. Kennedy was a bit more optimistic, saying a change in government in London might precipitate earlier admission, perhaps in 1966 or 1967.

Earlier in the year, External Affairs Minister Aiken had suggested to Ambassador

McCloskey that the United States should try to set up a meeting involving the United States, Britain, and France in an effort to end French objections to England's entry into the Common Market. Secretary of State Rusk, however, was cool to the proposal, saying success wasn't likely and that such a conference might end up offending other Common Market members.

Talk between Kennedy and Lemass turned to NATO. Ireland, of course, was neutral — though at one point Lemass emphasized the neutrality was more symbolic than real. Ireland, Lemass reviewed, had been unable to join the alliance because of the Northern Ireland situation. In essence, Irish political leaders considered it an untenable position to agree to a military partnership with Britain while that country persisted in its claims to the six counties. Partition, not addressed by Kennedy in public, occupied a significant part of the discussion between the two leaders.

Interestingly, Ireland had been assisting American efforts to keep Soviet offensive weapons out of Cuba. The Irish had been checking all aircraft from the Soviet bloc nations going through Shannon Airport. At the time of Kennedy's visit, such searches still were being conducted. The Irish wanted to end the checks, but the United States had persuaded them to keep conducting them.

Kennedy updated Lemass on U.S. efforts to secure nuclear test bans and nonproliferation agreements, and went into considerable detail about American military and political strategy in Europe, arguing that an answer to the common defense of the region needed to be found, even as it balanced competing European interests. Kennedy was trying to convince the Europeans that a sea-based force manned by NATO crews, their ships armed with nuclear missiles, was the most prudent response to the Soviet threat from medium-range ballistic missiles. The United States retained the authority to decide whether to use the weapons, a political problem in itself among NATO allies. The alternative of basing medium-range missiles in Germany presented all manner of other political complications on both sides of the Iron Curtain in Europe and would provoke higher anxieties in Moscow, the American government was sure.

France and its president were also discussed. It was de Gaulle who had played a major role in blocking England, and thus Ireland, from entering the Common Market, and he differed vehemently with U.S. views on military policy and European defense. Kennedy lamented to Lemass the lack of free and open discussion with the French leader about nuclear issues. And, despite the publicly chilly reception de Gaulle was giving Kennedy's European tour, the American president told Lemass he wanted to find a way to restore good relations with the French. Kennedy emphasized the United States was not trying to isolate or antagonize de Gaulle, but it appeared France's president just was in no mood to talk with Washington at the moment.

Ireland's participation in the Congo peacekeeping effort came in for praise from

Kennedy. The mission illustrated a larger point the president would elaborate on in his appearance before the Irish parliament the next day. "The president," the White House summary of the session with Lemass related, "said that the fact that Ireland was a small country, and officially neutral but dedicated to the interests and objectives of the West, conferred a considerable importance on her role."

The talk ended without fanfare or a press conference, unlike the custom of today. The two leaders briefly accommodated the photographers, but declined to reveal any details of their session.

Indeed, the substance of the discussion was hardly revealed to the public, and the White House notes of the session were kept classified for years. The *Irish Independent* speculated that Lemass may have discussed, among other subjects, "ending emigration, unemployment and partition."

The absence of substantive inquiry into the meeting seems all the more odd because of the significance that it held for the Irish government. Diplomatic historian Ian McCabe later wrote that Kennedy's talk with Lemass "was the highlight of the visit" for Dublin. "It represented," he said, "public acknowledgement that Ireland had been accepted back into the western fold despite the 'rejection' of NATO and military neutrality."

Forty years later, former White House assistant press secretary Malcolm Kilduff, who made all the advance press arrangements for Kennedy's trip, said there was a reason for not holding a news conference: partition.

"They didn't want the press bringing it up," Kilduff explained, referring to both the American and Irish sides.

The *Detroit News*'s Jerald terHorst and his fellow reporters were frustrated. "We had a heck of a time trying to find out anything that happened," he remembered years later. "We had a hard time making good copy. We were writing travelogues."

Tom Wicker, a *New York Times* reporter covering the trip, recalled that Salinger "did the press secretary's job very well," which was essentially to keep the press at arm's length or more from the president.

"Salinger, in his typical way, said he would keep us 'informed.' Of course, all these years later, I know better," Wicker said.

In truth, Kennedy's meeting with Lemass wasn't viewed by American reporters as material for good copy. Many were there because they hoped to have as much fun in Ireland as the president did. Wicker was asleep in a hotel room the night before the flight to Ireland when he was awakened by a telephone call. Sidney Gruson, the *Times*'s London bureau chief, needed a favor. "Can you get me on the press plane to Ireland?" he asked Wicker. Gruson had not been assigned to cover the Irish portion of Kennedy's European tour. "Oh, I can't manage that," Wicker recalled apologizing. The next day, when Wicker landed in Ireland, there was Sidney Gruson.

Among the opposition to Lemass in the Irish Parliament, the meeting with Kennedy aroused suspicions.

A Labour party member of the Dail, S. Coughlan, asked Lemass on the Tuesday after Kennedy's departure whether the possibility of American or NATO military bases in Ireland was discussed.

Lemass, of course, set the matter at rest with an answer "in the negative," as he put it.

♣ ♣ ♣ ♣

Kennedy was impatient to get on to Dunganstown. The day before, as he was approaching Dublin, he had asked O'Donnell about the schedule.

"Kenny, how soon will we be going back to see my cousins in Dunganstown?" the president inquired.

"Tomorrow," O'Donnell assured him. "They'll be all there waiting for you with a big spread of salmon and tea."

And now the day had come.

At 10:30 a.m., Kennedy's helicopter lifted off from the grounds of the American Embassy. His aircraft flew over the countryside at fifteen hundred feet, giving the president a chance to see the squared-off farmland and woodlands, punctuated occasionally by the bulk of a castle. He passed the Powerscourt waterfall, then crossed the Dublin and Wicklow Mountains and headed out over rolling country.

It had been raining in Dublin, but by the time Kennedy covered the roughly seventy miles to New Ross and hovered over Gaelic Field, the skies had broken a bit.

Among those who made the trip this day was Sinead Bean de Valera, the eighty-year-old, white-haired, erudite wife of the Irish president. And, of course, the president was with family: sisters Eunice Shriver and Jean Smith, and sister-in-law Princess Lee Radziwell.

The Irish, like most Americans, had never seen such an arrival. First came two helicopters carrying American and Irish reporters. About a half hour later, four more helicopters roared in, bearing more reporters, as well as White House security and some of Kennedy's aides. Then, about five minutes later, at last, the lone white-and-green helicopter of the president thundered into view.

As he approached his landing spot, America's chief executive saw children from the Christian Brothers School sprawled across the grass of Sean O'Kennedy Soccer Field (not named for JFK, but for a star of the Irish sport of hurling), their bodies, dressed in white and black, forming the word "*fáilte*."

But the rotor wash of the military helicopters was stronger than local planners anticipated: as Kennedy's chopper got closer to the ground, debris began to pelt the children and onlookers. The debris was, in fact, cow patties, which flew in the downdraft "like frisbees," as Kilduff later recalled. A lot of the kids were spattered.

"I hope you had nothing to do with this," Kennedy told Kilduff, who assured his boss he hadn't. The president couldn't contain his laughter at the scene, but he composed himself before alighting from the helicopter.

The president also had roared in delight at a debriefing Kilduff had given him as they approached New Ross. The centerpiece of the debriefing was Kilduff's previous encounter with Andrew Minihan, head of the New Ross Urban Council.

During his advance work for the trip, Kilduff told Kennedy, he had made a lot of demands of Minihan, asking for various changes and improvements that would help bring the president's visit off smoothly. When Minihan and Kilduff had reached the quay where Kennedy would speak, Kilduff calculated where the presidential limousine would stop to allow the president to get easily up to the speakers' platform. At about the right spot, Kilduff spotted a large pile of manure, awaiting shipment downriver to a processing plant.

"You're going to have to remove that pile of dung," Kilduff told Minihan.

Why? the New Ross leader wanted to know.

Kilduff explained that the manure just wouldn't be the right thing to have around for a presidential stop.

Minihan furrowed his brow.

"Remove it?" he exclaimed. "Christ now, I'm going to pile it twice as high and make that fucker think he's crossing the Alps."

"I don't think so," said the unflappable Kilduff, "not if you want the president here."

"Oh, all right," Minihan surrendered.

Upon hearing this story, Kennedy couldn't wait to get out of the helicopter.

On the ground, Kennedy was greeted by schoolchildren carrying American flags. A Dublin military school band played "For Boston," the victory song of Boston College.

Kennedy began shaking the hands of local leaders, beginning with Gerald Donovan, vice-chairman of the New Ross Urban Council. The president reached Minihan and greeted him warmly: "I've heard all about you, Mr. Minihan."

Minihan beamed.

Kennedy asked how well advance arrangements had worked out with Kilduff in charge.

"We've been getting along," Minihan assured Kennedy, adding, "well, famously, you might say."

Kennedy moved closer to Minihan: "Did you get all the manure picked up, or are you going to make this fucker think he's crossing the Alps?"

Minihan's smile fled. He blanched and nearly sank to the ground.

"Mr. President, I meant no disrespect," he stammered. He turned to Kilduff. "Mr. Kilduff, you shouldn't have told your man this." Back to Kennedy. "I hope you'll accept my apology."

Kennedy was laughing. "Nothing to apologize for," he insisted. "But did you remove all that so I won't have to cross the Alps?"

"It's all taken care of," Minihan said.

Donovan issued the formal welcome: "May I say, on behalf of New Ross and County Wexford, that we are honored, proud, and happy to welcome the president of the U.S.A., the leader of the free world. But I am sure the people of Wexford would like me to say to you that they have a special welcome for you as John Fitzgerald Kennedy, the great-grandson of our own Patrick Kennedy."

Ambassador McCloskey for some reason was anti-musical this day.

"Now I don't want any singing at the ceremony, understand?" he told Minihan.

Minihan turned to Kennedy: "Mr. President, would you like to hear some songs?"

"I'd love to," the president replied. Minihan cued the choirs near the platform.

Some of the children burst into song, serenading the president with his favorites, "Kelly the Boy from Killane," and "The Boys of Wexford." Asked by the nun directing the children if he would like to hear another selection, Kennedy answered: "Another verse of 'The Boys of Wexford' would be just fine."

Suddenly, Kennedy asked twelve-year-old Maura Hendrick, one of the schoolgirls, if he

At the Gaelic Field in New Ross on June 27, Kennedy reaches to the throng of mostly schoolchildren, with whom he sings. He appears to be holding a sheet of lyrics, not his speech, which is to come after a motorcade through town.

might borrow her paper slip with the words typed on it, and then he joined in the singing, as he directed the delighted children.

There was a reason Kennedy didn't normally sing in public. "He had a lousy voice for singing," recalled terHorst, a good judge, as he served as head of Washington's Gridiron Club, a tight circle of press people who annually staged satirical-political musicales for the president and select guests. "He could barely carry a tune. It was a gravelly monotone, not a baritone," he said. In Ireland, Kennedy pressed on, unembarrassed. The Irish savored every monotonal moment.

Officials tried in vain to truncate the singing to keep the president on schedule. Kennedy kept singing, the children enraptured. Eunice Shriver thought the whole reception was "beautiful."

As the music faded, Kennedy put the slip of paper in his pocket. He worked his way along a reception line of the young people, touching as many of the hands reaching out to him as he could. Pipe bands played, while dogs barked and howled.

In this nearly nine-hundred-year-old town of about forty-five hundred souls, three churches, sixty-five agents to take bets on sporting events, and an identical number of pubs (opened four hours early this day), a placid place through which farmers often drove their cattle, there were now some fifeen thousand people crowded into the narrow streets — about the population of the town at the time the Famine struck twelve decades before. Kennedy's motorcade crept down Mountgarret, College Road, John Street, North Street, and Quay Street. Surrounding him were centuries of Irish history: ruins of the old town walls, built in 1256; Three Bullet Gate, so named because Cromwell, in calling for the town's surrender, fired three shots into it; the ruins of a medieval parish church; and the Tholsel, center of town life, a graceful building dating to 1749 topped by a later-period cupola. Finally, Kennedy's car rolled to a stop at what is simply called the Quay.

The four-man pool of reporters, whose job it was to stay closest to Kennedy and be the eyes and ears for the hundred or so correspondents traveling with the president, had drawn a friendly driver who wanted to talk about the weather. The pressmen urged him to try to keep up with Kennedy's car. Meanwhile, James Rowley, head of the Secret Service, briefly was barred by Irish police from getting into his car. Security, you know. After some words, the misunderstanding was resolved, though Rowley was furious.

Up on a stage facing the quay from which the president's great-grandfather had left 115 years before, the podium was decked in green cloth and surrounded by vases of flowers. The "hot line" phone to Washington sat on a fancy little table near the platform steps. Among the throngs, signs read: *"Céad míle fáilte a Seán"* and some referred to Kennedy as "our 35th president." Among those on the platform, buffeted by a strong wind, were Irish Minister of External Affairs Aiken, U.S. Ambassador McCloskey, Clonmel Mayor Michael Kilkelly, Waterford Mayor Thomas Brennan, Kilkenny Mayor P. Kinsella, the Right Reverend Dr.

McAdoo, bishop of Ossory, and Msgr. J. Browne of New Ross. Dorothy Tubridy introduced Kennedy's sisters and sister-in-law to the wives of the local officials.

There was, Minihan made sure, no shortage of music. The Artane Boys' Band, a pipe band, a *ceili* band, a brass band, a male chorus, and the aforementioned children's chorus all serenaded Kennedy. The president requested "Grainvaile," a sixteenth century Irish ballad about a pirate named Grace O'Malley. The Loc Garman Brass Band played a new piece composed by member Jim Bolger, also a member of the Radio Eireann Light Orchestra, entitled "The Kennedy March."

The New Ross Holy Rosary Confraternity Band struck up "The Star-Spangled Banner."

Minihan, fifty-two, tall, balding, and sporting a reddish-gray beard, presided over the ceremonies. White House Press Secretary Pierre Salinger called Minihan "the most unforgettable character I ever met on an advance trip." Minihan, from Skibbereen in County Cork, had lived in Scotland before coming to New Ross in 1925. He ran for office in 1955,

"We are as one today": Andrew Minihan, the balding and bearded head of the New Ross Urban Council (at far left), listens to Kennedy, speaking on the quay from which his great-grandfather left for America. The president's sisters, Jean Kennedy Smith (in checked jacket) and Eunice Kennedy Shriver (second from right with back to camera), and his sister-in-law Princess Lee Radziwell (in the same row, between the sisters and two unidentified women), enjoy the humorous reception.

winning his seat on the council and, at the same time — this, surely, a testament to the force of his personality — the chairmanship. The father of six, who was fascinated with archaeology and read history, also was vice-chairman of the New Ross Harbor Commissioners and a member of the Wexford County Council. He came to be known as the best small-town politician in Ireland.

"We'll put on no frills or fancies for your young man," Minihan, whose company manufactured concrete mixers, told Salinger on his advance visit to New Ross. "He'll see us exactly as we are."

Indeed, there were reports of resentment in New Ross toward advice from the Irish Club of Chicago, which had helpfully suggested by letter that the village be well-scoured for the presidential visit. Some shopkeepers nevertheless made the most of the historic visit to spruce up. Kennedy's drape shop took a fresh coat of baby-blue paint, while down the block Gus O'Kennedy's radio store shined in canary yellow.

"I could use a dozen more men, if I could get them," the local painting contractor, James Stacey, complained in the days before the visit. "Twice last week I had to send to Dublin for more paint. I don't know what we'll do for work the next two years, so many places have been painted this past month."

One storefront across from the town hall displayed a large poster, bearing Kennedy's portrait, from the 1960 presidential campaign.

Some matters needed more attention that had to wait: motorists on the fragile bridge over the River Barrow — the sixth since the town's founding in the twelfth century — were limited to three miles per hour for fear the old structure would collapse.

Souvenirs were thick in the shops. Fifty cents could fetch a model of the Kennedy homestead, roofed in thatch. They were selling like "wildfire," reported Claire Kiely, who was peddling the little buildings alongside the cigarettes and candy in her shop. "I know the homestead actually has a corrugated iron roof," she apologized, "but I can't help it if the people make the model this way."

Minihan had skirmished with many to preserve his prerogatives. Not even the United States Secret Service intimidated him.

"Just listen to the bloody thunder," he said, referring to the fuss over presidential arrangements. "We will be the center of the universe for a few hours," he said, "and when the president leaves, the center of the universe will switch back to Rome and we'll be on about our business."

A problem arose when Minihan informed the president's security detail that the welcoming party would include the wives of town officials. And a marching band would be right next to the speaker's platform. The Secret Service wanted the stand moved back about five feet, the wives left out, and the marching band muffled. Minihan threatened to cancel all the festivities. The Secret Service surrendered.

Besides his political skills, Minihan applied what he knew from two decades in the FSA (Forsa Cosanta Aitiuil), the Irish defense forces. He put a fellow FSA member, Mike Fleming, in charge of arrangements in Dunganstown.

All this made Minihan the character-to-go-to for news reporters before and during the trip. Joked one citizen who knew Minihan well: "You'd think to hear him that he'd not only kissed the Blarney Stone but that he'd slept with the thing."

Town officials, as might be expected, were inundated with claims of Kennedy blood ties. The executive decision: the cutoff would be after third cousins.

Minihan spoke officially to the president as the ceremonies opened. Or tried to speak. The public address system was proving unreliable.

"Can you hear me?" an angry Minihan asked. When the crowd replied in the negative, Minihan turned red. "Oh, we're in trouble now. Some of the pressmen have walked on the cables," he huffed. "This will be a terrible anticlimax." Kennedy was greatly amused, laughing aloud with his hosts — other than Minihan — at the hitch in the proceedings.

As it was later learned, the Secret Service was worried about the routing of the wiring from a battery powering the address system to the stage, and, concerned it might be part of a bomb device, had unplugged it. The Secret Service had received an anonymous phone call in Wexford threatening Kennedy, but it turned out to be nothing.

The Secret Service needn't have worried. When Ambassador McCloskey asked Minihan why there didn't appear to be many policemen near the platform, the chairman reassured him. "They're all police out there," said Minihan, who had deployed a phalanx of plainclothes police around the podium. The officers all knew each other and therefore would have spotted an intruder.

The crowd took up the chant, "Ken-ne-dy, Ken-ne-dy!"

"Can ye hear me now?" Minihan bellowed. "Yes!" his countrymen shouted back. "Now we've got the pitch," he said in a satisfied air.

"I have heard the president speak before," Minihan told his fellow townsmen and their guests, "and I am sure he will be able to make himself heard without it."

"Mr. President," Minihan pushed on, reverting to the formal welcome, "on behalf of the people of New Ross, I wish you a *céad míle fáilte*.

"When you wrote to us on the day of your inauguration that you hoped to be with us in the near future, we thought it was too good to be true. When we heard that you and your beloved wife were coming, we were overjoyed. We would have been delighted to have the first lady's company, but fully appreciate the circumstances and wish you both God's blessing.

"Mr. President, this is a great day for Wexford and for the Irish. At this moment every Irishman and every Irish woman who is not on this quay (the spot from which your great-grandfather set sail over one hundred years ago) is glued to a television or radio set. Our exiles all over the world, the people in Ireland from Mizen Head to Fair Head in Antrim, from the Aran Islands to Ireland's Eye, from the Coal Quay in Cork to the Falls Road and Shankill in Belfast, despite our differences, we are as one today.

"Why can't we always be in this happy position? We all have a thrill of pride in us —

In the lenses of the cameras — and Ireland's young television network broadcast much of the American visitor's appearances live — a smiling Kennedy enjoys a pause in the proceedings in jammed New Ross.

pride in our nationality. We are proud of the fact that one of our race — you, Mr. President — has been chosen to lead the great American freedom-loving people. We are proud and grateful that, with all your glory, you have seen fit to visit the land of your forebears.

"We know that the affairs of state were never heavier than at present, and we thank you for giving us so much of your time and pray God that the present trials will pass off to your satisfaction. The Irish people, and especially the people of New Ross, are eagerly waiting to hear what you have to say to us, and have had enough of me.

"In conclusion, I would say: our late Holy Father will go down in history as John XXIII, the 'pope of peace.' We hope and pray that you, Mr. President, will go down in history as John Fitzgerald Kennedy, the president of peace. *Beannacht Dé ar an obair.* [God bless the work.]"

The president was presented with an eighteenth century Irish silver goblet, a handkerchief for Mrs. Kennedy, and a crochet lace bag for their daughter, Caroline, whom Minihan called "the real boss of the White House." Mrs. Kennedy's handkerchief was a piece of Venetian rose-point lace made at Mount Carmel Convent School in New Ross, exquisite artistry that once was known throughout the world but had since died out.

Minihan had a personal present for Kennedy: a chunk of rock.

"The president was unable to visit the Giant's Causeway," Minihan explained, "so from myself I would like to give you, Mr. President, a piece of rock from the causeway." He couldn't resist adding that "the mountain has been brought to Mahomet." (The rock, shaped in the form of a seat and mounted on mahogany, had been on the move. It was driven by a group of people from County Antrim in Northern Ireland down to Dublin, and dropped off at Iveagh House for the president. It was later helicoptered to New Ross.)

The president, feeling expansive and happy, asked a group of musicians playing violins and flutes to play some Irish reels. Kennedy's foot tapped time.

Minihan tried to keep control. During one local band's performance, the crowd got restless and noisy. Minihan stepped to the mikes. "Quiet!" he yelled.

When the men's chorus sang "Boolavogue," a rebel ballad from County Wexford, Kennedy soundlessly formed the words with his lips. He knew it well. "At Boolavogue as the sun was setting . . ."

The absence of pretense at this official welcome charmed the visitors and natives alike. "What a gloriously informal man," an Irish radio commentator said of Kennedy to his audience. (Kennedy's informality was contagious: members of the Irish government were heard calling the president "Jack," a liberty even close friends abandoned once he entered the White House.) Minihan said later it was clear Kennedy was "perfectly happy and perfectly at ease." In fact, Minihan laughed, "he was the only member on the platform that was relaxed."

A local shopkeeper shouted up to the president: "It's a great thing to see a man like you who is not ashamed of his humble origins!"

Finally, the president stepped to the restored microphones. The weather had reverted to drizzle.

"Mr. Mayor, I first of all would like to introduce two members of my family who came here with us: my sister Eunice Shriver, and to introduce another of my sisters, Jean Smith. I would like to have you meet American Ambassador McCloskey, who is with us. And I would like to have you meet the head of the American labor movement, whose mother and father were born in Ireland, George Meany, who is traveling with us. And then I would like to have you meet the only man with us who doesn't have a drop of Irish blood, but who is dying to — the head of the protocol of the United States, Angier Biddle Duke.

"See, Angie, how nice it is, just to be Irish!"

Duke later protested that he *did* have Irish blood: his great-grandmother was from Ireland.

"I am glad to be here," Kennedy continued. "It took 115 years to make this trip, and six thousand miles, and three generations. But I am proud to be here and I appreciate the warm welcome you have given to all of us.

"When my great-grandfather left here to become a cooper in East Boston, he carried nothing with him except two things: a strong religious faith and a strong desire for liberty. I am glad to say that all of his great-grandchildren have valued that inheritance.

"If he hadn't left, I would be working over at the Albatross Company, or perhaps for John V. Kelly." The Albatross Company was a fertilizer factory visible across the River Barrow, a Dutch-Irish firm that processed phosphates from Morocco. Kelly's was a local pub owned by the town auctioneer. The crowd laughed, and then laughed even harder as the microphone picked up the president's own chuckles.

"In any case, we are happy to be back here," Kennedy said.

"About fifty years ago," he then concluded, "an Irishman from New Ross traveled down to Washington with his family, and in order to tell his neighbors how well he was doing, he had his picture taken in front of the White House and said, 'This is our summer home. Come and see us.'

"Well, it is our home also in the winter, and I hope you will come and see us. Thank you."

New Ross was not quite through with its guest. Patrick Dolan, chairman of the New Ross Harbor Commissioners, presented Kennedy with a fourteen-inch-high Waterford decanter. The mouth-blown piece was hand-cut on the sides into four panels, one showing the White House, another the New Ross coat of arms, another a rendering of a ship like the one the president's great-grandfather had left on, and the last a depiction of the Kennedy ancestral home in nearby Dunganstown. Artisans had taken 150 hours to engrave the bowl.

"The light of the day shines through this glass," Dolan told Kennedy. "And we pray that through your efforts the light of freedom will shine through every nation on this earth."

The playing of the Irish national anthem concluded the official program. Local officials had been told by the American Embassy that the president wouldn't be shaking hands with the crowds because of his back injury. So, of course, Kennedy decided he wanted to shake hands with the crowd. "Right, sir. Come this way," his security men instructed. Kennedy didn't like to be directed. "Mayor," he told Minihan, "we go this way" — the opposite of where security wanted him. Kennedy waded into the hands. People clutched at the president. Those who were successful attaching themselves to him didn't want to release him. With his wary security detail in the crush with him, Kennedy reached into waving hands, again and again greeting the delirious faces with "Thank you" and "How are you?" People hollered to him, "How's Jackie?" and "Hello, John!"

Minihan pleaded with his countrymen: "Leave go his hand. . . . You can all die happy now."

One man didn't heed the advice. He held Kennedy's hand in a vise grip. The Secret Service jumped in, and an agent chopped on the man's wrist. "Let him go, let him go!" the agent ordered. Either the pain of the chops or the menace in the agent's voice did the trick, and the president was freed.

As Kennedy moved along in his car, people jogged alongside, yelling and cheering. Behind Kennedy, a brass band and a pipe band, with American flags stuck in the bagpipes, blared tunes.

John V. Kelly was asked by reporters what kind of job the president could get at his establishment.

"In New Ross today there is only one job — the job of barman, provided he doesn't drink. What would I pay him? About two pounds a week, I suppose. But I believe he has done better for himself."

Minihan shared with listeners Kennedy's delight at New Ross.

"He was charmed at the reception. I said to him, 'After your tour of Germany you must be very tired or very fit.' He said, 'Well, Mr. Mayor, I'm both.'" Kennedy had given Minihan an autographed picture and presented a silver cigarette box from Tiffany's, engraved with the presidential seal, to Minihan's wife.

♣ ♣ ♣ ♣

By the presidential limousine, Kennedy made the short drive to the family farm in Dunganstown, six miles from New Ross down the banks of the Barrow River. The eight-foot-wide road — what the Irish call a boreen — traversed a thickly wooded landscape of beech trees and lush ferns that seemed, like the people, to reach out to the entourage of seven black cars as it passed. Policemen guarded the road, where the usually unruly grass borders were cut short and the wild hedges trimmed. The procession passed through quaintly named bends in the road: Ely's Walks, Camblin, and Stokestown.

Dunganstown itself was but a cluster of about ten houses and outbuildings scattered across a few miles of farmland. A century before, the "town" in Dunganstown was more real: some fifty families had called it home.

Waiting in one of those houses was Mrs. Mary Ryan, the sixty-three-year-old third cousin to the president, and the hostess for this day, accompanied by twenty-five relatives and the parish priest. By all accounts, she was the ruler over the thirty-five-acre farm, its three cows, two sows and their twenty-four piglets, and seventy chickens. She raised corn and wheat in the surrounding fields. (Tommy Lennon, fifteen, helped with the pigs, which he much preferred to books. Asked what grade he was in, the diminutive youth replied, "Oh, I've finished school, sir.")

Blue-eyed, her hair in a bun, the Widow Ryan, as she was known locally, had resolved to adhere to her usual informality. She would call the president Cousin Jack, as she had when he first visited in 1947. Her grandfather, John Kennedy, was Patrick Kennedy's brother.

Her two-story, seven-room home was substantial by the standards of rural Ireland when it was built around 1870. But it had lacked an indoor toilet until Cousin Jack's imminent arrival. When the president's intention to visit was announced, the homestead won a major plumbing upgrade. Area residents took to calling it John's john. Mrs. Ryan also redecorated for her cousin. And she had a television antenna installed on her roof, the only one for miles around.

Backup for personal needs wasn't the only major installation at Dunganstown. The closest telephone was four miles from the farm. That would not do for the president's detail, which three weeks before had installed a secure line to Washington in a nearby cow barn. For more routine communications, fifteen telephone cables were laid between Dunganstown and New Ross.

Cousin James Kennedy, meanwhile, decided the old pillars holding the eight-foot-wide gate had to go. The entrance needed to be wider, but he insisted that was mainly so trucks could get through, not for the visit of the president.

And only a short time before Kennedy's visit, the dirt barnyard, which the Irish call a haggard, was paved over in concrete. Irish newspapers blamed the American government's taste for tidiness. American officials suggested the improvements were ordered closer to home. But apparently, the Philadelphia contractor, Ambassador McCloskey, was the culprit. ("How about putting some concrete in front of my farm?" JFK later joked in a handwritten P.S. to the envoy, thanking him for his efforts arranging the trip.) James Kennedy was concerned. How would his animals manage in the winter, when ice would glaze the now concrete yard?

Whatever the case, there was no manure pile here, either. The animals had been banished, too — almost. Word spread that the Ryan family cat, Beauty, had done its feline best for the president, snatching a rat in the yard not long before the distinguished guest arrived.

The sensitivity of the Irish to the stereotype of themselves as barefooted, hardscrabble wretches living off the land could not be denied. Even though few were wealthy, the nation was a far sight removed from abject poverty. And they cared little for media stunts that perpetuated the stereotype. One American television crew reportedly paid some boys to take off their shoes so they could be shown strolling down the road barefoot. Some American reporters could not disguise their disdain for the simple life they saw. One scribe, visiting Dunganstown shortly before Kennedy landed in Ireland, was overheard saying, "I can tell you one thing: Jackie wouldn't live here, that's for sure." Said another American, upon seeing Patrick Kennedy's cottage: "Is that it?" The remarks were noted in some of the Irish press, unfavorably.

The presidential limousine approached. Only minutes before, the rain had hammered the homestead, threatening to ruin the outdoor festivities. But now, the ever-changeable Irish weather turned back to sun and patches of blue sky. Across the lane stretched a colored banner: "Welcome Home, Mr. President."

Kennedy pulled up outside the whitewashed walls of the little farm compound not long after noon. A modest sign bearing the American and Irish flags announced the place: "The Kennedy Homestead." A banner over the yard carried the president's likeness and the greeting: *Céad Míle Fáilte*.

The president stepped out to walk through the gate, but before he could, his hands were grasped immediately by eager farmers and onlookers. Kennedy was delighted at the scene, pushing aside some of his protectors to invite more people to come nearer the commotion. "I want to meet some of the people to say hello, " the president explained. "God bless you, Mr. President," the people called to him. "May the road always rise with you," said some. He heard blessings and proverbs in Irish, too. A priest stretched his hand out over the president's head to give him a silent blessing. Most of the men wore ties, held to their shirts with PT-109 tie clips, gifts from presidential brother Edward M. Kennedy during a trip here in 1962. A junior honor guard from Ballykelly School, where great-grandfather Patrick Kennedy had learned reading and writing, cheered the president. He gave the children hugs and pats on the head.

Finally, Kennedy made his way through the gate to a waiting Mrs. Ryan, who was wearing a purple-and-white flowered dress.

"I'm glad to see you and I'm sorry for all the trouble I caused you," Kennedy told her. She answered with a smile and a kiss on the president's cheek. He beamed as if receiving the approval of a grandmother. Mrs. Ryan's two daughters, Mary Ann, twenty-three, a nurse at the Rotunda Hospital in Dublin, and Josephine, twenty-five, who helped on the farm, planted kisses on the president's sisters. Kennedy told Mrs. Ryan her daughters had grown up since his visit in 1947. "You were tots then," he told the two smiling young women.

"If only Mike Ryan had lived to see this day, God rest his soul," sighed a neighbor.

People could see the Kennedy likeness in the young Ryan women. But the girls were not about to scoot off to America to join the cousins.

Mary Ann was practical when asked whether she considered nursing in the United States.

"We have much more opportunity to do good work here, and we get enough salary to allow us to support ourselves decently according to the Irish standard of living," she said. "I would never want to leave Ireland."

The accompanying Washington press corps spotted a lot of familiar faces from the "Irish Mafia" wandering the homestead: Larry O'Brien, Kennedy's liaison with the Congress; O'Brien's assistant, Dick Donahue; presidential aide John McNally; Secret Service agent John "Mugsy" O'Leary, the president's former chauffeur; Richard Maguire of the Democratic National Committee; U.S. Rep. Edward Boland, from Springfield, Massachusetts; and of course, Dave Powers.

The yard got rather crowded. An Irish police inspector decided he wanted to clear it. His energetic entreaties were reinforced with a cane, which at one point punched at the chest of one of the most respected of White House reporters, Merriman Smith of United Press International.

"It was kind of a joke among the press," said the *New York Times*'s Tom Wicker. "The Irish cops were pretty rough. They had their rules and they wanted to enforce them."

Kennedy's semiprivate moments were inside the cottage, an interlude that began a bit formally. He was greeted by Rev. T.S. Power, of Horeswood, Rev. William Mernagh, of Ballykelly, and Rev. Brendan Kehoe, of Horeswood.

Finally, he sat down with Mrs. Ryan and her brother, James Kennedy, by a turf fire. The smell filling the damp air was familiar to the American president, a smell that would remind him where he was every day he was in Eire, a smell that is Ireland: the oakcy-sweet essence of burning peat.

"The fire feels good," the president remarked.

Kennedy somehow had seen a New Ross newspaper and noted that his cousins were planning a cattle auction the coming weekend.

"How is everything going with the farm?" he asked.

As they talked, James Kennedy poured the president a large shot of Irish whiskey. In the crowded room, the American cousin was able to pass off the elixir, behind his back, to Dave Powers, who quaffed the contents and quickly handed the empty glass back to his boss.

Dr. Martin J. Quigley, the area physician, presented the president with a wool fleece rug.

"Have this placed in the hospital room with your beautiful wife until the arrival of the twins in August," the doctor prescribed.

Kennedy burst into laughter. Everyone knew the Kennedys were not expecting twins.

He also was given a silver tray by his cousins, engraved with their initials; an Aran sweater; a handwoven blanket; a blackthorn stick known as a shillelagh, cut from the Kennedy land; a seventy-two-piece coffee set of Belleek china for his wife from fourteen

At Dunganstown on June 27, Kennedy returns to the courtyard he last saw in 1947. At the president's right are his second cousin, Mary Ryan; her daughter Josephine Ryan; Kennedy's sister Jean Kennedy Smith; Garda Michael Patrick Kirwan; and Margaret Kirwan. To the president's left are Mary Ryan's other daughter, Mary Ann Ryan; Margaret Whitty; Joan Kirwan; Margaret Kirwan; Matt Kirwan; Kitty Kennedy; the president's sister Eunice Kennedy Shriver; and an unidentified man.

The Dunganstown Kennedys: From left, Mary Ann Ryan, Josephine Ryan, Mary Ryan, and James Kennedy, standing in their front courtyard. James Kennedy was concerned the cemented-over yard — an "improvement" made for the president's visit — would be a problem for his cows, but it has remained for forty years. Behind is the hut where President Kennedy's great-grandfather Patrick once had lived.

Kennedy cousins; a handkerchief for Caroline; and a boat for little John-John. The president gave them all mounted pictures of the White House, signed by him and Mrs. Kennedy.

He sat by Mrs. Ryan. He sipped tea and looked through a family album. And the president asked James Kennedy if he still had the picture that he, then a congressman, had sent back after visiting in 1947. Cousin James did indeed have it. A copy had been hung on the wall.

The Irish cousins were taken by the president's utter informality. He had called James Kennedy by his name before being introduced formally.

Josephine and her family were tense before the visit, not knowing "who they were going to meet or what they were going to meet," as she put it.

"But I think he made them all just draw at their ease," she later said. "He came in. Here a lot of the neighbors that helped that day, they were in the kitchen and they weren't supposed to — they weren't on the official party. They were supposed to keep in the background and they had told some of the officials that they were to stay away. But they were in the kitchen there, and when he was going out they opened the door there. He went in and he chatted, chatted away with them. Some of them were shaking hands with him, for instance, three times. And he talked to them about what way they helped. . . ."

Kennedy was struck by the familiarity of the faces staring back at him.

"The president told me that I looked just like a sister," Josephine later said, "and said I have the Kennedy face."

Kennedy also inquired about the man who had directed him to the family homestead back in 1947. The president could not remember the man's name, but described him as big, with a round face. He used a walking stick. The Ryans knew whom he meant. He was a neighbor, Robert Burrell.

Someone went to fetch Burrell, but he wasn't at home. He was found on a little hill, watching the fuss made over Cousin Jack at the homestead. Asked if he wanted to meet President Kennedy, Burrell nonchalantly replied: "I met him sixteen years ago."

Kennedy proposed a toast, raising his cup of tea: "To all the Kennedys who went and all the Kennedys who stayed."

Josephine revealed to reporters that the president had invited them to the White House. Kennedy "said we should come whenever we could make it. We may go next year," she said. Mrs. Ryan was heard to tell the president: "We'd love it." The widow later slyly advised that if she went, she intended to "stay with the family at the family home."

The Irish Kennedys were numerous. Besides Mary Ryan and her daughters and James Kennedy, James's wife, Kitty, was in the cottage, as were their three children, Patrick, twenty-two, Peggy, twenty-one, and Kitty, eighteen; also crowded in were Anna Kennedy and her son-in-law, Michael Rowe; Margaret Kennedy Kirwan and her husband, William, and their children, Matt, twenty-one, Pat, twenty, Margaret, twenty-four, and Joan, seventeen; and the oldest of the cousins, Mrs. Margaret Whitty, eighty-six.

Eunice Shriver was impressed with the trouble her cousins had gone to.

"I remember going into the house there and thinking, 'Boy, they really hustled around here,'" she said. "It was quite a tiny little house. . . . But we all were very comfortable, very happy."

Refreshments were served in the farmyard, where some thought they detected the strong scent of disinfectant. Some of the women had to cover over their new dresses with aprons to serve from the tables, shaped in a U and loaded down with jams, cakes, brown bread, flans, fruitcake, pies, and sandwiches — all prepared by the neighbors. The Irish made sure their American guests knew they were drinking brewed tea, not tea from tea-bags common across the Atlantic. Kennedy took his tea with two lumps of sugar and milk.

"You know you are next to the pope," Dr. Quigley told the president. Kennedy grinned and thanked him for the compliment.

Across the yard stood a low shed, twelve feet by twenty-four feet. It was the family home when Patrick Kennedy had walked away down the lane to New Ross more than a century before. Over the years, it had been changed: about ten feet of the building had been chopped away to make room for the newer house; its red-painted walls were now a fresh white; instead of a thatched roof, it now wore green-painted tin, an upgrade made a decade earlier that also covered the hole where the chimney had come through; and the trim was covered in a fresh coat of green as well. The little building most recently had been used for storing potatoes and coal. As might be expected, there was some controversy about the shed's present appearance. Picture postcards had depicted it with its old, thatched roof. Some Irish officials thought it would be a good idea to put the thatch back, but Mrs. Ryan sternly resisted, pointing out that the tin roof stood up better to the elements. And, after all, it was her shed, and the government had ignored her earlier requests after Kennedy's election in 1960 to help out in the restoration of the little building.

But that was all past now. The family reunion was all smiles and chatter. Hundreds of happy onlookers who could not get into the yard watched from the lane in front of the house. Curiously, President Kennedy never went into the hut. His aides were hard-pressed later to explain why. Perhaps it was just all the commotion and Cousin Jack simply forgot to look.

There were no formal presidential remarks. This was family time. Strolling through the crowd, chatting with farmers, their wives and children, Kennedy spotted a microphone near the linen-and-flower-covered cake table. He teased the press, picking up the microphone and saying "Hello," and nothing else.

The president drank his tea and ate a salmon sandwich while talking.

"Did you catch this one, Jim? Or was it poached?" Kennedy teased his cousin.

James Kennedy replied that he couldn't take the credit. It was, in fact, caught that morning by a parish priest in Ballykelly.

Surveying the plenty before him, Kennedy wondered aloud, "What are we going to do with all this food? I just wish I could stay to eat it all."

He cut a white cake that was baked in the family home that morning. It was decorated with the Stars and Stripes, the Irish tricolor, and the outline of his own head.

"Don't cut yourself!" yelled a White House cameraman, a joking reference to an incident a few weeks earlier when the president revealed to a nationwide press conference he had cut a finger while slicing bread.

"You've cut yourself," cousin Mary Ryan (in flowered dress, back to camera) jokes with Kennedy as he cuts into a cake with his likeness on it. Grinning behind the president is Ireland's Minister of External Affairs Frank Aiken, who kept trying to prod a reluctant Kennedy to leave to keep to schedule.

The smile says it all: Kennedy takes a final look at his family homestead before boarding the helicopter at Dunganstown. Irish Minister of Foreign Affairs Frank Aiken, next behind the president, and U.S. Ambassador Matthew McCloskey who follows, don't look too put out, despite the fact the president was now behind schedule. Just over the heads of the two policemen in the dead center of the picture, smiling at her cousin, is Mary Ann Ryan.

Kennedy's cousin couldn't resist.

"You've cut yourself," Mrs. Ryan joked.

"I'm definitely cutting myself up," the president quipped.

Kennedy was enjoying himself immensely.

His kidding, relaxed manner was contagious.

One young girl walked up to the president to introduce him to another relative.

"Cousin Jimmy, meet up with Cousin Jack," the girl said.

But another cousin, a twenty-six-year-old member of the *gardai*, the police, couldn't shake his nervousness. When, at last, he neared the president, he reached out to shake the hand of his celebrated relation — and he missed. A second attempt proved the trick.

Kennedy ignored entreaties by Ambassador McCloskey and Minister Aiken to leave.

"Mr. Aiken wants me to leave all this beautiful brown bread," Kennedy announced.

"Don't mind Mr. Aiken. Stay where you are," Mrs. Ryan directed.

"I'm afraid we must go," the president finally surrendered.

Mrs. Ryan whispered in her cousin's ear.

"'Don't go?'" Kennedy repeated. "But Mr. Aiken says we have to."

"Don't take any notice of what Mr. Aiken says," Mary Ryan again advised.

The president chuckled.

Kennedy invited everyone within earshot to join in the food and tea.

"Why not partake of all this hospitality, you people?" he said.

The president was moved to again propose the toast he had given inside. Raising his mug of tea, while he was still chewing a cookie, he said: "We are going to drink a cup of tea for those Kennedys who went away and those who stayed behind."

The time for parting had come. "I've got to go," Kennedy apologized to Mrs. Ryan. "Thanks a lot, dear. I'll be back."

"This was a fine effort and we thank you very much," Kennedy told his relatives and new friends. "I promise you we won't come back oftener than once every ten years."

As the family walked with their cousin toward the rear of the farmhouse and the waiting helicopters, Mary Ryan scolded her nation's foreign minister: "You won't be hurrying him out of here until he plants a juniper tree in our garden so we'll have something to remind us of this day in the years to come."

This sounded like trouble to Kennedy's aides, who remembered the Ottawa tree-planting incident all too well.

But the president gamely went ahead without mishap: the tree was in the ground. Kennedy merely had to toss on some soil from a board, held up by an aide.

Mrs. Ryan gave her cousin a hug and a kiss. "Cousin Mary, the next time I come I'll bring Jackie and the children," the president told Mrs. Ryan.

"He said they were dying to come over here and that we would love them," Josephine

Ryan disclosed a couple of days later. "From the way he talked, we got the impression that we would not have to wait too long for the visit — maybe two years at most."

The presidential helicopter sat in a nearby field. The Ballykelly School junior honor guard again lined the way. Kennedy stopped and chatted with the children, again patting heads and giving encouragement.

A little boy grabbed the president and said something.

"What did you say?" Kennedy asked as he bent down to the youth. "What did you say your name was? What was it . . . Pat . . . Pat what?" The boy had frozen up under the attention. He could say no more.

"You are a good boy," the president said, putting his hand on the little fellow's head.

"This is one of the most remarkable tea parties in history," came the improbable commentary from one Irish television reporter. "Here is a president of the United States leaving an Irish farmyard in a jet helicopter."

Kennedy had spent some forty-five minutes — well beyond the schedule — at his ancestral seat. As he ascended the stairs to his helicopter, he kissed Mrs. Ryan on the cheek. She

From a field behind Mary Ryan's Dunganstown house, Kennedy's presidential helicopter lifts off, bound for Wexford. All the landing and takeoff spots were tested by military and Secret Service officials days before the president's arrival.

seemed surprised. Her eyes filled with tears. The president's sisters, noted O'Donnell and Powers, "stared in wide-eyed astonishment" at such a public display of affection. He was off to Wexford. In a few minutes, as the roar of the helicopters receded, Mrs. Ryan was seen back at the house, attacking the dishes.

"We were all very excited, but we regarded his coming as a cousin coming home," Josephine Ryan would later relate. Sure, he was the president of the United States, and they were delighted by that. But, she said, "we thought of him as being just a cousin. We liked to meet him that way and receive him that way. . . . We always felt very at home with him from the time he stepped out of the car. It was just as if he had been here the couple of days before."

And that is how she thought Kennedy felt, too. "No, he wasn't president when he was here, I don't think. . . . He wanted to be just one of ourselves."

🍀 🍀 🍀 🍀

That all this might have anything to do with unsentimental presidential politics across the Atlantic wasn't suggested much by observers. Sterling Slappey of the *Los Angeles Times* was among the handful of exceptions:

"Mr. Kennedy's team," he wrote, "is busy establishing that young Jack is at heart a man of the soil, a man of humble beginnings. This is the stuff of which political campaigns are made.

"And for all practical purposes," Slappey continued, "President Kennedy probably launched his campaign for re-election Thursday at Dunganstown, near Wexford.

". . . President Kennedy, who has indicated in dozens of ways that he has every intention of running for a second term, has now visited the old homestead, has been photographed with many distant cousins, has drunk tea and eaten homemade cookies.

"He has invited one and all to visit him in the White House, has shaken every hand thrust out to him, and spent the while talking about how wonderful it is to be Irish and to have such fine relatives.

"There are millions of Irishmen in the United States, as well as millions of others with similarly humble forebears, and such talk is music to their ears.

"In effect," the *Times* correspondent summed up, "the President has placed the Kennedy hut alongside Abraham Lincoln's log cabin in American political folklore."

Richard Wilson, a World War II combat correspondent and winner of the Pulitzer Prize, American journalism's highest honor, pointed out for readers of the *Minneapolis Tribune* and the *Des Moines Register* that Kennedy's entire European trip "will appear in a dramatic light at home in the year prior to the presidential election, thus eclipsing in national attention all his would-be competitors."

The *Newark Evening News* sent its Washington correspondent, George Kentera, on

Kennedy's trip. A former World War II fighter pilot who had been imprisoned by the Germans, Kentera had a wry wit and a keen understanding of politics, which he, too, thought certainly was an element of the presidential tour. Kennedy's strategists, he reported, "concede that there can be only a tenuous connection between a vote of kinship from Ireland or a vote of confidence from Germany and an increased vote from the American public next year. But they believe there is a connection and that Kennedy's current trip will turn out to be a political 'plus' at home. This view can be disputed, especially since the president's trip can hardly produce important international results for some time — if at all. But Kennedy's aides are convinced that their leader's public successes in Cologne, Bonn, Frankfurt, Berlin and Ireland will raise his standing with the U.S. voters as a world leader and help counter Republican criticism of his foreign policies."

Kennedy, Kentera said, showed he understood the political consequences, telling a small group during the trip that his receptions in Europe "have spoiled us" for the coming 1964 campaign.

"Now," Kennedy said, "if we don't get a million people out for a political speech in Worcester, Massachusetts, or Danbury, Connecticut, everyone — especially the reporters — is going to write that there are signs of apathy in the United States."

Prime Minister Lemass, while sure politics "wasn't very much" on Kennedy's mind, recalled a brief conversation they had during an appearance. "I said to him that probably everybody in that crowd had some relation in the United States of America and would be writing next week to report the fact that they'd seen the president. And he said this was going to do him no harm at all."

Though not oblivious of the tremendous boost Kennedy's visit gave to the prospects of Lemass and his government, Irish officials nevertheless were disinclined to see the trip connected to the 1964 campaign.

De Valera was representative of that Irish perspective: "My view was that it had nothing to do with domestic politics."

Nor global doings, insisted the *Carlow Nationalist*. "The purpose of the president's visit has nothing to do with power politics," the paper said.

☘ ☘ ☘ ☘

Kennedy's helicopter swept low over the verdant, undulating landscape on the fifteen-minute jaunt to Wexford. There, they did not use flexible children, but rather paint, to spell "*fáilte*" on the golf course as the president landed at the Wexford Gaelic Park. It had been cold and raining until just before Kennedy landed. Now the rain had halted. Among the thirty thousand gathered in a town normally of about twelve thousand souls, children sang the only song that logically could begin proceedings for the Irish-American leader of the free world: "The Boys of Wexford."

The motorcade assembled and moved through the crowd, beginning the mile-and-a-half trip along Summerhill Road, to Grogan Road, Roches Road, Bride Street, Stonebridge, King Street Lower, Paul Quay, and finally to Crescent Quay at the city harbor. Kennedy stood in the limousine acknowledging the cheers. Sometimes he stooped to ask questions of Wexford Mayor Thomas F. Bryne or Minister Aiken, who were riding with him. From the river, people in boats yelled out to him, and an amused president waved back. Children hollered and teenagers squealed. Many elderly people, perhaps sensing what this visit meant more than most, wept.

At Crescent Quay, with a U.S. Navy honor guard standing at attention and drums rolling, Kennedy laid a cypress wreath at the Barry Memorial, a bronze statue that looks out over the water. Given in 1956 by the United States government to the people of Ireland, the monument holds great significance to the Irish, because it commemorates the man responsible for the first American victory over the British by a commissioned naval vessel in the American Revolution. John Barry, born in Ballysampson, County Wexford, is considered by some the father of the American Navy. The message on Kennedy's wreath, made by William Coady, a carpenter from Rosslare, read: "Star of the Sea, guide all seamen safely home." Ringing the wreath were miniatures of Irish vessels lost in World War II: S.S. *Ardmore*, S.S. *Kylemore,* S.S. *Kylecare,* S.S. *Fintan,* S.S. *Irish Pine,* and the *M.V. Cymbric.* The president stood for some moments looking at the granite-base memorial, then scanned across the harbor to the sea. Ready to leave, the Navy man momentarily appeared to lose his bearings, walking in the wrong direction. An official corrected Kennedy, and the unbothered president joked with the official about his mistake.

What a tonic this was for poor Wexford. The local economy was sagging. Farm machinery, which Wexford made, wasn't selling. And shipping had disappeared from the harbor. Many tradesmen were working only part time, and others in small industries were losing their jobs. There was talk that if the trend persisted, Wexford would become a ghost town. Now, this brief respite from worry.

At 1:40 p.m. Kennedy was at Redmond Place, a plaza dominated by the railroad station. Greeting him in the official party, many in their red official robes, were Mayor Byrne, County Council Chairman James J. Bowe, and Minister Aiken. The people of Wexford had no need to fret about work on this day. The town had declared a holiday.

Mayor Byrne, an assistant in a shop, had served on the Wexford Borough Council since 1935 but had been mayor only four days, his name picked from a hat after the mayoral election had ended in a tie.

Byrne proceeded with the official welcoming speech. After an effusive expression of the city's pride upon the occasion, and regret at the shortness of the visit, he gave a brief history of the honor that was to be bestowed upon the president.

Wexford Town Clerk John J. Byrne read the resolution. Granting the status of freeman is a great Irish honor that dates from medieval times, entitling strangers, normally banished outside the town walls at sunset, to stay inside the gates and, should the need arise, to first dibs on a bed in the poorhouse.

The resolution, adopted on May 27 by the Wexford Corporation, read: "That by virtue of the Municipal Privilege Act (Ireland), 1876, the Honorary freedom of this, the ancient Borough of Wexford, be conferred on Mr. John Fitzgerald Kennedy, President of the United States of America, as a mark of our appreciation of his visit to our town, and as a token of our regard for a distinguished American of County Wexford extraction, who has labored indefatigably for the preservation of Democratic beliefs and for world peace."

Kennedy stepped up to sign the roll of freemen. Seamus O Gallcobhair, secretary of the

Paying homage to an early hero of the American Navy, Kennedy places a wreath at the Wexford memorial to Commodore John Barry, the Irish-born fighter in the American Revolution, on June 27. Wexford Councilor Thomas Byrne, the mayor, in his ceremonial robes, looks on with U.S. Ambassador Matthew McCloskey, far right, and Irish External Affairs Minister Frank Aiken, behind Byrne's shoulder. The president kept a Barry flag and sword in the White House Oval Office.

In Redmond Place, Wexford, with Mayor Byrne and Ambassador McCloskey (the white-haired gentleman) surveying the throng, Kennedy jokes with the crowd, "I am glad to see a few cousins who didn't catch the boat."

Wexford County Council, handed Kennedy the scroll to sign. It was hand-painted and written out by the Sisters of the Perpetual Adoration Convent. The president, enjoying himself, pretended to take an interest in the secretary's badge. Wexford rocked with laughter. After Kennedy put his signature to the roll, the town clerk read out the certificate of enrollment, and the document was placed in an engraved silver-and-gold box lined in cedar and bearing the coats of arms of Wexford and the Kennedys and the official seal of the United States government.

On cue, the Wexford United Pigeon Flying Club released a flock of two hundred of its best.

The pride of the moment got the better of Mayor Byrne and Council Chairman Bowe, who seemed to be vying over the honor of giving the president the scroll granting him the freedom of the borough. The president appeared greatly amused by the officials' little tiff. Bowe hung onto the scroll, briefly.

Bowe then presented Kennedy with a gift for Mrs. Kennedy, a tablecloth of the best Irish linen. He was pleased, he said, that so many had turned out to welcome "this great man who had to take a risk only a few months ago of war or peace. His decision was the right one and he took it unflinchingly. And because of his bravery in doing so we now have peace."

In Irish and English, O Gallcobhair delivered the county council's welcoming address.

"The members of Wexford County Council extend to you, on behalf of the people of Wexford, a most cordial welcome on this most auspicious occasion of your return to the county from which sprang your paternal ancestry. The townland of Dunganstown will forever occupy pride of place in the affections of Irish people and in the annals of our history as the birthplace of an illustrious son who set forth in a less fortunate time to seek his fortune in the New World. His success is manifest in your presence today, a century later, as the First Citizen of the great republic of the West. We salute you as the modern champion of liberty in a world enmeshed in bondage. Your evident love of freedom — both national and individual — in itself blazoned forth your Irish heritage, the heritage of a nation which survived centuries of bondage and oppression through the unfailing strength of its faith and that same love of freedom which never brooked defeat. County Wexford and the Republic of Ireland join with the free world in wishing you every success in your mighty undertaking and pray God's blessing on those shoulders which seem fully capable of bearing the burden of your high endeavors, of such immense import to all humanity."

Then Kennedy, the thirteenth freeman of the borough, got up to speak. After lusty cheering, the crowd hushed to hear the president. In that moment of expectant silence, a voice yelled out "Welcome home!" The cheers began again. Kennedy smiled and said, "Thank you."

"Mr. Mayor, Chairman of the Council, Mr. Minister, my friends," the president began. "I want to express my pleasure at being back from whence I came. There is an impression in Washington that there are no Kennedys left in Ireland, that they are all in Washington, so I wonder if there are any Kennedys in this audience. Could you hold up your hand so I can see?"

About a half-dozen hands floated skyward.

"Well, I am glad to see a few cousins who didn't catch the boat," the president went on.

"And I am glad to take part in this ceremony this morning for John Barry. I have had in my office since I was president the flag that he flew and the sword that he wore. It is no coincidence that John Barry and a good many of his successors played such a leading part in the American struggle, not only for independence, but for its maintenance. About two months ago I visited the Battle of Gettysburg, the bloodiest battlefield in the American Civil War, and one of the monuments to the dead was to the Irish Brigade. In Fredericksburg, which was another slaughter, the Irish Brigade was nearly wiped out. They went into battle wearing a sprig of green in their hats and it was said of them what was said about Irishmen in other countries: 'War battered dogs are we, gnawing a naked bone, fighting in every land and clime, for every cause but our own.'

"It seems to me that in these dangerous days when the struggle for freedom is worldwide against an armed doctrine, that Ireland and its experience has one special significance, and that is that the people's fight, which John Boyle O'Reilly said outlived a thousand years, that it was possible for a people over hundreds of years of foreign domination and religious persecution — it was possible for that people to maintain their national identity and their strong faith. And therefore those who may feel that in these difficult times, who may believe that freedom may be on the run, or that some nations may be permanently subjugated and eventually wiped out, would do well to remember Ireland.

"And I am proud to come here for another reason, because it makes me even prouder of my own country. My country welcomes so many sons and daughters of so many countries, Irish and Scandinavian, Germans, Italian, and all the rest, and gave them a fair chance and a fair opportunity. The Speaker of the House of Representatives is of Irish descent. The leader of the Senate is of Irish descent. And what is true of the Irish people has been true of dozens of other people. In Ireland I think you see something of what is so great about the United States; and I must say that in the United States, through millions of your sons and daughters and cousins — 25 million, in fact — you see something of what is great about Ireland.

"So I am proud to be here. I am proud to have connected on that beautiful golden box the coat of arms of Wexford, the coat of arms of the kingly and beautiful Kennedys, and the coat of arms of the United States. That is a very good combination.

"Thank you."

A single Irish tenor sang "The Soldier's Song," the Irish national anthem, to the accompaniment of a band, a stirring moment.

In the motorcade, Kennedy took his by-now customary waves. But at the gates of Loreto Convent, where schoolchildren and nuns joyously waved flags to greet him, Kennedy ordered his car to stop. He stepped out and, with another man, walked into the convent. Everyone else in the motorcade waited.

He had stopped to see Mother Superior Clement, a third cousin, or, as she told another nun, "the relation nobody knows about." She was the former Florrie Ward, from County Cork, a cousin through her mother, who was a Fitzgerald.

"This is one of the greatest moments of my life," Kennedy greeted her, shaking her hand. "I am very glad to have met you, another member of the family."

Middle-aged, small and shy, the mother superior declined to say exactly what Kennedy said to her, other than that he thanked her and the twenty-seven other nuns in the convent for greeting him. They had to get special permission from their order to stand at the gates to welcome Kennedy.

"The president signed autographs for the nuns," the mother superior allowed to reporters afterward. "I got the visitor's book signed. I only managed that for myself."

"I have never seen him in the flesh before," she added. "The poor president must be very worn out. We all think he is a wonderful man and we are very proud of him. . . . The welcome must have given him great pleasure."

Had she ever written the president? Mother Superior Clement had a political answer:

On his way out of Wexford, Kennedy visits another cousin, Mother Superior Clement, at Loreto Convent. She thought "the poor president must be very worn out."

"I try not to answer those questions," she said.

Back in his car, Kennedy stopped twice more, despite being behind the official schedule. First, he pulled up to get out and talk and shake hands with St. John of God nuns and a crowd of nurses from the County Hospital. Not far down the road, Kennedy halted the motorcade again, this time to see some two hundred orphan pupils at the Convent of Mercy. He walked into the children, patting them on their heads and hugging them.

"Never before in this country," declared one astonished onlooker, "has a nun been seen waving a flag."

As Kennedy headed north back to Dublin, the press encountered unexpected excitement. One of the reporters' helicopters developed engine trouble. The craft put down in a field, none the worse for wear.

♣ ♣ ♣ ♣

Back in the capital, Kennedy was feted at a garden party at Aras an Uachtarain, the Irish president's house, hosted by President and Mrs. de Valera. The pillared, white Georgian house — once the viceregal lodge when the British ruled Ireland, a sort of getaway from Dublin Castle — sits in its own enclosure within the nearly two thousand acres of Phoenix Park, where deer wander among the trees and fields, and sometimes into traffic on the roads that traverse the green expanse.

The weather having turned again, with rain dampening hopes that the outside could take the overflow, the stately house became jammed with humanity. Kennedy was outside in the fifty-degree weather, hatless as usual, then inside, buffeted to and fro by the who's who of Ireland — and Northern Ireland (the sympathetic ones, anyway) — from the mayor of Sligo, James Gannon, to Joseph Stewart, Nationalist M.P. from East Tyrone. About nineteen hundred people, women in brocade gowns, and men in cutaway coats, striped pants, and gray top hats, all wanted to squeeze into the same space near Kennedy. With their dripping and splayed umbrellas. De Valera pleaded with the throng at one point, "Move back, move back, please."

Mrs. de Valera had made a last-minute switch in deference to the elements.

"I had planned to wear a lovely silk sheath dress with a huge cartwheel hat," she informed a society reporter. Instead, she opted for a charcoal-gray dress, with a mauve chiffon scarf, covered by a black linen coat. She sported a shocking-pink hat and matched that with good cheer.

"What a store of knowledge she has," Eunice Shriver marveled. "She has just been reciting a poem to me here. I wish I had her memory."

De Valera recalled the weather later as "unfortunate for us."

"It was very wet, so the people weren't able to meet him as they wished," the Irish president explained. "The danger there was that there was a mob that was crushing in upon him, and the security men were trying to keep them back, but of course they were being pressed in with the crowd. And he was anxious anyhow to go out and meet the people."

Women were pushed out of their high-heeled shoes. Some left them where they were, stuck in the mud. One man became entangled in a bishop's scarlet cape, and the sound of rending of cloth broke the din. Chairs went over. Hats were crushed.

An embarrassed attendee declared: "What disgusting behavior at a garden party!"

"At Buckingham Palace," lectured one Irishman, spiffy in his cutaway coat, "at a garden party everyone is lined up and an attendant comes along to about every one in four and says, 'You may speak to the queen.' It is all very proper — but this!"

"If half these people stayed home," an incensed woman complained, "I would have got to meet the president."

And the refreshments . . . well.

"I'll have a Power's Gold Label," one man confidently informed a waiter.

"Sorry, sir," the waiter replied, "there is no drink, only tea."

"Ah, sure what sort of a garden party is this?" the man exclaimed as he turned away.

"No eruption of mass orgasmic excitement exceeded that of a historic day when Jack Kennedy presented himself at Aras an Uachtarain," a writer sniffed. "The blooming shrubs were crushed to pulp when Kennedy appeared with blind old Eamon de Valera to meet with the cream of pushy Irish society — stockbrokers, building contractors, lawyers, nuns, priests, bishops, politicians, horse trainers, and reformed gunmen, who, in their attempt to touch the hem of the hero's garment, mounted a charge of such determined wild-eyed ferocity that Jack skipped back nimbly to the drawing room."

"Top society in Ireland did not behave well," Education Minister Hillery later wryly recollected. "They did not have the courtesy of people down in the country." It should be noted that Hillery's constituency, in County Clare in Ireland's west, was made up of "people down in the country."

De Valera tried to calm the crush, only to find himself in it. At one point, he turned to the milling sea of high fashion and tried to speak. A band nearly drowned him out. "Mr. Kennedy," the aging Irish leader said, "is very sorry he cannot meet you all. You will have to take it that he has shaken hands with you all. He will have to say good-bye for the moment."

Kennedy was brought around to a side of the residence — to the great trepidation of his aides who worried about his back — to plant a California redwood. Kennedy turned one shovelful of earth, then handed the tool to Patrick Buggy, one of the groundsmen. "Now let's see the expert do it," the president joked. De Valera planted a tree, too. And he spent more time on the shovel than did his young guest. "You are making me look awfully bad, Mr. President," Kennedy chided.

Despite the chaos in the garden, Kennedy was able to rendezvous with Mrs. Ryan and her daughters and introduce them to President de Valera.

The ever-dignified Eamon de Valera becomes an unwilling participant in a wet and wild garden party on June 27 at his Dublin house, Aras an Uachtarain, where guests in all their finery trample grass and flowers and overturn chairs to get to Kennedy.

Lord Longford, de Valera's old friend, witnessed the "unforgettable atmosphere" and emotion firsthand at the garden party. "The overwhelming point is that the fervor was two-way, mutual," he later wrote. "In Berlin, a million or so beleaguered citizens had hailed their savior; but there was no suggestion of his being one of their number. He was the one man who could guarantee their physical security. In Dublin Kennedy had nothing to bring the Irish people except himself, and himself as profoundly Irish, in all respects one of them. He felt it; they felt it; they felt that he felt it; he felt . . . the rapport was total and beyond comparison or description."

Pierre Salinger, cigar in hand, made an appearance in the Gresham Hotel's Aberdeen Hall, press central for the trip.

He was there to relay one of those routine White House announcements of nominations. The business of the presidency churned away, regardless of the president's whereabouts. And so came word on this day in Dublin that Kennedy intended to nominate an old political foe as ambassador. Henry Cabot Lodge, Jr., the man JFK defeated for a seat in the United States Senate in 1952, a former ambassador to the United Nations and Richard Nixon's running mate in 1960, was to be the new American envoy to South Vietnam.

Reporters, especially those from Ireland, pressed the White House spokesman on whether there were plans for a full-scale presidential press conference while Kennedy was in Dublin. There were not, Salinger said, explaining that on a trip such as this in Ireland, a press conference wasn't held. But there had been one in Germany, reporters pressed.

"Sometimes he gives one and sometimes he does not," Salinger said. "I'll take the matter up with the president."

"We really leaned on Salinger," terHorst recalled. It just seemed curious the White House was so resistant. "We never got a good answer" why, ultimately, there was no press conference, he said. "It was treated wholly as sort of a family trip, a non-[international] security trip, a non-governmental trip, a homecoming, a uniting with his Irish roots."

The press took solace in Dublin's eating and drinking establishments. Ireland's capital struck Wicker of the *New York Times* as "a very modern city," even if there were no traffic signals on O'Connell Street. The American press ate a lot of salmon, Wicker recalled. "They had it everywhere," he said.

The president's back needed tending after all this activity. He had taken to hot baths for some relief. But on this night, or the next — memories have grown a bit fuzzy on the timing — Kennedy discovered it didn't pay to be last in line. Returning to the American Embassy, he discovered that his sisters had bathed ahead of him and there was no hot water. "Here was the president of the United States, sitting in the bathtub, and they had to bring up pots of hot water and pour them in there," White House staffer Lenny Donnelly remembered. Her boss, Dave Powers, told her about it. He was one of those who had to carry the water upstairs to the chief.

In the evening, Kennedy was center stage at a dinner for seventy-five at Iveagh House given by the prime minister and Mrs. Lemass. With his sisters and sister-in-law, the president walked into the house across a green carpet. The tables were decorated with red and white carnations and roses. There weren't many blue flowers; they were scarce at this time of the season, the florists said. M. Pierre Rolland, chef at Dublin's Hotel Russell, made a special table ornament out of sugar: a reproduction of PT-109. Back outside, the Irish Transport and General Workers Union band played and a children's choir sang from nearby St. Stephen's Green.

The Minihans came up from New Ross for the reception. But one of their sons, Eoin, watched proceedings from behind a rope with his pal, Desmond Carroll. The two young men were at Dublin's Bolton Street College of Technology, and this was their chance to see Kennedy. Eoin Minihan had no strings to pull: the reception was for officials and spouses only. So he and Carroll had to settle for a presidential handshake. "I'm one of the fellows that barely touched him," Minihan laughed four decades later.

After dinner, there was a reception for five hundred — at 10 p.m.! The invitations had caused great consternation in Dublin: it was difficult to find that many suits of white tie and tails in the Irish capital city. It was, the *Irish Times* said, "one of the gravest crises in Hibernian sartorial history." White tie and tails were passé, the newspaper scolded. A spokesman for the Department of External Affairs was pretty unyielding on the point: "White tie is the prescribed dress. To depart from that is entirely up to oneself, but there is no official encouragement to do so. If one wants to come in a dinner jacket, one might by chance, be outstanding." Well, why not, the *Times* riposted. Irish men had attacked such fashion problems through history with "panache and elegance"; since ancient times, the Irish had "a reputation for daring to be different." "Is this to be dashed in the dust by a returned exile?" Well, yes. Kennedy looked elegant and dashing in his white tie and tails.

During the celebration, the American president was given a fourteenth century document linking the Kennedy name and Irish history. On this vellum was the treaty, written in Latin, between the Earl of Ormond, James Butler, and O'Kenedy, at Nenagh, County Tipperary, on March 5, 1336. The document bears the O'Kenedy seal.

The Irish remained continuously amused by presidential security. At one point during the Iveagh House reception, a very conspicuous Secret Service agent, in a raincoat, wandered into a room full of sharply dressed partygoers. He reached into a palm tree and pulled out a red telephone, spoke into the receiver for a moment, then returned it to the tree.

Also targets of Irish curiosity — and generosity — were any staffers connected to Kennedy.

Jean Price Lewis, who worked in the White House's congressional relations office, was stopped in Dublin traffic in a car bearing a sign that said "White House Staff." A woman came up to the vehicle and knocked on the closed window. Price rolled it down. "Have you seen himself today?" the woman asked.

Lenny Donnelly was enticed with some other staffers to a new establishment on Dublin's Sarsfield Quay called the Bark Kitchen Lounge. Just after the 11 p.m. closing time, a Dublin woman rushed Donnelly into the lounge's ladies' room and told her to stand on a toilet seat behind a closed stall door. Within minutes, a local policeman was in the restroom, tapping the stall doors with his nightstick. He scolded the Dublin woman and told her to go home. "You can stay," he whispered to Donnelly, having somehow become aware she was with Kennedy.

The president's appearances, meanwhile, were taking on the enthusiasm and hysteria usually associated with movie and pop music stars.

At evening's end, outside Iveagh House, Kennedy walked toward a crowd of some five thousand, among whom were screaming teenage girls. The security cordon couldn't contain the mass of young women, who broke through the police line and surrounded Kennedy, reaching for his hands and clothes. The scene alarmed police and Secret Service, who pushed into the mob to get to the president. In the process, some girls were pushed against walls and railings. Eight were reported to have fainted, and some were carted off by ambulance.

One young lady made a sprint for the president's empty limousine, with the apparent intent of getting in it. Police intercepted her.

After Kennedy reached his car, the crowd pushed forward again, surrounding him. For a few moments, the limousine couldn't move. Only the persistence of his motorcycle escort finally cleared a path, and the star of the show moved off into the Dublin night.

The security officials later described the frenzy as "a near panic."

This was but one of several incidents of what one writer later described as "hospitality verging on assault."

four

June 28, 1963:
Cork and Dublin

Our weapons were the weapons of the conquered: a dogged ability to endure and preserve our culture, a sense of humor and, most of all, words.

Leon Uris
Trinity: A Novel of Ireland *(1976)*

O**n this morning**, at nine o'clock, Kennedy flew by Army helicopter to the drill square of Collins Barracks in Cork, 166 miles from Dublin. His craft during the one-hour flight was accompanied by four additional helicopters bearing members of his family and the extensive presidential entourage. Lenny Donnelly and her colleagues laughed when the helicopter crew handed them earplugs. They thought it was a joke.

"We didn't laugh when they started their engines," Donnelly said. "Oh my God. We put those in [and] our ears were still hurting."

Because of the rain and mist, the choppers flew low. "I'll bet you no cow in Ireland gave milk for a week after," Donnelly laughed. "All the cows were running like mad."

On the ground, and again in cold and mist, the president was greeted by the pipers of the Fourth and Twelfth Battalions, both of which had served as part of the Irish peacekeeping force in Congo.

For all the meticulous preparations for a presidential trip, the machinery didn't always cooperate: just before Kennedy arrived, the Secret Service discovered his limousine was out of commission. An electrical problem of some kind. The Secret Service asked town officials if they could locate a car with running boards. Kennedy would ride in the car that security normally used. In minutes, a Cork company had produced almost what the Secret Service ordered: a black 1937 Rolls Royce, with running boards. They took it.

Again in a motorcade, the Kennedy procession took fifteen minutes weaving its way for a mile and a half through the steep streets of the second-largest city in Ireland, from Collins Barracks to Dillon's Cross, St. Luke's, Summerhill, MacCurtain Street, Patrick Street, Grand Parade, and South Mall. In the din of cheers and impromptu street corner bands, Kennedy waved under a rain of rose petals and confetti. In this "rebel city" of eighty thousand on Ireland's south coast, the crowds were estimated at more than a hundred thousand. According to some officials, nearly every resident of the city and of towns for miles around were out to see Kennedy. Schools and stores had been closed for the day; bowing to the appeals of officials desperate to keep city streets clear, customary morning deliveries by the milkmen and breadmen had been completed the night before. "Anything Dublin can do, Cork can do better," city residents had boasted before the president's arrival. Out in Cork Harbor, the U.S.S. *Norris* patrolled while private craft blared their sirens.

Skibbereen played a part after all. A large contingent of residents parked themselves strategically, and none better than the St. Fachtnas Silver Band, thirty members strong, camped out on Patrick Street, entertaining the masses with an Irish air, followed by a John Philip Sousa march, then another air. "His maternal ancestors came from Skibbereen and this is one of Skibbereen's great tributes," said Frank Fahy. He and his friends Seamus Ryan, Joe O'Neill, and Joe and John Donovan were parked in place at 7 a.m. "This is the Skibbereen visit Cork is having," Fahy joked.

It was a raucous outpouring, and it would get worse. Some people were hurt as they were pushed up against the locked arms of police, who were trying to keep a line that was moving back and forth like waves on a beach. Lifeguards stood near the River Lee opposite the city hall, ready to pluck the overly boisterous from the water. Others patrolled back and forth in boats in the river. They weren't called upon.

After landing at Collins Barracks in Cork, Kennedy shakes hands with Alderman Sean Casey, mayor of Cork, flanked by mace bearers. Casey was allowed to stay in office beyond his term so he could preside over the day. Irish External Affairs Minister Frank Aiken is wearing his homburg for the damp weather, while Col. W. Donagh of the Irish Army's Southern Command clutches an umbrella at the ready.

Kennedy delighted in the signs people waved over their heads. One read: "JFK and Dev" [many Irish called de Valera that], We came from a land beyond the seas, from Boston and New York. And the boys who beat the Black and Tans are the boys from County Cork." Another poster assured the president, "Do not worry, Jack. The Iron Curtain will rust in peace."

At 10:15, Kennedy, damp from the soft rain, pulled up to the Mansion House, Cork's city hall. There he was joined by the lord mayor of Cork, Alderman Sean Casey — his term of office having been extended so he could preside over this day —External Affairs Minister Aiken, Minister for Industry and Commerce John Lynch, as well as clerics of the major faiths of the city. As in Wexford the day before, many of these dignitaries wore their red robes of office.

"Everybody in Kerry, Tipperary, Kilkenny, and Wexford is here today," Casey told the presidential party. "And a few spies from Belfast, too."

The ceremonies were held in the main concert hall inside the city hall. One thousand people

One of Cork's bridges undergoes an impromptu weight test as every spot is taken for a view of Kennedy's passing motorcade.

had been invited to attend. And to participate: besides the usual ferocious applause and ear-splitting cheers, the audience stomped the floor to signal particularly strong agreement.

On his way into the hall, Kennedy was introduced to four distant cousins from Skibbereen: Richard D. and Patrick D. Fitzgerald, who were brothers, and Richard P. and Patrick Fitzgerald, cousins.

"What do you do there?" the president asked his relatives.

They were farmers, they replied.

"Good," said Kennedy.

The Fitzgeralds then unfolded a copy of the *Sunday Independent* to a page featuring side-by-side photos of Richard D. Fitzgerald and John Fitzgerald Kennedy at age twelve. The president nodded his head as he studied the photos of the two boys, who could have been brothers.

"I am very glad to have met you," Kennedy told his relations. "I'll see you again on the way out."

At Cork City Hall, the red carpet and the military honor guard await Kennedy and his party.

The president's arrival was heralded by a fanfare of trumpets from the Southern Command Army Band. The huge room of the city hall into which Kennedy strode, down a red carpet that stretched all the way back outside to the middle of the street, was resplendent in red, white, and blue flowers. In front of the dais, red and white roses and blue cornflowers formed a large American flag. Red flowers hung in bouquets from the balcony. The scene was lit by floodlights, to accommodate the television cameras.

While many of the powerful, elected and connected, had won chairs in the hall, Cork showed some democracy. Here and there in various sections sat the people who had cleaned the hall in preparation for this event.

The ceremony was piped over loudspeakers to the rest of Cork waiting outside. Lapps Quay opposite city hall was an ocean of people. As in other cities and towns, some of the more adventurous had found rooftop perches. The parapets and support beams of nearby Parnell and Clontarf bridges were strung with people.

This being an official meeting of the Corporation of Cork, Assistant Town Clerk Patrick Clayton read the roll and noted a quorum. One unfortunate wretch was ill and unaccounted for. Lord Mayor Casey, in English and Irish, recited the traditional prayer that opened every meeting.

The freedom of the city, on a scroll and housed in a gold-and-silver box engraved with the American eagle and the Kennedy family crest and mounted on a plinth of Connemara's famous marble, was conferred on Kennedy. The president was being honored, the scroll said, "in token of our pride that this descendant of Irish emigrants should have been elected to such an exalted office, and of appreciation of his action in coming to visit the country of his ancestors; as a tribute to his unceasing and fruitful work towards the attainment of prosperity and true peace by all people of the world; and in recognition of the close ties that have always existed between our two countries." Kennedy was the second president to receive the honor: Woodrow Wilson was given the freedom of the city in January 1919 for his contributions to world peace after World War I. Wilson, however, did not come to Cork personally to pick it up.

Lord Mayor Casey made the presentation, in a speech of considerable length, in Irish and English.

"Throughout its long history, Cork has received many famous visitors from many parts of the world, but I can confidently say that no man has ever come within our walls who is more welcome than John Fitzgerald Kennedy, thirty-fifth president of the great republic of the West, leader of the powerful nation to whom we all owe so much," Casey said. ". . . Mr. President, you have reached the highest point in American public life which any Irishman or any man of Irish descent has reached. In honoring you today in Cork we honor not alone yourself personally and the great American nation, we also honor the Irish race at home and beyond the seas.

"We honor all those who crossed the Atlantic from this island, who made their new homes in the United States and who have contributed so much to that country throughout the years. You, sir, in our eyes represent all that is best, all that is honorable, all that is valiant in our people."

He concluded: "Mr. President, John Fitzgerald Kennedy, thirty-fifth president of the United States of America, distinguished author, valiant fighter for peace, fighter for freedom, fighter for democracy, for me it is a great honor indeed on behalf of my fellow citizens to welcome you here today, to tell you of our great regard for you, and to offer you the highest honor that this city can confer on any man — the freedom of the city of Cork."

The president had a surprise for some of the fifty White House staffers who had flown to Ireland to join him on his trip and were now looking on. He had assigned an aide to research which staffers still had relatives in Ireland. And so it was Lawrence O'Brien, Kennedy's White House liaison with the Congress, saw his aunt, Julia Sweeney, from nearby Dunmanway, sitting in the VIP section with neighbors. Dave Powers's cousins were there, too.

"Mr. Mayor, members of the City Council, Mr. Aiken, ladies and gentlemen," the president began.

"I am honored by this generous gift and also once again am reminded that the Irish have not lost their ability to speak. That was a beautiful welcome.

"I would like to ask how many people here have relatives in the United States? Perhaps they could hold up their hands, if they do."

Many hands waved above the crowd.

"Well, I want to tell you they are doing well," Kennedy went on. His listeners cheered. From outside, cheers rolled easily through the thick walls of the hall.

"I would like to introduce two or three Irishmen who came with me. One is the appointments secretary — the greeter at the White House, Dave Powers, who has, I think, seven first cousins here and they are sitting in the front row. Perhaps he would stand up and all of his Irish cousins. He looks more Irish than they do. Do you want to stand up and turn around so they can see you, Dave?

"And then I would like to introduce to you the pastor at the church which I go to, who comes from Cork — Monsignor [Jeremiah] O'Mahoney. He is the pastor of a poor, humble flock in Palm Beach, Florida!"

This was a reference to St. Edward's, where the Kennedy family worshipped when staying at the family home on the ocean. Their section of Palm Beach was among the wealthiest communities in America.

"And then I would like to have you meet — I don't think he comes from Cork — his family — but, nevertheless, he is our legislative assistant at the White House who came over with us — Larry O'Brien. Perhaps he could stand up. That is his cousin from Cork who is sitting next to him.

"Also, a congressman who represents about eighty-five members of the House of Representatives who are Irish — Congressman Boland from Massachusetts, who came with us.

"I don't want to give the impression that every member of this administration in Washington is Irish — it just seems that way.

"In any case, we are delighted to be here.

"Coming in, I met four rather angry Fitzgeralds. They said they are tired of hearing about the Kennedys in New Ross — and what about the Fitzgeralds? I said that was because my grandfather, who was mayor of Boston, John F. Fitzgerald, used to tell everybody he was from Limerick, Donegal, Donnybrook, anywhere!

"I want to have another Irishman, Jim Rowley — come out here, Jim. He is head of the United States Secret Service. Those members of the Secret Service who aren't Irish are embarrassed about it, but we will make them honorary freemen today, too, Mr. Mayor, if that is all right with you.

"I want to bring you greetings today from the people of Galway, New York; Dublin, New Hampshire; the people of Killarney, West Virginia; Kilkenny, Minnesota; the people of Limerick, Maine; and the people of Shamrock, Texas.

"Most countries send out oil or iron, steel or gold or some other crop, but Ireland has had only one export and that is its people. They have gone all over the United States, and the United States has been generous to them. And I think it not unfair to say that they have been generous themselves and with their sons and daughters to the United States.

"What pleases me most about coming here is not only this connection which all of us in America feel with Ireland, even though time and generations may have separated us from this island, but also because I find here in Ireland those qualities which I associate with the best not only of my own country but of all that we are trying to do and all that we are trying to be.

"The world is a small place today and it is, it seems to me, important that we recognize the kinship which exists between all free people.

"We are in a most climactic period, in the most difficult and dangerous struggle in the history of the world, with the most difficult and dangerous weapons which have ever been devised which could annihilate the human race in a few hours.

"So I think it is important that those of us who happen to be of Irish descent who come to Ireland recognize an even stronger bond which exists between Ireland and the United States, between Europe and the United States, between Latin America and the United States, between the people of Africa, the people of Asia, between all people who wish to be free. That is the most important association, the most important kinship. And I come to this island which has been identified with that effort for a thousand years, which was the first country in the twentieth century to lead what is the most powerful tide of the twentieth century — the desire for national independence, the desire to be free. And I come here in 1963 and find that strong tide still beats, still runs. And I drive from where we arrived to here and am greeted by an honor guard on the way down, nearly half of whom wear the Blue Ribbon, which indicates service in the Congo. So Ireland is still old Ireland, but it has found a new mission in the 1960s, and that is to lead the free world to join with other countries of the free world to do in the sixties what Ireland did in the early part of this century and, indeed, has done for the last eight hundred years — and that is associate intimately with independence and freedom.

"So I must say, Mr. Mayor, that when I am retired from public life that I will take the greatest pride and satisfaction in not only having been president of my own country but a freeman of this city. Thank you."

Walking back outside, Kennedy tripped over something on the steps of city hall, but didn't fall. The crowds strained against the police and pushed closer and closer to Kennedy.

Kennedy addresses Cork from inside city hall. Among the officialdom are ordinary citizens, including the people who had cleaned and readied the hall for the visit. The president surprised some of his White House staffers by making sure some of their Irish relatives were at this event.

Their enthusiasm was impossible to contain. Despite the security, the people of Cork were determined to push past the tight cordon around Kennedy as he moved, quite deliberately, into the mass of men, women, and children struggling mightily to see him, to touch him, to say something to him.

The president was not alarmed.

"You're really a great people. This is really something," he told the crowd.

Then the leader of the free world was pinned against a wall by the crush. The police got a little more forceful, trying to extract the president. Kennedy smiled and was heard to say, "It's all right — these are my people." His security men forced a wedge, and the president helped with a bit of shoving of his own.

"We're all good friends here," he told his well-wishers, "and I'm very happy at this tremendous reception you've all given me. . . . Now I am in a terrible hurry. Will you let me out please?" The crowd parted.

A young girl screamed out to Kennedy: "Please shake my hand!"

He reached through his guards and touched one of her fingers.

"Will that do?" the apologetic president asked.

A half dozen nuns in their habits were spotted crawling under a wooden barricade to get closer to Kennedy.

The vast crowd chanted, "We want Kennedy! We want Kennedy!"

The mayhem resumed. People kept grabbing at his outstretched hands as he stood in his limousine. The frenzied mass closed in again. This time, a man ran up to the president's car and grabbed Kennedy's right hand with both of his. He did not let go. The car moved forward, the grasping man did not. Secret Service agent Jerry Blaine put his arm around Kennedy and tugged, breaking the grip but upsetting the president's balance. Kennedy fell down in the back seat, looking surprised. He was even more surprised when, seconds later, the agent lost his balance, too, and landed on top of his charge. Neither was hurt. The president laughed off the incident when he returned to the American Embassy in Dublin. "My trip to Cork was wonderful," he said, "and I am looking forward to reading about it in the newspapers."

But Kennedy stopped reaching out to shake hands in delirious Cork. He settled for waving.

As his motorcade crawled through the city to the Victoria Road playing field and his waiting helicopter, it seemed the entire city tried to follow, streaming behind his entourage and running and jostling along parallel side streets. Jerald terHorst of the *Detroit News* watched the pushing and shoving. "It was very frenetic," he said. "It may have been scary to people who were security-minded. But it was another expression of joy. It was sort of their way of saying, 'Here I am! Let me recognize you!'"

With the president at the helicopter at last, the enthusiasm nearly turned tragic.

An estimated thirty thousand people had jammed onto the field, and as the Army aircraft prepared to lift off, the throng broke through the police barriers. In the melee, "We were afraid to get left behind," said White House staffer Pauline Fluet. Lenny Donnelly shared the same fear: "We were fighting through the crowd to get into the helicopters."

The helicopter pilots were unable to get going. "The pilots kept saying, 'We can't start. We can't start the helicopters. It's too dangerous — there are too many of them close by the blades,'" Donnelly recalled. "We were yelling, 'Stop those people! Somebody is going to get killed!'" Fluet said.

The American leader's security detail tried to enlist Irish help. "They had a heck of a time getting . . . the Irish cops, getting people back," terHorst said. There was a less-than-obvious reason: "The Irish security people were as anxious to be as close to Kennedy as they could be, just like everybody else," the journalist explained.

Finally, the presidential helicopter's big rotor and the smaller, aft stabilizing rotor began whirling. The pilot attempted a taxiing maneuver, but the crowd still remained dangerously close. Only the racket of the helicopter, the force of the backwash it was creating and the beating of the ominous blades kept the crowd from trying to hold the president to the earth. Even so, it took fifteen minutes for the field to be sufficiently cleared for a safe departure.

"Gee," said another worried White House press veteran who watched the helicopter finally leave the ground, "that was the most dangerous takeoff I've ever seen in many years of covering American presidents. . . . My message home will be of this one helluva hooley we had in Cork."

Connor Coughlan came from Mallow to see the president. Kennedy, he said, was a man who put truth into action. Elsewhere, seventy-two-year-old Mrs. Margaret Gillity came from her house on Temple Avenue and waited three hours for the president. "I am one of the few real Irish colleens he saw," she said. "This was the biggest welcome I have ever seen anyone get in Cork, and it's just as it should be. Because he is a good man and a good Catholic. I hope he will be all right."

☘ ☘ ☘ ☘

Eunice Shriver and Jean Smith did not go with their brother to Cork. The two Kennedy sisters instead visited mentally retarded children at Dublin's St. Augustine School for Boys and the Holy Angel School for Girls. Shriver had visited three such schools on the German leg of the trip, and the cause of the mentally retarded was close to her heart. Her own sister, Rosemary Kennedy, 43 in 1963, was institutionalized. Shriver had been appointed by her brother as a special consultant to a presidential committee dealing with mental retardation. Her family also established the Kennedy Foundation to aid the retarded. She and her husband operated an annual three-week summer camp for retarded girls and boys at their home in suburban Maryland.

President Kennedy "was very good about it" when she asked to break off from the Cork trip to visit the schools, Shriver told a reporter. ". . . When he learned what I wanted to see, he said to go ahead."

The police are no match for the enthusiasm of Cork's crowds, who nearly block Kennedy's way. The president is riding in the Secret Service's Cadillac, which had to replace one of the malfunctioning limousines Kennedy was to use. The security detail is following in its last-minute replacement car, a 1937 Rolls Royce volunteered by a Cork company.

At the schools, the children sang and danced.

"The Irish dances were wonderful," she told the boys. "Why don't you come to the White House? Will you all come?" The answer was obvious.

Shriver said they had come to the boys' school because "the Order of St. John had been nominated for a special award from the Kennedy Foundation."

Nearly ready to go, she begged the children for a lesson in Irish dancing. As they showed her, she danced with them.

Mrs. Smith admired a collection of animals the boys had made from shells. Young John O'Keeffe gave her a rabbit.

At the girls' school, Shriver made apologies for her brother. "I'm sure the president would have come to see you, except that he had to go to the County of Cork," she explained. "So he asked me to visit you instead."

"*Erin go bragh,*" she told the cheering girls as she left.

♣ ♣ ♣ ♣

Returned to the comparative calm of Dublin, Kennedy hustled off his helicopter and into the American Embassy.

"Come quick and we can see ourselves on television," he told Dorothy Tubridy and his aides.

Kennedy entertained his Irish hosts with an embassy luncheon for President and Mrs. de Valera, Prime Minister and Mrs. Lemass, members of the Irish government, and a who's who of Ireland. Mrs. Shriver was hostess for the forty guests.

The women from Bunratty Castle's nightly medieval gatherings, wearing their fifteenth century finery, were flown by military helicopter across the country to Dublin. They sang "The West's Awake," "A Jug of Punch," "Pucae Boille" and "Roisin Dub." The president had a request: "Danny Boy." As the women offered an encore, Kennedy joined in.

"We were absolutely thrilled," said Ruth Hill, producer for the singers. "We had a wonderful time. President Kennedy asked to meet us after the lunch and chatted and shook hands with us all."

The Ireland-America Society presented Kennedy with a special poem, written by Liam Gogan and printed on vellum, celebrating the president's return to Eire.

The contrast between the young president and Ireland's legendary leader was stark. Kennedy was relaxed and informal; de Valera was a bit aloof, and attended to almost constantly by a hovering aide, presumably to ensure the nearly blind and aged man kept a steady course.

After a rain, Kennedy motored to the Arbour Hill Memorial Garden in Dublin, next to the Church of the Sacred Heart. It was in the notorious provost's prison here in 1798 that Theobald Wolfe Tone, the Irish patriot, slit his own throat to deny the British hangman his job.

But Kennedy had come to pay homage to patriots of more recent history. Here the president of the United States became the first foreign head of state to lay a wreath on ten graves of de Valera's comrades in arms, ten of fourteen leaders of the Easter Rising of 1916 who all were executed by the British. They were buried in a common grave in what had been the prison yard.

It is one of those ironies of history that the five-day rebellion in April 1916 caused puzzlement, then irritation among much of Dublin's populace, upset over the disruptions, then destruction, in their city. There was no general rising, and Padraig Pearse, James Connolly, and the other leaders were forced to surrender.

Then, as had been their history in Ireland for centuries, the British overplayed their advantage. They began shooting the rebels. Pearse and Connolly were executed first. Then Thomas Clarke, Sean MacDiarmada, Thomas MacDonagh, Eamonn Ceannt, Joseph Plunkett, Edward Daly, Michael O. Hanrahan, William Pearse, John McBride, Con Colbert, Sean Heuston, and Michael Mallin. The executions shocked Dublin and Ireland. From those

On a damp Dublin afternoon, Kennedy and the official party arrive at Arbour Hill, which the president later would say was the "highlight" of his visit. Prime Minister Sean Lemass walks with Kennedy. Just after the group of military officers are U.S. Ambassador Matthew McCloskey and Irish External Affairs Minister Frank Aiken.

deaths sprang to life the determination that Ireland would be independent at last.

Next to the common grave, in the church, is a wooden altar believed to have been fashioned by an Irish political prisoner in the nineteenth century.

A plaque by the altar tells a poignant tale: "Before this altar in Kilmainham Jail, men and women, who served for their patriotism and of whom a number gave their lives for Ireland, assisted at Holy Mass. Among them, before their execution, were leaders of the 1916 rising. At this altar also, Joseph Mary Plunkett, one of the seven signatories of the Proclamation of the Republic, was married to Grace Gifford on 3rd May, 1916, the eve of his execution. Pray for the souls of those who died for Ireland."

De Valera, the rebel who had commanded Boland's Flour Mills and had barely escaped the executioners' bullets himself, walked with Kennedy to the gravesite, now bordered by a curved wall of Irish limestone, bearing a cross and the text of the independence proclamation, in English and Irish. Lemass, another veteran of the Easter Rising, was there, too, with Lt. Gen. Sean McKeown, chief of staff and former commander-in-chief of the United Nations forces in Congo.

The respects paid were no mere ceremonial duty. Like Kennedy's visit itself, this was a closing of an historical circle.

"The fact that he, as the president of the United States, the greatest nation in the world, of Irish origin, performed the ceremony had to have a tremendously emotional effect upon the Irish people," Lemass explained.

Kennedy sensed this immediately. He felt what the Irish felt. His face was set as if he were attending the funerals of dear friends. The Irish army band played Chopin's "Funeral March" and "Flowers of the Forest" as Kennedy stood at the wall. The last post was sounded, then the Irish tricolor, previously at half-mast, was hoisted to the top of the staff.

Kennedy watched the guard of honor from the Irish Army Cadet School perform drills so impressive that he asked his hosts afterwards for details of what they did. And he requested a film of the ceremony, so something like it could be conducted at the Tomb of the Unknown Soldier in Arlington National Cemetery across the Potomac River from Washington. Kennedy confided that he did not think American drills performed for such solemn ceremonies measured up.

He had a chance to read the wall at Arbour Hill.

"We declare," part of the proclamation read, "the right of the people of Ireland to the ownership of Ireland and to the unfettered control of Irish destinies, to be sovereign and indefeasible. The long usurpation of that right by a foreign people and government has not extinguished the right, nor can it ever be extinguished except by the destruction of the Irish people."

The president walked over to speak to some of the cadets, who were two weeks away from being commissioned, and to greet a group of military nurses.

Kennedy would later say that the Arbour Hill commemoration was the highlight of his tour in Ireland.

♣ ♣ ♣ ♣

When the Irish leader Charles Stewart Parnell visited Washington in 1880, he was granted a rare honor: he was invited to address a joint session of the United States Congress.

At long last, Ireland now could reply in kind. Kennedy would address a joint session of the Dail and Seanad, the two houses of the Irish Parliament.

Riding in the limousine through the rain-soaked streets on the way to Leinster House from Arbour Hill, Kennedy scribbled changes in the margins of his prepared text. As he made corrections, he acknowledged the cheers of the throngs along the route. "It's a pity he couldn't wave his foot," joked Minister Aiken.

Lemass, sitting with the president and Aiken, was impressed at how Kennedy moved

At Arbour Hill in Dublin on the rainy afternoon of June 28, Kennedy honors the executed leaders of the 1916 Rising. Prime Minister Sean Lemass, himself a veteran of the Rising, stands to Kennedy's right, while Lt. Gen. Sean McKeown, chief of staff and former United Nations commander in chief in Congo, salutes to the president's left. Kennedy called the ceremony the "highlight" of his Irish visit and asked for a film of the Irish Army Cadets' drill.

from the script to the crowd and back again. The prime minister told Kennedy he often made changes to speeches, too, but then discovered he couldn't read his own writing.

"Neither can I," Kennedy replied. But he explained further: "This way, in the margin, it puts points in mind, and helps me to find the words that I want to use in addition to the script."

The president was crossing out entire paragraphs and adding new thoughts all during the short ride.

At the steps leading into Leinster House, the major figures of the two governments met. Then those with Kennedy were escorted to what is called the distinguished strangers gallery.

In the vestibule of the Dail chamber, Kennedy signed the visitors' book. Around him in urns and boat-shaped vases were freshly cut chrysanthemums, peonies, iris, delphiniums, and bridal gladioli. The president joined Lemass for the walk down the main hall and up the stairs to the Dail itself.

The superintendent of the Houses of the Oireachtas, S. O'Leary — much like the sergeant at arms in the U.S. House of Representatives — introduced the president. He spoke four Gaelic words never before uttered to announce a visitor to the chamber: "*Uachtarán stáit aonlaithi mhericeá.*" Of course, these words were: "The President of the United States of America."

At 4:18 p.m., President Kennedy entered the Parliament. Usually, visiting dignitaries used the back entrance to the chamber. Kennedy was escorted through the front entrance by Lemass; Deputy James Mathew Dillon, leader of the Fine Gael party; and Deputy Brendan Corish, leader of the Labour party. The members of Parliament stood and applauded as Kennedy made his way to the dais, where he met Padraig Hogan, Speaker of the Dail, the *Ceann Comhairle.*

Among those sitting with the 144 deputies and 60 senators jammed into the intimate chamber, with horseshoe-shaped rows of seats and mahogany benches, was de Valera. From the distinguished strangers gallery above the Dail floor peered figures from a half century of Irish history: Domhnall O Buachalla, the *Seanascal*; Sean T. O'Kelly, former president of Ireland; and William T. Cosgrave, first president of the Executive Council and a former prime minister, stepping into the Dail for the first time in two decades. The presence of O'Kelly and Cosgrave, as well as their demeanor toward each other, was almost as much a sensation as Kennedy's appearance. The two had been on opposite sides of Ireland's brief and bloody civil war after independence was obtained forty years before: O'Kelly was among those pushing for a pure republic, while Cosgrave backed keeping Ireland's dominion status with the United Kingdom. Cosgrave's side prevailed when the strife ended in 1923, but O'Kelly's turn came in 1948 when Ireland formally withdrew from the British Commonwealth and proclaimed itself a republic. Cosgrave, 83, had entered and taken his seat first. O'Kelly, 81, had come in a little later. He stopped behind Cosgrave's chair, squeezed Cosgrave's arm, and the two shook hands, to the delirious ovations of onlookers.

Kennedy was breaking new ground this day. His was the first speech in a parliamentary session to be televised. And he was the first foreigner to address the Irish body. And for the first time, the wire mesh that protected Irish lawmakers from projectiles launched from the visitors gallery was removed.

Hogan greeted Kennedy after the president sat next to him on the special dais erected for the event.

"Mr. President," the Speaker said, "it is indeed a great honor to have the privilege as *Ceann Comhairle* of *Dáil Éireann* of welcoming you on behalf of my colleagues and myself to the Parliament of Ireland. For generations, the people of Ireland and the people of the United States of America have been closely and intimately associated in times of trial and in times of triumph.

"The emigrants from our shores have tasted the sweet air of freedom and opportunity sweeping across the broad plains of that hospitable land, and we are proud — very proud indeed — to know that these emigrants were effective and potent factors in the development of that great country. Thus in ordinary circumstances it would be an occasion of pride and privilege for any Irishman to welcome the president of the United States of America to an Irish Parliament.

"But, Mr. President, this is not an ordinary occasion. Your great personality elevates it far above that level. It is an occasion unique as an event in Irish history — it is an international gesture of kindness and goodwill of inestimable value. When the citizen who presides over the great American people of the United States shares with the people of Ireland the heritage of blood, of name and tradition, then the event is enhanced almost beyond measure.

"May I therefore hasten to extend to you, Mr. President, on behalf of my colleagues and myself a sincere and hearty welcome to the Parliament of Ireland, and I respectfully request you to address your eager audience."

Education Minister Hillery watched Kennedy closely from his seat near the front of the Dail. One of the American leader's trouser legs, Hillery noticed, "was shimmering a bit" from rapid movement. It wasn't so much nervousness, the minister thought, but more "like a horse, a thoroughbred waiting to go out in a race." As Kennedy spoke, the shimmering went away.

"Mr. Speaker, Prime Minister, members of the Parliament," the president began, "I am grateful for your welcome and for that of your countrymen.

"The thirteenth day of [December], 1862, will be a day long remembered in American history. At Fredericksburg, [Virginia], thousands of men fought and died on one of the bloodiest battlefields of the American Civil War. One of the most brilliant stories of that day was written by a band of twelve hundred men who went into battle wearing a green sprig in their hats. They wore a proud heritage and a special courage, given to those who had long fought for the cause of freedom. I am referring, of course, to the Irish Brigade. Gen. Robert

E. Lee, the great military leader of the Southern Confederate forces, said of this group of men after the battle, 'The gallant stand which this bold brigade made on the heights of Fredericksburg is well known. Never were men so brave. They ennobled their race by their splendid gallantry on that desperate occasion. Their brilliant though hopeless assaults on our lines excited the hearty applause of our officers and soldiers.'

"Of the twelve hundred men who took part in that assault, 280 survived the battle. The Irish Brigade was led into battle on that occasion by Brig. Gen. Thomas F. Meagher, who had participated in the unsuccessful Irish uprising of 1848, was captured by the British and sent in a prison ship to Australia, from whence he finally came to America. In the fall of 1862, after serving with distinction and gallantry in some of the toughest fighting of this most bloody struggle, the Irish Brigade was presented with a new set of flags. In the city ceremony, the city chamberlain gave them the motto, 'The Union, Our Country, and Ireland Forever.' Their old ones having been torn to shreds by bullets in previous battles, Capt. Richard McGee took possession of these flags on December second in New York City and arrived with them at the Battle of Fredericksburg and carried them in the battle. Today, in recognition of what these gallant Irishmen and what millions of other Irish have done for my country, and through the generosity of the 'Fighting Sixty-ninth,' I would like to present one of these flags to the people of Ireland."

The presentation was a surprise. The Irish lawmakers, of course, were delighted. Kennedy unveiled the huge green battle flag, embroidered with a gold harp, placed behind him to his left. The standard carries this inscription: "69th Regiment N.Y.S.V. — presented by the citizens of New York to the 69th N.Y.S.V. (1st Regt. of the Irish Brigade), Brigadier General Thomas Francis Meagher, commanding. In grateful appreciation of their gallant and brilliant conduct on the battlefields of Virginia and Maryland in the war to maintain the national domain and the American Union, Nov. 1862."

Kennedy had had the flag mounted and put behind glass with a gilt frame. A small metal plate on that frame reads: "*Don a Shoilse, Eamon de Valera, Uachtarán na hÉireann* [To His Excellency, Eamon de Valera, President of Ireland], from President John F. Kennedy, June, 1963." (The flag now occupies a prominent place just inside the public entrance to Leinster House.)

"As you can see, gentlemen," Kennedy continued, "the battle honors of the brigade include Fredericksburg, Chancellorsville, Yorktown, Fair Oaks, Gaines Mill, Allen's Farm, Savage's Station, White Oak Bridge, Glendale, Malvern Hill, Antietam, Gettysburg, and Bristow Station.

"I am deeply honored to be your guest in the free parliament of a free Ireland. If this nation had achieved its present political and economic stature a century or so ago, my great-grandfather might never have left New Ross, and I might, if fortunate, be sitting down there with you."

The chamber laughed.

"Of course," Kennedy went on, "if your own president had never left Brooklyn, he might be standing up here instead of me!" Now, even louder laughter.

"This elegant building, as you know, was once the property of the Fitzgerald family, but I have not come here to claim it," the president said. "Of all the new relations I have discovered on this trip, I regret to say that no one has yet found any link between me and a great Irish patriot, Lord Edward Fitzgerald. Lord Edward, however, did not like to stay here in his family home because, as he wrote his mother, 'Leinster House does not inspire the brightest ideas.'"

This line would subsequently prove ill-advised.

"That was a long time ago, however. It has also been said by some that a few of the features of this stately mansion served to inspire similar features in the White House in Washington. Whether this is true or not, I know that the White House was designed by James Hoban, a noted Irish-American architect, and I have no doubt that he believed by incorporating several features of the Dublin style he would make it more homelike for any president of Irish descent. It was a long wait, but I appreciate his efforts.

"There is also an unconfirmed rumor that Hoban was never fully paid for his work on the White House. If this proves to be true, I will speak to our secretary of the treasury about it, although I hear this body is not particularly interested in the subject of revenues."

Kennedy was jokingly referring, of course, to the recent, bitter battle over a sales tax.

"I am proud to be the first American president to visit Ireland during his term of office, proud to be addressing this distinguished assembly, and proud of the welcome you have given me. My presence and your welcome, however, only symbolize the many and enduring links which have bound the Irish and the Americans since the earliest days.

"Benjamin Franklin — the envoy of the American Revolution who was also born in Boston — was received by the Irish Parliament in 1772. It was neither independent nor free from discrimination at the time, but Franklin reported its members 'disposed to be friends of America.' 'By joining our interest with theirs,' he said, 'a more equitable treatment . . . might be obtained for both nations.'

"Our interests have been joined ever since. Franklin sent leaflets to Irish freedom fighters. O'Connell was influenced by Washington, and Emmet influenced Lincoln. Irish volunteers played so predominant a role in the American army that Lord Mountjoy lamented in the British Parliament that 'we have lost America through the Irish.'

"John Barry, whose statue we honored yesterday and whose sword is in my office, was only one who fought for liberty in America to set an example for liberty in Ireland. Yesterday was the 117th anniversary of Charles Stewart Parnell — whose grandfather fought under Barry and whose mother was born in America — and who, at the age of thirty-four, was invited to address the American Congress on the cause of Irish freedom. 'I have seen since

I have been in this country,' he said, 'so many tokens of the good wishes of the American people toward Ireland. . . .' And today, eighty-three years later, I can say to you that I have seen in *this* country so many tokens of good wishes of the Irish people towards America.

"And so it is that our two nations, divided by distance, have been united by history. No people ever believed more deeply in the cause of Irish freedom than the people of the United States. And no country contributed more to building my own than your sons and daughters. They came to our shores in a mixture of hope and agony, and I would not underrate the difficulties of their course once they arrived in the United States. They left behind hearts, fields, and a nation yearning to be free. It is no wonder that James Joyce described the Atlantic as a bowl of bitter tears. And an earlier poet wrote, 'They are going, going, going, and we cannot bid them stay.'

"But today this is no longer the country of hunger and famine that those emigrants left behind. It is not rich, and its progress is not yet complete; but it is, according to statistics, one of the best-fed countries in the world. Nor is it any longer a country of persecution, political or religious. It is a free country, and that is why any American feels at home.

"There are those who regard this history of past strife and exile as better forgotten. But, to use the phrase of Yeats, let us not casually reduce 'that great past to a trouble of fools.'"

Yeats's son, Sen. Michael Yeats, was in the audience.

"For we need not feel the bitterness of the past to discover its meaning for the present and the future," Kennedy went on. "And it is the present and the future of Ireland that today holds so much promise to my nation as well as to yours, and, indeed, to all mankind.

"For the Ireland of 1963, one of the youngest of nations and the oldest of civilizations, has discovered that the achievement of nationhood is not an end but a beginning. In the years since independence, you have undergone a new and peaceful revolution, an economic and industrial revolution, transforming the face of this land while still holding to the old spiritual and cultural values. You have modernized your economy, harnessed your rivers, diversified your industry, liberalized your trade, electrified your farms, accelerated your rate of growth, and improved the living standards of your people.

"The other nations of the world — in whom Ireland has long invested her people and her children — are now investing their capital as well as their vacations here in Ireland. This revolution is not yet over, nor will it be, I am sure, until a fully modern Irish economy fully shares in world prosperity.

"But prosperity is not enough. Eighty-three years ago, Henry Grattan, demanding the more independent Irish Parliament that would always bear his name, denounced those who were satisfied merely by new grants of economic opportunity. 'A country,' he said, 'enlightened as Ireland, chartered as Ireland, armed as Ireland, and injured as Ireland will be satisfied with nothing less than liberty.' And today, I am certain, free Ireland — a full-fledged member of the world community, where some are not yet free, and where some counsel an acceptance of tyranny — free Ireland will not be satisfied with anything less than liberty.

"I am glad, therefore, that Ireland is moving in the mainstream of current world events. For I sincerely believe that your future is as promising as your past is proud, and that your destiny lies not as a peaceful island in a sea of troubles, but as a maker and shaper of world peace.

"For self-determination can no longer mean isolation; and the achievement of national independence today means withdrawal from the old status only to return to the world scene with a new one. New nations can build with their former governing powers the same kind of fruitful relationship that Ireland has established with Great Britain — a relationship founded on equality and mutual interests. And no nation, large or small, can be indifferent to the fate of others, near or far. Modern economics, weaponry, and communications have made us realize more than ever that we are one human family and this one planet is our home.

" 'The world is large,' wrote John Boyle O'Reilly.

" 'The world is large when its weary leagues two loving hearts divide,

" 'But the world is small when your enemy is loose on the other side.'

"The world is even smaller today, though the enemy of John Boyle O'Reilly is no longer a hostile power. Indeed, across the gulfs and barriers that now divide us, we must remember that there are no permanent enemies. Hostility today is a fact, but it is not a ruling law. The supreme reality of our time is our indivisibility as children of God and our common vulnerability on this planet.

"Some may say that all this means little to Ireland. In an age when 'history moves with the tramp of earthquake feet' — in an age when a handful of men and nations have the power literally to devastate mankind — in an age when the needs of the developing nations are so staggering that even the richest lands often groan with the burden of assistance — in such an age, it may be asked, how can a nation as small as Ireland play much of a role on the world stage?

"I would remind those who ask that question, including those in other small countries, of the words of one of the great orators of the English language: 'All the world owes much to the little "five feet high" nations. The greatest art of the world was the work of little nations. The most enduring literature of the world came from little nations. The heroic deeds that thrill humanity through generations were the deeds of little nations fighting for their freedom. And oh, yes, the salvation of mankind came through a little nation.'

"Ireland has already set an example and a standard for other small nations to follow.

"This has never been a rich or powerful country, and yet, since earliest times, its influence on the world has been rich and powerful. No larger nation did more to keep Christianity and Western culture alive in their darkest centuries. No larger nation did more to spark the cause of independence in America, indeed, around the world. And no larger nation has ever provided the world with more literary and artistic genius.

"This is an extraordinary country. George Bernard Shaw, speaking as an Irishman, summed up an approach to life: Other people, he said, 'see things and . . . say: "Why?" . . . But I dream things that never were — and I say: "Why not?"'

"It is that quality of the Irish — that remarkable combination of hope, confidence, and imagination — that is needed more than ever today. The problems of the world cannot possibly be solved by skeptics or cynics, whose horizons are limited by the obvious realities. We need men who can dream of things that never were, and ask why not. It matters not how small a nation is that seeks world peace and freedom, for, to paraphrase a citizen of my country, 'the humblest nation of all the world, when clad in armor of a righteous cause, is stronger than all the hosts of Error.'

"Ireland is clad in the cause of national and human liberty with peace. To the extent that the peace is disturbed by conflict between the former colonial powers and the new and developing nations, Ireland's role is unique. For every new nation knows that Ireland was the first of the small nations in the twentieth century to win its struggle for independence, and that the Irish have traditionally sent their doctors and technicians and soldiers and priests to help other lands to keep their liberty alive.

"At the same time, Ireland is part of Europe, associated with the Council of Europe, progressing in the context of Europe, and a prospective member of an expanded European Common Market. Thus Ireland has excellent relations with both the new and the old, the confidence of both sides and an opportunity to act where the actions of greater powers might be looked upon with suspicion.

"The central issue of freedom, however, is between those who believe in self-determination and those in the East who would impose on others the harsh and oppressive Communist system; and here your nation wisely rejects the role of a go-between or a mediator. Ireland pursues an independent course in foreign policy, but it is not neutral between liberty and tyranny and never will be.

"For knowing the meaning of foreign domination, Ireland is the example and inspiration to those enduring endless years of oppression. It was fitting and appropriate that this nation played a leading role in censuring the suppression of the Hungarian revolution, for how many times was Ireland's quest for freedom suppressed only to have that quest renewed by the succeeding generation? Those who suffer beyond that wall I saw on Wednesday in Berlin must not despair of their future. Let them remember the constancy, the faith, the endurance, and the final success of the Irish. And let them remember, as I heard sung by your sons and daughters yesterday in Wexford, the words, 'the boys of Wexford, who fought with heart and hand, to burst in twain the galling chain and free our native land.'

"The major forum for your nation's greater role in world affairs is that of protector of the weak and the voice of the small, the United Nations. From Cork to the Congo, from Galway to the Gaza Strip, from this legislative assembly to the United Nations, Ireland is sending its most talented men to do the world's most important work — the work of peace.

"In a sense, this export of talent is in keeping with an historic Irish role — but you no longer go as exiles and emigrants, but for the service of your country and, indeed, of all men. Like the Irish missionaries of medieval days, like the 'wild geese' after the Battle of the Boyne, you are not content to sit by your fireside while others are in need of your help. Nor are you content with the recollections of the past when you face the responsibilities of the present.

"Twenty-six sons of Ireland have died in the Congo; many others have been wounded. I pay tribute to them and to all of you for your commitment and dedication to world order. And their sacrifice reminds us all that we must not falter now.

"The United Nations must be fully and fairly financed. Its peace-keeping machinery must be strengthened. Its institutions must be developed until some day, and perhaps some distant day, a world of law is achieved.

"Ireland's influence in the United Nations is far greater than your relative size. You have not hesitated to take the lead on such sensitive issues as the Kashmir dispute. And you sponsored that most vital resolution, adopted by the General Assembly, which opposed the spread of nuclear arms to any nation not now possessing them, urging an international agreement with inspection and controls. And I pledge to you that the United States of America will do all in its power to achieve such an agreement and fulfill your resolution.

"I speak of these matters today not because Ireland is unaware of its role — but I think it important that you know that we know what you have done. And I speak to remind the other small nations that they, too, can and must help build a world peace. They, too, as we all are, are dependent on the United Nations for security, for an equal chance to be heard, for progress towards a world made safe for diversity.

"The peace-keeping machinery of the United Nations cannot work without the help of the smaller nations, nations whose forces threaten no one and whose forces can thus help create a world in which no nation is threatened. Great powers have their responsibilities and their burdens, but the smaller nations of the world must fulfill their obligations as well.

"A great Irish poet once wrote: 'I believe profoundly . . . in the future of Ireland . . . that this is an isle of destiny, that that destiny will be glorious . . . and that when our hour is come, we will have something to give to the world.'

"My friends: Ireland's hour has come. You have something to give to the world — and that is a future of peace with freedom.

"Thank you."

After thirty-five minutes of decorating Kennedy's words with truncated applause and shouts of "Hear, hear" at every mention of Ireland's fight for liberty, the Irish Parliament at last stood in tribute, filling the chamber with sustained clapping and cheers.

Liam O Buachalla, the chairman of the Seanad, then spoke, in Gaelic, and then in English:

"It is my privilege, as chairman of the Seanad, to convey to the president of the United States of America, John F. Kennedy, the profound thanks of this joint assembly of the Houses of *Oireachtas Éireann.* President Kennedy has done us a high honor by accepting our invitation to visit and to address us here today. We assure him of our deep appreciation of the sentiments and of the high ideals enshrined in that address. May I also say we thank him from the bottom of our hearts for the generous gift he has bestowed on us? We assure him that this flag will serve to strengthen still further the bonds of friendship that exist between our two nations.

"This, indeed, is truly an historic occasion and, in addition, unprecedented in the annals of our parliamentary institutions. This is the first time, since the foundation of the state, a visitor has been accorded the distinction of addressing us, in joint session, from the floor of the House.

"Today, Mr. President, your responsibilities are many and they are heavy. The great cause of truth and liberty is being assailed. The battle for the rights of man, for his economic, social and political uplift, is being waged in every land and in every clime, regardless of creed or color. To you, sir, has fallen the task of leadership in this desperate struggle. The members of *Dáil Éireann* and of *Seanad Éireann* are proud of you. In common with true lovers of freedom and progress everywhere, we repose, fully, our confidence in you. We assure you of our steadfast support and we pray that God will sustain you and that He will crown your efforts with success.

"In conclusion, may I once again assure you how deeply we have been honored by your coming and how deeply we are inspired by your address, which we shall be privileged to record in our official proceedings. Mr. President, as you leave us, you carry with you the warm affection of the members of this Parliament and, indeed, of Irishmen and of Irishwomen all over the world. *Go gcuire Dia gach beannacht ort agus go dte tú slán* [May God's blessing be upon you, and goodbye]."

President Kennedy then departed the chamber with his escorts as his hosts stood and applauded him one last time.

Kenneth O'Donnell was stopped by an Irish woman who pointed out two lawmakers chatting in the hall.

"Those two are political enemies," she said. "This is the first time they've spoken together in twenty years. All of us love your President Kennedy, and that's the only thing that all of the people in Ireland have completely agreed upon since the British passed the Conscription Bill of 1918."

Then came an amusing little sidelight that delighted the Irish, who had bristled a bit at some of the take-charge attitude of the security advance teams that had tromped through city and farm before Kennedy had arrived.

On the move from event to event, the president of the United States paused for a side

The *Irish Press*, Saturday, June 29, 1963

The Irish Press

State, civic and academic honours for President Kennedy

CLIMAX TO HISTORIC VISIT

CROWDED, MOVING EVENTS

YESTERDAY was a crowded day of historic events as President Kennedy, on the third day of his Irish tour, created history in Dáil Eireann, received the freedom of the State's two greatest cities, had honours conferred on him by two universities and paid homage at the graves of the 1916 leaders in Arbour Hill.

In speech after speech there was a fierce pride and glowing joy in his Irish descent, and Irish people throughout the world who witnessed the day of history awoke to a new appreciation of their nation.

It was a day of great solemnity and dignity, of affairs of State and academic occasion, a day when Mr. Kennedy delved deep in the history of Ireland—a day on which he showed for all the world to see just how much he thinks of the country of his forebears.

In world's great forum

He spoke of freedom and liberty, of the role of Ireland in the cause of the free world, of the Congo and the Irish soldiers who died there, of the Council of Europe, of the United Nations and the country's work for peace.

The major forum for your nation's greater role in world affairs is that of protector of the weak and voice of the small, the United Nations," he said. "From Cork to the Congo, from Galway to the Gaza Strip, from this legislative assembly to the United Nations General Assembly, Ireland is sending its most talented men to do the world's most important work — the work of peace."

And again he said: " Ireland is part of Europe, associated with the Council of Europe, progressing in the context of Europe, and a prospective member of an expanded European Common Market."

Hope and imagination

Or again: " It is that quality of the Irish — that remarkable combination of hope, confidence and imagination — that is needed more than ever today. Ireland is clad in the cause of national and human liberty with peace.

the 'Boys of Wexford, who fought with heart and hand to burst in twain the galling chain and free our native land '."

At Arbour Hill he saw the graves where the 1916 leaders lie and read their names and the Proclamation of the Irish Republic. It was following his tribute at this hallowed spot that he said later in the Dáil: " This has never been a rich or powerful country and yet, since the earliest times, its influence on the world has been both rich and powerful. No larger nation did more to keep Christianity and Western culture alive in their darkest centuries. No larger nation did more to spark the cause of independence in America and around the world. And no larger nation has ever provided the world with more literary and artistic genius."

In the magnificent St. Patrick's Hall in Dublin Castle he was truly appreciative of the honours conferred on him when he received the freedom of the city of Dublin and the honorary degrees of Doctor of Laws from both the National University and Dublin University. But he provided the welcome note of light-hearted humour when in his speech of thanks he said that if ever he is at a Gaelic football match between Trinity and U.C.D. he would " cheer for one and pray for the other."

South's greatest ever

The South, not to be outdone by Dublin and Wexford, gave President Kennedy a welcome reception never before experienced by any visitor to the City of Cork. His address here was in marked contrast to the Dáil speech and, while he did not forget to pay stress on the matters that counted to Cork people, he delighted the attendance in the City Hall with his light approach in replying to the Lord Mayor's speech.

Everywhere he went, both in Cork and Dublin, there were the same enthusiastic crowds who forsook work and business for the brief time it took to see him pass along the route.

Last night there was a welcome respite for Mr. Kennedy when he was the guest at a private dinner of

Pope thanks Taoiseach for message

THE following is the text of the telegram received by the Taoiseach from His Eminence Cardinal Cicognani, Vatican Secretary of State, in reply to the message of congratulation sent on the occasion of the election of His Holiness Pope Paul VI.:

" Right Honourable Sean F. Lemass, Taoiseach Dublin. Holy Father, touched by your moving message on his election, expresses to you and colleagues in Government and Irish nation heartfelt gratitude. "Imparting particular Apostolic Benediction.

" CARDINAL CICOGNANI"

TODAY'S TIDES

An historic picture — President Kennedy addressing a joint session of both Houses of the Oireachtas yesterday. On the front benches is the centre of the picture are the Taoiseach and members of the Government and in the benches at the bottom of the picture are the members of the Opposition, seated in the centre near the President are the Ceann Comhairle, Mr. Hogan, and the Cathaoirleach of the Seanad, Prof. O Buachalla. In front of them are Dáil officials.

trip to the men's room. Somehow, the Secret Service missed the exit. For a few harrowing moments — for the Secret Service, but not for the amused hosts — the leader of the Western world was missing.

♣ ♣ ♣ ♣

Not a word about partition had been spoken in Kennedy's most important speech in Ireland.

"To most residents of this independent-minded republic the most sensible thing he could say would be that he would do everything possible to unify the six counties of Northern Ireland, with their strong Protestant, pro-British leanings, to the Erin governed out of Dublin," reported the *Dallas Morning News*. "In an address before a joint session of the Irish Parliament, however, Kennedy said nothing of the kind. Nobody in his right mind would have expected him to."

That omission was, indeed, deliberate.

The White House position, enumerated in internal communications before the trip, was that in American relations with Ireland, there were "no real substantive problems, except perhaps partition, which the president should avoid." That meant avoid in public, for, as Kennedy had already made clear with Lemass, he was eager to discuss the matter privately.

In the context of what would be euphemistically termed the "troubles" in Northern Ireland at the end of the decade, Kennedy's public silence on the matter might seem puzzling. But at the time, partition was a dormant, though certainly not forgotten, matter. Far from it.

Ireland's minister of external affairs in 1951, as in 1963, was Frank Aiken.

"We'll settle the matter of Ireland and the six northern counties in a logical, orderly manner, and not by force," he had said twelve years before Kennedy's visit.

There were rumbles for a time from new dissenters from the status quo, young people mostly, referred to by some as "thugs," by others as "young lads," who appropriated the banner of the Irish Republican Army to let their presence be known. A new IRA had become active in Northern Ireland in 1956. Violence on both sides claimed eighteen lives over five years. By some estimates, there were about two hundred IRA partisans by the early 1960s. But they won little public backing, and when both the British and de Valera began imprisoning IRA members without trial, the pressure forced the IRA to disband in 1961.

"Irridentism — the movement for recovery of lost territories — is not a strong political force in Ireland today," reported Robert H. Estabrook for the *Washington Post and Times-Herald*. "Although virtually all politicians champion reunification, few advocate achieving it by violence."

And in subtle ways, the Republic of Ireland refused to even acknowledge the island was divided. In a booklet the government distributed to visitors, the Irish population figures combined North and South without distinction. The six counties in the North, the booklet noted in passing, were run separately from the Republic.

In the euphoria after his visit, Kennedy was seen as a potential mediator in the partition debate. If only he had gone to the North and tried to "heal the breach between us," writer Donald S. Connery heard often.

"I have always remembered this as an exquisite example of Irish pipe-dreaming," he scoffed in 1968. "Kennedy might have been able to do some good in the North, even as a Catholic, and Prime Minister O'Neill hoped he would come, but healing the breach is something else. Having just flown in from the relative simplicities of divided Berlin and divided Germany, Kennedy was not anxious to hurl himself into the bottomless pit of the divided-Ireland question."

Others were less reticent. A group called the Border Protest Committee dropped a resolution by the American Embassy for Kennedy. It isn't known whether he ever saw it. The document, signed by the committee's chairman and secretary, Leo McCann and G.K. Scott, respectively, asked for the American leader's backing for efforts to end "the mutilation of our island home."

"Relying on the claims of your Irish ancestry and realizing your power and influence, we appeal to you personally to use your good offices," the resolution stated, "in pressing upon the British prime minister the necessity of seeking a solution to the partition question, failing which that the assistance of the United Nations be invoked and a committee of that body be set up to examine the whole position. Actions such as these would make your term of office a period never to be forgotten by the Irish people from whom you have sprung."

Belfast's Nationalist newspaper, the *Irish News,* was not reluctant to raise the partition issue in the context of Kennedy's visit, even if its neighbors in the South were.

"In Ireland," the paper said, "the only dark cloud is the fact that he finds on this soil a country which is denied full nationhood."

The Irish government was keen to see Kennedy take a stand as president on partition. But Dublin also was cognizant of the warm relations the United States enjoyed with London. They would have to settle for symbolism. "The visit of an American president with roots in Ireland is a propaganda weapon of tremendous value for those in the Republic of Eire to whom the six counties of the island are a bone in the throat," an American observer pointed out.

"I would like to have seen him be a bit more active in getting a solution for partition," Aiken later said. "We urged him to do it. He perhaps did it quietly, but he didn't disclose that fact."

Kennedy, Aiken pointed out, had been behind resolutions while in Congress urging an end to partition.

"But I appreciate also that an American president has a long list of problems," the minister acknowledged, "and over the years, the relations between Great Britain and the United States have been very close, and they felt a great need to keep together so, in those circumstances, great powers don't take any public action that might upset that relationship."

That was precisely the point, agreed columnist W.A. Newman in the *Irish Press:* "Those of us who hoped that he *might* throw out some expression of anti-partitionist sentiment should have known better. As head of a nation friendly to and in the closest alliance with Britain, he could not have been expected — indeed, it would have been in the worst of diplomatic bad taste."

In the view of opposition leaders in Fine Gael, the Lemass government hadn't laid the proper groundwork for productive relations with the Kennedy administration.

Sen. Maurice Manning, a Fine Gael leader in the 1990s, described the "flat-footed ineptitude" with which an offer from Attorney General Robert F. Kennedy to significantly increase the number of visas for Irish immigrants was rebuffed by Ambassador Kiernan. Lemass and Aiken did not wish to be perceived as fostering emigration, but the rejection from Dublin, Manning said, "was conveyed to Robert Kennedy in a brusque, almost ill-mannered way, and when President Kennedy himself intervened the answer was the same and with no effort to deliver it in any more palatable way." This early misstep was, Manning said, "the blowing of a great opportunity."

As planning for Kennedy's Irish visit was being finalized, Ambassador Kiernan had had a talk with the president about Northern Ireland.

"I said, of course, that I'd never troubled him to take any line or make any intervention with Mr. Macmillan in the matter of the partition problem, which is our major problem," the envoy recalled. "And he said he understood that. It would embarrass him because, naturally, with the special relationship between the British and American governments, that would have put the American government . . . perhaps it could have got him in a difficulty."

The Dail speech would have been an obvious opening for the American president to lay out a more active policy on partition. But Dublin declined to apply any pressure.

"I told him . . . that we didn't expect him to make any reference to the matter when he was in Ireland in his speech," Kiernan said. "Presumably, he would talk privately to the ministers here, but that was another matter."

In a "personal and secret" cable to Hugh McCann, secretary of the Department of External Affairs, Kiernan related his relay of Aiken's wish for an American initiative to Kennedy, and Kennedy's response. "His reaction was typical of his pragmatic political philosophy," Kiernan wrote. "He is convinced that no British minister would feel able to make a public statement of the kind suggested. . . . It should be stated that he is by temperament, which is calculating, inclined to avoid the too direct approach in any confused issue, i.e., where there are conflicting interests. His political method is completely unemotional, avoiding the right-wrong dilemma, and making probes to find an opening where compromise success may be achieved. He is by his education, British inclined. And in the present international conjuncture, he makes no secret of his firm attachment to Britain. So that, to raise a new issue (or renew an old issue) now when Britain has so many pressing problems to solve, is something he would avoid and would seek an alternative. He would, therefore, regard our suggestion as embarrassing to the British at this troubled stage in their history."

"In the brief conversation which is all I could have with him" Aiken reported, "it was possible by mentioning partition with precise suggestion, to see that his undoubted goodwill to Ireland will be exercised in our favor so long as he is fully clear that he can take a line which can be persuasively put to the British, with a chance of leading to results."

On the eve of his European trip, Kennedy was "in an unusual state of irritation and nervousness," Kiernan thought, largely because of the criticism of the entire tour. The ambassador assured him that Ireland was approaching hysteria in its anticipation of his visit.

"Is it understood that I am not expected to refer publicly to partition?" the president asked Kiernan as the ambassador was leaving the Oval Office. Kiernan told Dublin "I assured him, to his relief I think, that this was so."

Kennedy did spend some time with Prime Minister Lemass on the subject of partition during formal talks on the morning before the Dail address.

"The president inquired if any progress is being made on partition," Lemass wrote privately. "I explained that, while there is some evidence of a modification of old attitudes, the position is much as it was."

Lemass told Kennedy that Ireland's eventual entry into the Common Market could change the dialogue about partition and even make Ireland's joining of NATO possible. The Irish leader shared with Kennedy his view that international pressure on London over partition would not be productive. (Taking the matter of partition to the United Nations, interestingly enough, did not appeal to Lemass. Asked about such an approach once, Lemass replied that it could be done, "If you are willing to accept the results." That was an obvious reference to Britain's veto power on the Security Council.) Lemass hoped that in time England could be convinced that partition was an "Irish concern." It would be the shared economic interests of Northern Ireland and the Republic, Lemass believed, that would produce pressures for unification.

Lemass said Dublin even was willing to maintain a separate governmental entity in the North to reassure the people there that their interests would be recognized and protected.

"I said I had detected some change of attitude in British government circles," Lemass noted afterwards, "but that, in their present political situation, this was unlikely to find public expression."

Kennedy wondered whether a change in the British government, to the Labour party, would aid in Ireland's effort. Lemass was doubtful. Dealing with the Conservative party was, in some respects, easier, because they knew how far they could push the issue, the prime minister explained. Labor, on the other hand, was more tentative on partition, he said.

The matter of the blow-up over Captain O'Neill's invitation to Kennedy to visit the

North drew sympathy from Kennedy and Lemass. Both agreed that the Northern Irish leader's intentions were to try to improve relations, not to cause trouble. Lemass thought highly of O'Neill and shared that with Kennedy.

The president, Lemass later remembered, offered no solutions to the problems of Northern Ireland. But "he certainly was interested in them and asked of them" during their talks, the Irish leader said.

Lemass had hoped that Kennedy might be helpful as an intermediary with London on the Northern Ireland problem, but the time never came for the president to act.

At a different time, the Irish ambassador, Kiernan, had what he considered a very revealing exchange with Kennedy about Northern Ireland.

The president had asked Kiernan what he thought could be done.

"Well," Kiernan replied, "what do you think is the issue?"

"Well, of course it's an Irish issue," the president returned.

"Well, that is the British line very good," the ambassador bravely retorted. "But partition was enforced against the wishes of both parts of Ireland by the British. No country cuts itself in two."

Still, Kennedy's response had paralleled Lemass's characterization of partition as an Irish issue; Lemass hardly could be accused of spouting the British line.

Kennedy, it was Kiernan's impression, was taken aback by the ambassador's alternative analysis.

"That's quite true, of course. It is a British issue," the president corrected himself, according to the envoy.

The door having been opened, Kiernan pressed on.

"The fact that the British are constantly in financial difficulties," he said, "and yet subsidize the position in Northern Ireland at the rate of a hundred to a hundred and fifty million dollars a year indicates that they have an interest in perpetuating it."

Kennedy asked for more elaboration, and he was obliged. Kiernan said it was hard "to get rid of old notions" that Britain required a foothold on Ireland for her self-defense — notions "that disappeared with the atomic bomb, with modern weapons of defense and offense."

What Ireland wanted was a declaration from someone in London that it was not against British interests to see Eire united. That was, Kiernan thought, putting the issue "in a very minimum way."

Kennedy was confused.

"Well, why, why would you — what value is that?" the president asked.

"The value," Kiernan remembered explaining, "is that partition remains because the junta in the six counties feel that they have — they know they have — the moral support of Britain. If a statement were made by the British government that it would not be contrary to imperial or British interests if the country became united under a single government, they'd begin to get shaky in the moral support, quite apart from the financial support."

Kennedy, as Kiernan saw it, was unconvinced.

"Well, you know it's very hard," the president told him. "I can see the British difficulty. It's very hard to say that on account of the past history."

Kiernan and the American leader ended the conversation without resolution. In the end, the Irish envoy decided, Kennedy, "apart from his Americanism, which was a hundred percent, was more British than Irish."

But on this day of Kennedy's speech to the Dail, that definitely was a minority opinion.

♣ ♣ ♣ ♣

Back through the narrow streets Kennedy and his hosts drove, the crowds happy for just a glimpse of their American cousin.

Then, only minutes after the end of his parliamentary address, at 5 p.m., Kennedy was in St. Patrick's Hall at Dublin Castle, a half dozen blocks from Leinster House, to be honored by the city and its two universities, the National University of Ireland, which is Catholic, and Trinity College of the University of Dublin, which is Protestant. Both schools conferred upon him honorary degrees of doctor of laws. De Valera did the honors for National, where he was the university chancellor. In the castle's throne room, Kennedy was clothed by Ireland's president in National's purple, green, and scarlet robes, as well as a large black-velvet hat. Kennedy, who by now had sent the hat business into steep recession back in the United States, obviously felt this medieval-style headgear was wrong, wrong, wrong. He put it on out in the hall, then took it off, then put it on again for the processional, then, as quickly as it seemed prudent to do so, removed the offending lid for good.

Dr. Michael Tierney, vice-chancellor, presented Kennedy, first in the Irish tongue, then in English.

"In offering him this honorary degree of the National University of Ireland," Tierney concluded, "we all join in praying that he may succeed in his great task of preserving peace, ensuring freedom, and maintaining honor, both in his own mighty nation and in all the nations of the world which look to it and to him for the fulfillment of their brightest and fondest hopes."

As he was given the degree, Kennedy shook hands with de Valera, then both signed the scroll with a quill pen dipped in a gold inkpot.

When it came Trinity's turn, the National audience filed out, as did Kennedy, replaced by the guests of the Protestant institution. Then Kennedy, who had gone into the Birmingham Room behind the dais, re-emerged, this time cloaked in the scarlet and rose colors of Trinity, with a hood of a doctor in laws of the university. The Earle of Rosse, who lived in Birr Castle in County Offaly, seat of the O'Carrolls who had sometimes fought with the Kennedys in centuries long past, presided over his school's ceremony.

Dave Powers couldn't resist. When Kennedy passed, Powers said to him, "Is this the real John F. Kennedy?"

The president was absolutely serious about the honors and did not appreciate the joking, shooting his aides, they remembered, "that quick disapproving look, which meant 'Knock it off.'"

The presentation was made in Latin by Dr. D.E.W. Wormell, the Public Orator. Kennedy was addressed as "Johannes Fitzgerald Kennedy, Praesses Civitatum Foederatum Americanarum."

"I introduce the president of the United States of America," Wormell said in the language of the Romans, "the first citizen of a people to whom Irishmen everywhere are bound by special ties of kinship and friendship, by common memories and traditions, by common beliefs and hopes. We greet in him one whose parents were both of Irish origin; and on that day on which he becomes a Dubliner, the University of Dublin is proud and happy in its turn to confer on him its highest honors."

The citation on the degree, in Latin, read in part: "Now summoned to the highest office in years of peace no less critical and perilous than those of war, he reveals the same dauntless spirit, the same unflinching acceptance of responsibility, the same qualities of initiative and leadership. A staunch champion of human rights and individual liberty, he seeks to erase the bitter legacy of the past, to promote unity, concord and understanding amongst those of differing color, race and creed, not only in his native land, but throughout the world. These are aims which can be fully realized only by a sharing of educational purposes and ideals. . . ."

After the vice-chancellor conferred the degree, Kennedy signed the roll, not with a quill this time, but a fountain pen, and again left the hall — briefly. He returned moments later in his gray business suit.

Dublin Lord Mayor Sean Moore, in the blue-and-gold robes of the Corporation of Dublin, made the president an honorary freeman of the city. Kennedy joined a long list of distinguished visitors so honored: Ulysses S. Grant was made a freeman during his world tour after leaving the presidency; Daniel O'Connell, the "Liberator," was put on the roll; so were Irish playwright George Bernard Shaw and British Prime Minister William Gladstone, the nineteenth century leader who had known sympathies for the Irish condition.

"To us," the lord mayor said, "you are the personification of that earlier dedication of your illustrious predecessor — who held certain truths to be self-evident, the principal of which was that all men are created equal in their right to the pursuit of happiness. . . . We think kindly of the American people . . . and we would like them to think kindly of us. We would like them to come and judge us personally and not take us as we are too often depicted on stage and screen."

Moore gave Kennedy a pair of decanters and a pair of vases, all Waterford crystal. For the Kennedy children, Moore offered two dolls dressed in traditional Irish costumes.

Kennedy looked out on the eighteenth century hall, its white, gold, and blue set off by the banners and crests of knights, and all bathed in blinding television lights.

"Mr. Mayor," Kennedy began, "faculty and officials of these two great universities, ladies and gentlemen: This city, these schools — this country has certainly done more than it should have to show friendship for my own people and to honor my country. I must say, as the recipient of this outpouring of good will for the United States, I am most grateful to you all. I feel most indebted, not only to all of you here who hold positions of responsibility, but to all the people of this city, which has welcomed us so generously, and this country, which has made us feel so very much at home.

"So, Mr. Mayor, I want to thank you for the honor you have done me this afternoon,

In St. Patrick's Hall in Dublin Castle on June 28, Eamon de Valera signs the scroll as Kennedy receives an honorary degree from the National University of Ireland, which is Catholic. He also is given a degree from Trinity College of the University of Dublin, which is Protestant. The president jokes that if the schools ever square off in Gaelic football or hurling, "I shall cheer for Trinity and pray for National."

and also, through you, to express our thanks to the people of Dublin. I can imagine nothing more pleasant than continuing day after day to drive through the streets of Dublin and wave, and I may come back and do it.

"I want to also say how pleased I am to have this association with these two great universities. Now I feel equally part of both, and if they ever have a game of Gaelic football or hurling, I shall cheer for Trinity and pray for National."

The quip filled the hall with laughter.

"It is appropriate," Kennedy continued, "to have this opportunity to form this association because Ireland and education have been synonymous for nearly two thousand years. For so many hundreds of years this country had colleges and universities of two thousand, three thousand, and four thousand students in the darkest ages of Europe, which served as the core, as the foundation, for what became the enlightenment and the religious revival of Europe. This country was wise enough to see in days that were past, that when it finally became independent, that it would need educated men and women.

"Democracy is a difficult kind of government. It requires the highest qualities of self-discipline, restraint, a willingness to make commitments and sacrifices for the general interest, and also it requires knowledge.

"My own country, in its earliest days, put the greatest emphasis on the development of education for its citizens. In the Northwest Ordinance, which was drafted by Thomas Jefferson and John Adams, it was provided that a section of land would be set aside in every thirty sections in order to educate the people. Thomas Jefferson once said, 'If you expect the people to be ignorant and free, you expect what never was and never will be.' And in the heights of the Civil War, when the outcome was most uncertain, and the results in doubt, the United States Congress, under the leadership of Abraham Lincoln, passed the Morrill Act, which established our land grant colleges, and which set aside public land in every state in order to maintain a state college and state university. We have just recently celebrated the hundredth anniversary and we now have in every one of our states universities which have educated our sons and daughters and helped make it possible to maintain self-government.

"So education, these two great schools, the city of Dublin, the country of Ireland, the future of the West — all are closely intertwined. And I can assure you that there are no [greater] honors that you could give me, as the president of the United States, than to have received the three distinctions which I hold today and shall always value. Thank you."

The warm feelings the appearance before the Parliament and then the honors from the schools generated on both sides were undeniable.

"It is doubtful if any single address in the last fifty years gave the Irish people such a sense of unity and such consciousness of destiny," declared the *Midland Tribune,* based in Birr in County Offaly.

Kennedy's Dail address, the *Cork Examiner* said in its praise, "pointed the way to a role of growing influence for our country in the realm of world affairs where we are, as yet, only finding our feet."

But de Valera felt warmly, and not in a good way, about one moment in Kennedy's speech in the Dail. The quotation from Lord Fitzgerald about nothing good ever coming out of Leinster House had stuck in the old Irish president's craw. At Aras an Uachtarain, during the dinner for his American guest, de Valera told Kennedy he had done Irish politicians no favor by reviving Lord Fitzgerald's observation.

Apparently, de Valera subsequently had something to do with attempting to change history. The Lord Fitzgerald line was, according to Lemass, left out of audio and film versions of the speech produced by Irish radio and television.

Prime Minister Lemass later marveled at de Valera's crafty handiwork: "How he managed this complete suppression of this sentence, I do not know."

If that was the only sour note, it apparently passed without casting any gloom on Kennedy or the boisterous proceedings to follow.

That de Valera spoke frankly was a measure, no doubt, of the level of comfort the Irish and Americans felt with each other.

Kennedy spoke frankly, too, about a subject the Irish cared much about: the efforts to revive the Irish language.

"He thought this was such a waste of national effort," Lemass recalled.

His Irish hosts tried to convince him the language issue was part of a broader national revival, but the president didn't appear entirely won over. Eunice Shriver was more sympathetic.

"He said, 'You cannot have a strong culture without a strong language,'" she remembered.

But on the whole, the evening with the de Valeras was lively and happy. At one point, Kennedy asked his host why he had been the only leader of the 1916 rebellion who had not been shot. Kennedy, with all his readings on Irish history, must have known the answer to this, but undoubtedly wanted to hear a firsthand account. De Valera obliged, pointing out that although he had lived in Ireland since a youth, his birth in New York City gave the British pause. Executing an American citizen was a different matter from shooting the native Irish, in the British view.

"But there were many times when the key in my jail cell door was turned and I thought my turn had come," de Valera told Kennedy. The Irish leader recounted his involvement in the push for independence and his frustrations with the British. Kennedy got a different take on America's ally from de Valera.

"If you are weak in your dealings with the British, they will pressure you," Ireland's president declared to his guest. "If you are subject to flattery, they will cajole you. Only if you are reasonable will they reason with you, and being reasonable with the British means letting them know that you are willing to throw an occasional bomb into one of their lorries."

There were many light moments, too. Kennedy asked Dave Powers to tell some Irish jokes, an easy task in Boston but quite another, intimidating matter in Dublin. But Powers hit home with the story of two Irishmen reading the gravestones in a Boston cemetery where British soldiers killed in the Battle of Bunker Hill during the American Revolution had been buried. One headstone read: "Here lies an Englishman and a good man." Said one of the Irishmen to his companion: "Now, Mike, sure that grave doesn't look as if it had room enough for two people, does it?"

Kennedy's interest in Ireland was intense and constant. During the dinner, Kennedy and Sinead de Valera ranged over Irish writing and poetry. When he told her his last stop was at Shannon Airport, she recited from memory a poem about the River Shannon. Kennedy took it down on place cards.

"He was very taken with her," Eunice Shriver said of her brother and Mrs. de Valera. "She was terrific. I thought she was sensational."

Indeed, she was. Her husband, advocate of the Irish language, learned it from her. She was nearly sixty when she launched a writing career, publishing poetry and children's plays in Irish, as well as works in English.

Ireland's president noticed the chemistry between his wife and his American guest. "They got on very well together," Eamon de Valera conceded.

Out on the tours of the country, Kennedy peppered Irish officials with questions about the nation's economy, about the history of towns he was visiting and their particular problems.

De Valera was struck by his guest's grasp of Ireland and its history.

"Oh, he seemed to be interested and seemed to know a good deal about it," the Irish leader recalled. "He was very quick, you see. He was very quick on the uptake. He was a good listener. . . . He was able to size things up all right."

Ambassador Kiernan agreed, and in fact felt that Kennedy's constant queries had, perhaps, a personal purpose. On a helicopter jaunt, the envoy said, the president "was constantly asking about places. We were low enough to see large-sized houses. He was costing houses. 'How much would a place like that cost with a certain amount of land attached?' I assumed he was wondering just what it would be like to live in Ireland or to have a pied-à-terre where he could come or send the children occasionally. . . ."

Kennedy's two sisters, meanwhile, had an urge to experience a more prosaic corner of Irish life: they wanted to visit a pub. So they were taken to Gerry Carthy's Ivy Leaf Lounge on Upper Dromcondra Road. They were accompanied by high-level Irish government guides: Minister for Justice Charles Haughey, Minister for Industry Jack Lynch, and Minister for Education Dr. P.J. Hillery. The sisters each had a vodka and lime juice.

It's not clear that the excursion produced the goods the sisters were looking for.

Mrs. Shriver allowed that she thought what she saw "was a little luxurious," according to Carthy.

Meanwhile, President Kennedy returned to the American Embassy in a downpour that somehow had not deterred five hundred hardy souls. As his limousine, flanked by motorcycles, speeded toward the entrance of the embassy grounds, a man rushed out. One motorcycle was forced to swerve to avoid hitting him. The man reached toward the limousine's open window. Kennedy leaned toward his driver, apparently suggesting he slow down so people could shake hands. But the police had had enough of this fervor. They rushed Kennedy along and loudly banged shut the embassy gates before some of the crowd could step into the grounds. The man who had started it all claimed to have achieved his objective. "I touched his sleeve," he bragged.

The aura cut a wide swath through Kennedy's entourage. Any American associated with the president was treated by the Irish almost like yet another Kennedy cousin.

Or, in the case of terHorst of the *Detroit News*, a Kennedy himself.

Finishing up an evening's work, terHorst and three colleagues, one of whom was NBC-TV's John Chancellor, hailed a taxi outside the Gresham Hotel to go to a restaurant.

The driver glanced several times into the back seat.

"You're one of them, aren't you?" the cab driver finally said to terHorst.

"Pardon?" the reporter answered.

"You're a Kennedy. Aren't you related to the man?" the driver pressed.

TerHorst in fact had been mistaken a few times in the United States for a Kennedy relative.

"No, no. I'm just a journalist from America," terHorst assured the man. "As a matter of fact, I'm Dutch."

The driver barely spoke the rest of the ride. He had been hoping he had snagged the fare of fares. He was crushed.

Not far from all the official duties that were keeping President Kennedy occupied were the fond memories of other happy times in Ireland. He had indulged himself on the helicopter trip back to Dublin from Cork, asking the pilot to circle low over the crenelated bulk of Lismore Castle. He had stayed there with his beloved sister, Kathleen, in 1947, a visit on which he began searching out his relatives. The presidential copter circled once, twice, three times. But there was no time to land.

five

. . . A flow of nostalgia and sentiment

When I went to those great cities I saw wonders I had never seen in Ireland. But when I came back to Ireland I found all the wonders there waiting for me. You see, they had been there all the time; but my eyes had never been opened to them.

George Bernard Shaw
John Bull's Other Island *(1904)*

Germany had invaded Poland on the first day of September 1939, triggering the cataclysm that would be World War II. But for a brief time immediately after the invasion, most of the world outside Poland had a last moment to breathe, to prepare for what looked to be a very dark future indeed.

Seventeen days after the German invasion, a scrawny yet handsome twenty-two-year-old American arrived at the tiny Irish village of Foynes perched on the River Shannon in County Limerick, about two dozen miles southwest of the city of Limerick. It is doubtful the young man had more than the time it took to stretch one's legs to look around. John Fitzgerald Kennedy was headed home.

In the Foynes graveyard is buried Sir Stephen de Vere, an obscure figure to Americans and, really, to most Irish. But he and Charlotte O'Brien, buried on a nearby hill called Knockpatrick, had a kind of connection with this young American.

De Vere and O'Brien had been in the unenviable position, at a time in the nineteenth century when Ireland was emptying of its poorest inhabitants, of advocating against the so-called coffin ships sailing to America. These seekers of better conditions for wretches who would never set eyes again on Eire could not have imagined that, in just three decades after their deaths, transatlantic travel would be, by almost any measure, luxurious. And for the exclusive few, the trip could be made by air. Right from Ireland.

Such was the case for Jack Kennedy, great-grandson of an Irish emigrant who had left by slow sail for the United States ninety-nine years before.

This young Kennedy had just concluded travel through brooding Europe, and had spent time with his father, Joseph P. Kennedy, the American ambassador to the Court of St. James's. Now the second-oldest of the envoy's nine children needed to return to Harvard University and to the manuscript of a thesis that would be a book in 1940, *Why England Slept.* He also may have been urged to leave by his father. Only days before hostilities broke out, the ambassador had issued a statement saying that, given the tense international situation, it was "advisable for American travelers to leave England."

Jack Kennedy booked passage on the Pan American Airways flying boat, the *Yankee Clipper.* Presumably, he had flown to Foynes from London. He would fly nonstop from Foynes to New York.

Foynes was a new venture in Ireland. It had been set up as a seaplane base for flights to the United States the previous April. De Valera himself dedicated the facility.

What Kennedy thought of what he saw or the flight down the Shannon estuary to the Atlantic is unknown. But he would return to Ireland, and each time he would be more intrigued.

Of course, as is well known, Kennedy joined the U.S. Navy and commanded a patrol torpedo boat in the Pacific in World War II. When PT-109 was cut in half one murky night by a Japanese destroyer, Kennedy swam for hours with his surviving crew to safety. In short order, the story of his exploits made him a war hero.

Once back at home, recuperating, Kennedy seemed to be thinking more about his family's roots and Ireland. In February 1944, Kennedy referred to himself as "the Irishman" in a letter to his close friend, Paul "Red" Fay.

The offhanded reference to his Irishness may be an insight into Kennedy's mindset on the eve of his political career.

The Kennedy household under Rose Fitzgerald Kennedy and Joseph P. Kennedy talked about Ireland "at times," recalled Eunice Shriver. But it was Honey Fitz, Rose's father, who was the repository of Irish pride and family stories. "Any time Honey Fitz would come down to the house for dinner, he would talk about it with us," Mrs. Shriver said.

"And he was very Irish in his personality," Jean Kennedy Smith said of Honey Fitz.

Jean and Eunice's mother, Rose Fitzgerald Kennedy, also talked a lot about "how 'the Irish need not apply,'" and how she started the Ace of Clubs [a Boston-based charitable society originally for Irish women], which still exists," Jean Smith recalled. "We were well aware of the prejudice against Irish Catholics growing up."

Sen. Edward Kennedy remembered Honey Fitz as "sort of a second father." Before Sunday luncheons with his grandfather in a Boston hotel, the senator said, they would go into the kitchen to meet all the workers there before sitting down to eat. "And then afterwards, he would walk me around Boston," Kennedy said, talking about the history of the Irish in America.

Their own father had what might be called a love-hate relationship with his Irish background. He used it when it suited him, and rued it when it frustrated his ambitions. The eventual Kennedy family seat ended up at Hyannisport, Massachusetts, because of prejudice. "Dad had come there because he couldn't get into the clubs around Boston," Mrs. Smith explained.

Yet one senses that, at bottom, the Kennedy patriarch had a pride in being Irish: he was showing those Brahmin highbrows he could beat them at their own game.

And Kennedy père also knew the value of the Irish vote in Boston. He reportedly encouraged John to cross the Atlantic and take a measure of Ireland.

"Jack delighted in his Irish heritage," his mother, Rose, wrote. "And, perhaps, took a more than ordinary interest in it because of stories he had heard from his grandparents, handed down to them by their parents, about the miserable conditions under which the immigrants of the 1840s and '50s had arrived in Boston, and the poverty and social disdain they suffered there as 'muckers' and the like, a condition from which they could rise only by hard work and ingenuity."

John Kennedy returned to Ireland shortly before the end of the war, in July 1945. The fighting in Europe had ended in May. At the time, he had not committed to a political career. He was contemplating pursuing the reporter's craft. He went to Europe to cover the British elections, and in the middle of that assignment crossed the Irish Sea to assess how Ireland had weathered the war.

The ambassador's son and war hero arrived in Dublin on July 23. He stayed with David Gray, the American minister to Ireland from 1940 to 1947 and a first cousin to President Franklin D. Roosevelt, at the U.S. legation. The American government had not yet elevated the legation to full embassy status.

Gray had a rather dim view of Eamon de Valera, telling Kennedy the Irish leader was "sincere, incorruptible, also a paranoiac and a lunatic." At the time, de Valera was out of favor with many Americans because he had kept Ireland neutral during the war. Gray was in that group, having advocated a British takeover of Irish ports, a move de Valera vehemently opposed.

In Gray's view, de Valera believed everything was tied to the issue of the partition of Ireland.

"He joined neutrality in this war with the independence of Ireland," Kennedy wrote in his diary, although it's not clear whether Kennedy was summarizing Gray's view of de Valera or recording his own perception. "Either you were for neutrality and against partition, or if you were against neutrality you were for partition."

Later, in the 1950s, Gray would be even harsher, writing that de Valera manufactured the issue of partition "as a grievance and excuse" to divert attention from, in Gray's view, backing "the wrong horse" — Adolf Hitler — during the war. To say that Gray was unsympathetic to the Republic's stand on partition would be an understatement. He asserted that Ireland, in fact, had no claim on the North and unification; for the North to join the Republic would be "economic suicide," and if it was forced, it would be "economic murder." Perhaps these sentiments make it clearer why the United States made little headway with de Valera during the war years with Gray in Dublin.

In a separate travel diary entry for the same day, Kennedy eloquently captures postwar Dublin:

"Arriving in Ireland from England, you see sharply the blessings of peace. The people are cheerful — there is none of that chronic fatigue that sharpens tempers in London. Food is plentiful, what rationing there is, is applied with Irish tolerance and good humor; there are none of the queues of London.

"In Dublin there are few cars, petrol is difficult to get, but the people walk or ride their bicycles. The streets are scrupulously clean and the famous doors of Dublin are freshly painted and the brass is shining.

"But the appearances are superficial. Ireland, which has escaped the devastation and bombing of Europe, has had its casualties. More than 250,000 of its population crossed to England to serve in the armed forces or to [work] in the factories. How many of these went direct into the armed forces has not been disclosed, but the fact that residents of Southern Ireland received seven Victoria Cross[es] while people in the North received none has caused some satisfaction among the people in the South.

"In direct contrast to the political situation, Ireland's economic ties with England are closer than they have ever been."

Kennedy did not know de Valera, having met him years earlier merely as one of Ambassador Kennedy's sons. But on July 25, 1945, John Kennedy and de Valera sat down to talk. It is not entirely clear what the two talked about — Kennedy did not divulge much even in private notes to himself — although some months later he recalled that de Valera forcefully defended Ireland's neutrality in the war "at some length."

"There is no compromise in de Valera's firm, ascetic face," Kennedy said. "He has a passionate intensity and single-mindedness in the course he is taking that brooks no opposition."

In a piece he wrote for Hearst newspapers, Kennedy deftly dissected the then-boiling quarrel between de Valera and James Dillon, leader of the opposition, over the issue of ending the partition of Ireland.

The matter had come to a head because de Valera had responded to a question about Ireland's constitutional status by declaring: "We are a republic." This utterance came despite Ireland's membership in the British commonwealth of nations. After a week of further thought, de Valera's answer on the commonwealth question was, in essence, "Yes and no." The real issue, Kennedy pointed out to Hearst readers in a story written from London, was the Irish desire to end the political division of their island.

"De Valera is determined to end this partition, as it is called, and to that cause he has dedicated his life," Kennedy wrote.

"In this cause, all Irishmen of the south are united.

"On this, there is no dispute between Dillon and de Valera.

"The dispute concerns the method to be followed.

"Dillon and Gen. [Richard] Mulcahy, leader of the Fine Gael Party, Ireland's second largest political party, argue it is time to bury old hatchets.

"England and Ireland are bound together by the closest economic ties.

"Militarily, England will never consent to see a completely neutral and weakly armed power on her vulnerable western flank.

"Only if England has a guarantee that this and other bases are put at her disposal, in case of war, will she consent to give up her great base of Ulster, which served her so well in this war.

"By cooperating and the building of mutual trust, the partition can be broken and all Ireland united.

"So argue Dillon and a substantial section of the Irish populace.

"But ranged against this group is the powerful Fianna Fail Party, led by the brilliant, austere figure of de Valera, born in New York, the son of a Spanish father and an Irish mother.

"De Valera is fighting politically the same relentless battle they fought in the field during the uprising of 1916, in the war of independence and later in the civil war.

"He feels everything Ireland has gained has been given grudgingly and at the end of a long and bitter struggle.

"Always it has been too little and too late.

"He is surrounded by men of the same background in his government. They include Sean Lemass, deputy prime minister, Sean MacEntee, chief of the local government, Gerald Boland, minister of justice, and Dr. [James] Ryan, minister of agriculture.

"Many were in the abortive uprising of 1916. All fought in the war of independence against the Black and Tans and later in the civil war of 1922.

"All have been in both English and Irish prisons, and many have wounds which still ache when the cold rains come in from the west. They have not forgotten nor have they forgiven.

"The only settlement they will accept is a free and independent Ireland, free to go where it will be the master of its own destiny.

"Only on these terms will they accept the ending of the partition.

"Thus," Kennedy even-handedly summed up, "there are two splits."

That neatly summed up Kennedy's personal dilemma, too: should he follow journalism and perhaps become a historian, or pursue public service?

By the third time he visited in Ireland, beginning on September 1, 1947, Kennedy had made his choice and set his life course. He was a new congressman, elected the previous year in the Boston district once represented by his grandfather Honey Fitz.

On this trip, Kennedy stayed for three weeks. His base was imposing Lismore Castle in County Waterford, a magnificent structure of battlements and turrets on the River Blackstone. His sister Kathleen spent part of the year there — an irony, really.

Lismore Castle (Lismore means "great place or enclosure") was built eight hundred years earlier by Prince John of England, son of Henry II. During one of the many outbreaks of war sweeping across Ireland in the twelfth century, the Irish clans and their religious leaders were called to the castle for one of their many pledges of loyalty to the Crown. Many years later, Sir Walter Raleigh, a bloodthirsty enemy of the Irish, held the fortress, built and rebuilt several times over by then. Eventually, Lismore became the property of the Dukes of Devonshire. Much of the medieval appearance of the edifice was added in the mid-nineteenth century. In a grand ballroom converted from a ruined chapel are words Kennedy would hear much in 1963: *Céad Míle Fáilte.*

Kathleen "Kick" Kennedy in 1944 had married the oldest son of the Duke of Devonshire, "Billy," the Marquis of Hartington. The duke and duchess were related to the wife of future British Prime Minister Harold Macmillan and to David Ormsby-Gore, the future British ambassador to the United States and a close friend of the future president.

Billy Hartington was a Protestant, and this caused a great — and uncharacteristic — rift in the Kennedy clan that truly was never repaired. Rose Fitzgerald Kennedy, matriarch of the family and a staunch Catholic, vehemently disapproved of Kathleen's choice for a husband. After the union went forward anyway, mother and daughter rarely spoke. Then Billy was killed in action in France just four months after the wedding.

Kathleen, a Britisher more than an American by this point, had tried to live back in the United States. But the deep divide with her parents never could be crossed. Her in-laws, on the other hand, were welcoming and understanding. And so she returned to Europe, and enjoyed Lismore, where she liked to entertain.

And on this September visit, her brother John, quartered in the Queen's Room overlooking the river, was just one of several guests, including former British foreign secretary Anthony Eden, Pamela Churchill (then the wife of Randolph Churchill), Hugh Fraser and Tony Rosslyn, both members of the British Parliament, Charles Johnson, who would later become British high commissioner in Australia, and Sean Leslie, a writer.

John Kennedy, now intent on knowing more about his familial ties to Ireland, had made queries of relatives in Massachusetts. His aunt and godmother, Loretta Kennedy Connelly, wrote down directions for her nephew to New Ross, some fifty miles from Lismore Castle.

The congressman acquired a green, softcover guidebook and studied it. Reading the *Irish Tourist Directory,* he scrawled his name in ink on the inside title page, then went about marking places he wanted to check out. At the entry for New Ross in County Wexford, he underlined the town and county and placed an "x" next to them. For some reason, he also circled the New Ross Motor and Engineering Company and, for possible research, the local newspaper, the *New Ross Standard.* At Wexford, he penned hashmarks next to White's Hotel. Before or after his visit to Ireland, he may have contacted the Irish consul in Boston, Galway Foley, because he circled his name under "Irish Free State Representatives Abroad." When he reached the Irish Tourist Association's motto on page 138, he punctuated it with quotation marks so it would read: "See Ireland First."

Kennedy borrowed his sister's American station wagon — an unusual sight in the Europe of the time — and, with Mrs. Churchill at his side, embarked on his search for his roots.

Once in Dunganstown, Kennedy came upon Robert Burrell, a longtime resident who knew what the young American was looking for. He directed Kennedy down the unpaved road to a thatched-roof cottage with whitewashed walls and a dirt floor. The house was by a stream.

"I'm John Kennedy from Boston," he told the startled family. "I believe this is the old Kennedy homestead."

Kennedy was disappointed to discover that these Irish Kennedys didn't know much about the family history. They did remember a Patrick Kennedy visiting some three decades earlier. That would have been John Kennedy's grandfather.

"It sounded from their conversation as if all the Kennedys had emigrated," the congressman would later recall for biographer James MacGregor Burns. But young Kennedy was delighted with the relatives he found, who offered him and his lady friend tea.

To lighten the awkwardness, Kennedy gave the seven or eight children around the place rides in the station wagon.

"I spent about an hour there surrounded by chickens and pigs, and left in a flow of nostalgia and sentiment," he recalled.

Lady Churchill was far less smitten. "That was just like Tobacco Road!" she huffed. Kennedy fought the temptation to make his guest walk the fifty miles back to Lismore.

There is some historical confusion here: by some accounts, Kennedy first was directed to the home of James Kennedy, who was a second cousin to Joseph Kennedy. James Kennedy then took him to the home of Mary Ryan, in Dunganstown, who would host the young congressman as president of the United States sixteen years later.

That is the way James Kennedy remembered it in 1963.

When Joseph P. Kennedy had been made ambassador to Great Britain, it had not occurred to the Dunganstown Kennedys there was any familial link. And Ambassador Kennedy didn't come in search of them.

The "tall, thin American" man James Kennedy met in 1947 told him his Boston aunt had advised him to check around Dunganstown and he would find his family roots.

"Well," James Kennedy related, "I remembered my father had corresponded with his sister in Boston. We mentioned names and decided John Kennedy's great-grandfather, Patrick, had come from here. So I called my wife and daughter and they said they would take him to see my sister [Mary Ryan] and the place where Patrick was born."

"He didn't look well at all," Mrs. Ryan later remembered.

"Begod, and he was shook-looking," James Kennedy agreed.

Kennedy was wan. He may have been still suffering the effects of malaria he contracted in the South Pacific during the war. But he also was battling Addison's disease, which a London doctor diagnosed not long after Kennedy left Ireland. The disease is a gradual failure of the adrenal glands that breaks down the body's ability to fight infection. It had been considered fatal until drugs were developed in the 1930s to control it. Kennedy would keep the affliction under wraps as he pursued his political career.

"They got into the car. Kennedy gave me his card," James Kennedy said. "I read it as they drove off. It said, 'John Kennedy, Congressman, Massachusetts,' or something like that. Only then did I realize we had something big in the family."

Whichever way he went first, Mrs. Ryan's daughter Josephine would recall years later that Kennedy had bit of a lead foot, driving up and driving away speedily.

Mrs. Ryan later remembered that the congressman "took photographs all over the place." Kennedy considerately shared his efforts with his cousins, sending them copies of the pictures he took. The photos were placed by the Ryans in a family album.

Kennedy repeated the story of his trip to his distant relatives to Dave Powers and Ken O'Donnell in 1963 as they flew aboard Air Force One toward Dublin.

The president said he remembered that evening after the trip to Dunganstown. He was sitting in the sumptuous surroundings of the castle, dining with distinguished figures of British society.

"I looked around the table," Kennedy recalled, "and thought about the cottage where my cousins lived and I said to myself, 'What a contrast!'"

Kennedy's interest in family relations was not shared by his sister. "Did they have a bathroom?" Kick asked. No, they didn't, her brother and Pamela Churchill told her.

This trip also included forays into Dublin. On one jaunt, Kennedy visited the *Irish Press* and asked a lot of questions about Irish politics and history. He also quaffed refreshment at John Mulligan's on Poolbeg Street. Wasn't this the Mulligan's in which James Joyce had placed much of his story "Counterparts," in *Dubliners*? the congressman asked. Indeed it was. Patrick Flynn, then Mulligan's manager, recalled the visitor as pleasant and friendly. If only he'd known what the future was to bring, "we would have taken down every word about him," said Flynn in 1963.

The 1947 visit also would be a bittersweet memory for Kennedy. His beloved sister Kick died on May 14, 1948, in a plane crash in southern France. She was twenty-eight.

In the summer of 1949, Kennedy made his fourth visit to Ireland, this time with many other members of his family. They stayed in Dublin at a house rented by Frank More O'Ferrell, a friend of the family from London. The family vacation, O'Ferrell later recalled, was "a really hilarious week."

Kennedy made it clear he had ambitions. After first toying with the idea of running for governor of Massachusetts and rejecting it, the young politician decided to move to the upper house of Congress. And he, too, knew the value of the Irish vote in the Bay State.

Rep. John E. Fogarty recalled that Kennedy used the Irish connection in his 1952 campaign against Henry Cabot Lodge for the U.S. Senate. Kennedy asked Fogarty to pose with him with a map of Ireland in the background.

The pair had worked in the House in 1951 on a resolution backing the unification of Ireland.

"And I was sure it wouldn't do him any harm in Massachusetts, with all the Irish that were there at that time," Fogarty remembered.

In 1953, Sen. John Kennedy, then one of Washington's most eligible bachelors, married Jacqueline Lee Bouvier. She, too, had Irish immigrants in her family, though the perception of the day and later was that she was of solely French lineage.

Jackie had been to Ireland in 1951 and had been quite enchanted.

So, in 1955, she arranged a trip to Ireland with her husband, his fifth visit since 1939.

They arrived on September 30 and stayed three days.

The couple had lunch with Ireland's then-minister of external affairs, Liam Cosgrave, a member of Fine Gael in a coalition government. They lunched at Dublin's elegant Shelbourne Hotel, overlooking the flowers, ponds, and palm trees in St. Stephen's Green; the senator was having back trouble and using crutches, making it difficult to move from place to place. Father Joseph Leonard, a Vincentian priest at All Hallowes College and a friend of Mrs. Kennedy's, joined the luncheon with some others.

Kennedy had arrived at a time of the year when "things are rather slack," Cosgrave recalled later. "The universities and colleges are closed. Senator Kennedy . . . was, I think, anxious to make a speech or meet some students."

That afternoon, Kennedy spoke at Father Leonard's college in Drumcondra, discussing how the Catholic Church was faring in then-Communist Poland, where he had recently been. The senator noted that churches in Poland were crowded. And Catholicism posed a serious obstacle to Russian domination of that nation, he added.

Cosgrave, son of W.T. Cosgrave, a longtime political rival to de Valera, liked Kennedy.

"He was very friendly, matter-of-fact, devoid of pretense of any sort, good sense of humor, clear grasp of the essentials, the current international political situation, [and] was reasonably familiar with conditions [in Ireland]," the younger Cosgrave recalled.

The man who would become Irish prime minister in the early 1970s had a writer's eye for his American subject.

The "boyish appearance" of the young Kennedy was deceptive, Cosgrave felt.

"When you were nearer to him, he didn't look quite so young," the Irish minister explained. "In fact, his face showed certain signs of the suffering he'd undergone. Probably [there were] two things that gave him the boyish impression: one was that he was tall, and although not very light, he was not heavy, and he had a very fine shock or head of fair hair, which, of course, gave him an impression of [youth]. . . . But I did notice on that first occasion that he looked somewhat worn."

The up-and-coming senator "gave you the impression of being a man who had a serious outlook and was concerned with not merely American problems, but world problems," Cosgrave said.

John and Jackie Kennedy were a relatively anonymous couple then, despite the big splashes their marriage made on the social pages of American newspapers. In the Dublin evenings, the pair did what many Dubliners did then and do to this day: they went to the pubs. But they were not alone: Jackie telephoned Irish journalists to invite them to meet her husband.

A brief newspaper account of the Kennedys' visit to Dublin stated that the senator hoped to go to the horse races. It is not known for certain that he did. But some Dubliners later swore, after Kennedy became president, that they had spotted the senator at the Curragh, the horse track, in that fall of 1955.

Kennedy's feeling for Ireland, sparked in the early days by his grandfather Honey Fitz, and fed by his own visits, was well-nourished well before the crowded days of 1963.

"He was rooted there forever," wrote Hugh Sidey, the veteran White House watcher who covered Kennedy.

Kennedy's Harvard intellectualism, his cool demeanor in public and his sophisticated style and tastes, didn't play into the stereotypical image of the Irish politician as some kind of backslapping, slightly clownish, boozy ward-healer.

Even some Irish didn't "get" Kennedy's affinity for the country of his forebears.

Ambassador Kiernan didn't think Kennedy had particularly strong sentiments toward Ireland or his Irish background until the June 1963 trip. "The turning point did come on his visit to Ireland," the envoy said. "I doubt it came very much before that. . . . He had a sort of affection or friendship for me. . . . perhaps because I didn't bother him too much, because we reacted well together, but there was nothing specially pro-Irish."

Kiernan's analysis indisputably was filtered by his diplomatic experience as the odd man out in the British-American relationship, amplified by the familial ties between Kennedy and Macmillan.

In his younger years, Kennedy, in Kiernan's view, "wanted above all things to be a good New Englander." When he visited England and observed its diplomatic and political intrigues, it was "very much as an English American with English people."

At the same time, Kiernan subscribed to Carl Jung's theory of a racial unconscious that, in the ambassador's words, "comes out in moments of stress or strain and which really is at the basis of everything we do."

"We have our cultures superimposed on it," Kiernan said. "I feel myself that that was in Kennedy, that one could apply that to Kennedy himself, this racial unconscious and the reaction coming from it. Now, the culture superimposed upon it is a hard culture, a culture of living up to Boston's Harvard, which for an Irish person treated as they were. . . . And I was surprised how often Kennedy mentioned 'No Irish need apply.' It wasn't just superimposing a culture directly on a German or an Italian. It was superimposing it against a terrific obstacle, the obstacle being the hatred I believe was felt for the Irish in America.

"I have no sentimental idea that there's any love lost for the Irish in America," the ambassador said in 1966. "I think there's a tremendous amount of not only antagonism but

Kennedy surprises nurses at a window at St. Vincent Hospital, Dublin.

really almost hatred which you don't get for other nations. And it's probably built in with their religion. It may be. It's also built in with the fact that we dared to stand up against another nation which has spread its tentacles all over the world.

"Kennedy couldn't divide that Irish heritage, but what was superimposed upon it made him, I imagine, often wish, as I think it makes many Americans often wish, that they could avoid it. He couldn't avoid it because it was there in his blood."

Understanding Kiernan's inner thoughts on Kennedy shed light on his dispatches to Dublin before the American leader's June 1963 visit. (See account on Page 128.)

Prime Minister Lemass, on the other hand, had an entirely different sense of Kennedy. He saw the American leader as "intensely interested in his Irish ancestry. I think there was no question about this." The O'Kenedy treaty the Irish gave Kennedy, Lemass noted, sat on a table behind his desk in the Oval Office.

Not far outside the Oval Office was another artifact Lemass would have appreciated. A sign on a basket on the desk of Lenny Donnelly read: Only Irish Need Apply.

The evidence, from family, friends, and those who worked with him and knew him, was that John Kennedy celebrated his ancestry and greatly enjoyed talking about it and, in some cases, ribbing others about their lineage.

Once, in May 1963, Kennedy teased his wife, along with *Newsweek* Washington Bureau chief Benjamin Bradlee and his wife, Tony, about how "mongrelized you all are." He and his brothers and sisters were one hundred percent Irish, he boasted.

When Dorothy Tubridy visited the Kennedys, "We always sang Irish songs and played Irish tunes on the piano and generally had a lot of Irish evenings," she said.

Kennedy, it came to be known, traveled with Irish records to keep him amused and distracted when he could afford to be. As his Ireland trip showed, he had absorbed a lot from the records, even if his singing never would be studio quality.

Ireland reciprocated the connections, early on.

"We have felt this way toward him from the beginning," an Irish government official's wife told reporters in 1963. They didn't name her. "On your presidential election day I boarded a bus and the motorman asked, 'How is he doing?' I knew right away whom he meant by 'he.' There was only one 'he' in the world that day."

When Kennedy was inaugurated president in January 1961, New Ross sent him a telegram of congratulations and threw a party for itself.

"We had celebrations at exactly the same hour as the president was being inaugurated," New Ross Urban District Council Chairman Andrew Minihan recalled. Kennedy took the time to tape a personal message to the people of New Ross. The tape was to be flown to Ireland but was held up by weather. When it finally reached Dublin, too late to make it to New Ross, government officials read the message over the phone to the celebrants. Kennedy thanked New Ross for the best wishes and said he hoped to be with the people of the town within weeks or months. "That was naturally the first word that we had in Ireland that he intended to visit Ireland," Minihan said.

Theodore C. Sorensen, who went on the trip to Ireland, thought that when it came to his chief's feelings for Ireland and Irish affairs, "the interest was always there." He wasn't sure that, at the personal level, the trip changed much about Kennedy's feelings. "It would be difficult to measure intensification [of interest] since it was always there," Sorensen said.

Sen. Edward Kennedy remembered his brother reading Irish history. The harsh experience of the Irish people, and the struggles of Irish Americans, the young president "felt . . . kind of deep in his soul," his brother said. And thus it was no surprise President Kennedy was quite familiar with the Irish writers and poets, and quoted them often. Decades after the Irish trip, the president's youngest brother privately published a collection of favorite JFK quotations, entitled *Words Jack Loved*. It is replete with Irish sources.

In 1961, President Kennedy was given a specially designed Kennedy coat of arms by the Chief Herald of Ireland. He was so pleased with it that Jacqueline Kennedy had a seal ring made for him bearing the coat of arms. Kennedy did not wear rings. But he took the coat-of-arms ring out of his desk one day and used it, telling his wife with a grin: "I used my Irish seal on a letter today — to the Queen of England!"

Eamon de Valera found no mystery in the Irish-Americans' abiding affection for the island their ancestors had left. Once, while traveling in the United States, he was asked how it was possible a person could love two countries.

"Now look here," he remembered answering, "a man can love his wife and love her best in the world, but that doesn't prevent him at all from having a very deep love for his mother. And for us, as for a lot of our people, this was the mother country."

SÍX

June 29, 1963:

Galway, Limerick, and Shannon Airport

I have put away sorrow like a shoe that is worn out and muddy, for it is I have had a life that will be envied by great companies.

John Millington Synge
Deirdre of the Sorrows *(1910)*

Kennedy launched his last day in Ireland in a wistful mood. At breakfast in the American Embassy with Ambassador McCloskey, the president confided that in the 1968 campaign for the White House (1964 being spoken for by himself), he would back whichever candidate agreed to make him the next American envoy to Dublin.

He bounced the idea off Dorothy Tubridy, too. "How do you think the people of Ireland would like me as an ambassador when I retire from the presidency?" he asked her.

As he readied to leave, Kennedy went to the embassy's dining room — now accompanied by President de Valera — to thank the waiters and the chefs for their doting on him during his visit.

"President Kennedy's visit here has given joy not merely to the Irish people at home but the Irish race wherever they are throughout the world," de Valera told the embassy staff. "We are sorry he has to leave, but we know that he has great work to do in his own country."

Time running short, Kennedy also thought of cornering some souvenirs for his family — not more official ones, nice as they were, but personal ones, from him. Of course, the president of the United States cannot stroll into department stores or shops without attracting a mob and, without meticulous planning, throwing off his schedule. So he detailed Evelyn Lincoln, his personal secretary, to go on a mission. Before boarding the helicopter for Galway, Kennedy asked Mrs. Lincoln to find some sweaters for Mrs. Kennedy and the children at Shannon Airport, where she would go to await the president's departure.

As he walked to the helicopter to leave Dublin for the last time, Kennedy was accompanied by the man who had welcomed him to Ireland, President de Valera, and by External Affairs Minister Aiken. Some veteran White House reporters thought Kennedy was subdued, not solely because of the emotion of the moment, but because it appeared that the spill the day before in Cork was, indeed, bothering him. The president, the correspondents were sure, was in some pain.

In this somewhat intimate setting, at least compared to most of the places where he had spoken publicly, Kennedy told the small gathering that he was grateful to the American community for what they had done to help. Turning to the embassy people, the president said: "You did a great job for us and did much to make our stay so pleasant and comfortable.

"I will be back again," Kennedy said. "I do hope to be back."

A reporter for the *Evening Herald* in Dublin moved close to Kennedy to ask him about his trip.

"I have enjoyed myself wonderfully," Kennedy said. "It has been great."

And the highlight?

"The highlight? That was the memorial service at Arbour Hill yesterday," the president answered. "It was very impressive. And I must say, too, that the people everywhere have been wonderful. We had a tremendous welcome."

Strolling past the U.S. Marine Corps honor guard, Kennedy suddenly broke all the farewell formality. He had forgotten to say goodbye to de Valera's wife, Sinead. He quickly strode back through the honor guard to Mrs. de Valera, hugged her and kissed her on the cheek.

And in that little gesture, even the hardest hearts in Ireland were won.

As Kennedy's helicopter flew off, Dorothy Tubridy and Kennedy's sisters waited in the drawing room of the embassy to be escorted to their helicopter. They heard the second helicopter land. After a few moments, they heard it take off. A third helicopter landed. And, to the women's astonishment, they heard that helicopter leave, too. "Nobody came for us! They left us!" Tubridy recalled. "I think Eunice was a bit upset." Tubridy was supposed to provide some commentary for RTE from Shannon. The network found a plane and got her, along with Eunice and Jean, to the other side of Ireland.

♣ ♣ ♣ ♣

Approaching a damp and chilly Galway, Kennedy was treated to more innovation among Irish greeting planners: the Irish flag, formed by 320 children from the Convent of Mercy School, standing in ranks dressed in green, white, and gold.

Touching down on the sports grounds, it was more of the same adulation and vast crowds — some eighty thousand in the gracious and picturesque city of about twenty-one thousand souls.

Kennedy was greeted by, among others, twenty-four members of a local American Legion post. The amused president told Kenneth O'Donnell: "You can't get away from the American Legion no matter where you go. I'll bet they have a post at the South Pole."

The connections to America were strong in all of Ireland, but nowhere did they seem quite as close as in this region. For here and in the rolling mountains to the west in Connemara, people were fond of saying, "The next parish over is New York." Out in Galway Bay, fishing trawlers flew signal flags spelling out "Kennedy." The Irish naval corvette *Cliona* rode at anchor, festooned in signal flags.

The president approached the children dressed in the Irish tricolors.

"Can they sing?" he asked.

As if on cue, a hundred-voice children's choir sang "Galway Bay."

If you ever go across the sea to Ireland,
    Then maybe at the closing of your day,
You will sit and watch the moon rise over Claddagh,
    And see the sun go down on Galway Bay.

The delighted Kennedy applauded. "Very good. . . . That's the stuff," he said.

He stood in his car as he motorcaded into one last Irish city. As he reached Forster House, the residence of the mayor, Kennedy ordered his driver to stop. The president got out and greeted the mayor's mother, Mrs. Catherine Ryan, and the mayor's five children, ranging from eight years to five months — Margaret, Deirdre, Anthony, Patrick, and Elizabeth — all gathered around the flower-covered entrance to the house. Mrs. Ryan asked Kennedy to autograph an old American history book.

The motorcade arrived in Eyre Square, where the president strode toward the ceremonial stand through a vast sea of outstretched hands. Women appeared to outnumber the men

Dressed in green, white, and orange, children from Galway's Convent of Mercy School get the close-up treatment from Kennedy as he arrives at the sports grounds on June 29. The president constantly was talking to kids, shaking their hands, and patting their heads during his time in Ireland.

His hand fiddling with his jacket in one of his trademark gestures,
Kennedy chats with nuns at Galway's sports grounds.

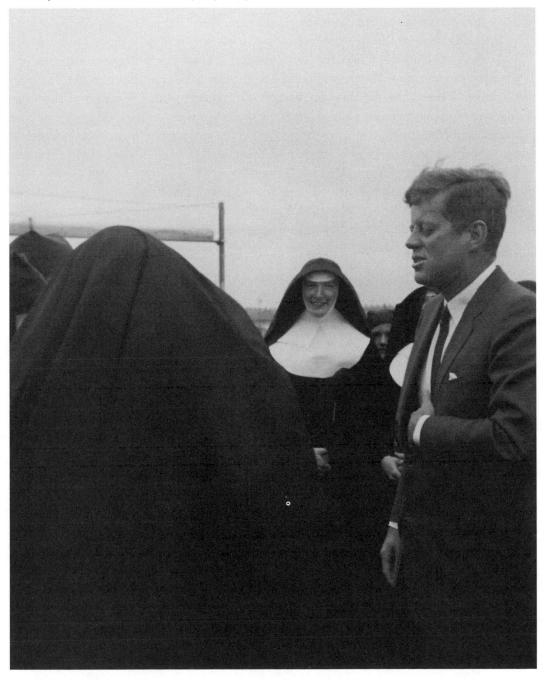

in the gathering by three to one. He did his best to touch, touch, touch, as he kept moving. "Galway loves you!" a girl yelled. An Irish police sergeant decided he needed reinforcements. "Quick, or they'll be wanting to carry him shoulder high through the town!" The nearest in the crowd began the chant, and it spread outward: "Shoulder him! Shoulder him!"

The bells of Saint Nicholas's Collegiate Church, where Columbus is reputed to have heard Mass before one of his voyages to the New World, rang out "The Star-Spangled Banner."

Galway's lord mayor, Alderman Patrick Ryan, wearing his red robes of office, had greeted President Kennedy and ridden with him through the city streets. The members of the Corporation of Galway met their guest at the Browne Doorway leading to Eyre Square. Lemass, Kiernan, and McCloskey also were there. The president inspected a guard of honor from Dun ui Mhaoiliosa, Renmore, to musical background from the City of Galway Pipe Band and the Western Army Command.

The American leader was treated to children in traditional kilts dancing an Irish reel. Harpist Ruth Bradley, seventeen years old, played and sang "Men of the West," a Galway ballad. The Patrician Brothers School Choir sang "You Are Welcome Home."

A picture postcard scene, complete with thatched-roof house, of an uncrowded moment along the motorcade route into Galway.

Standing on a platform with the statue of poet Padraic O'Conaire behind him, Kennedy was made the ninth freeman of the City of the Tribes. The scroll was cradled in a silver gilt casket bearing the coats of arms of Galway and the Kennedy family. His face grew solemn as he signed the official scroll. In Gaelic, the lord mayor spoke of the importance of the president being in this part of western Ireland, which laid claim to the Fitzgerald wing of his family.

"We are honored today that John Fitzgerald Kennedy has accepted from us the freedom of our city," Ryan said. "We renew to him our welcome extended to him first as a distinguished visitor and now extended to him as an Honorary Freeman of Galway. . . . We have today wrought one more link in the centuries-old chain of friendship which binds the great American nation with Ireland."

Ryan spoke for a half hour in Irish, flying the linguistic flag of the old tongue in a nation that, in most places, already had abandoned it in daily speech, no matter what de Valera wanted. Kennedy was given a translation, but even the strongest supporters of the Irish language thought the effort was excessive.

"He went on and on," remembered Randa Murphy, an Irish speaker who was in Eyre Square to see Kennedy. She and her husband, Gay, now run a charming hotel and pub just outside Ennis in County Clare. "We thought he'd never stop."

"The reading of a long address in Irish to a person of prominence who understands only three words of Irish shows little consideration of him," J.F. Doyle complained to the *Connacht Tribune*. "It has been said to me by many and I agree that more harm was done to the movement for the revival of Irish in five minutes on Saturday than by any previous single act."

The city's chamber of commerce gave the president a silver replica of the Great Mace of Galway, with badges of Ireland, Scotland, England, and France on it, while the County Council presented their guest with an Irish linen banquet cloth. Kennedy also was given a silver replica of the sword King James of the Boyne had given to Galway.

At noon, the president got his chance. He looked out over faces jammed into a little park that, had he not been who he was, he could have strolled across in about a minute. The square was, and is, surrounded by mostly three- and four-story buildings with shops on the ground floor and apartments on the upper levels. At the far end of the square, facing Kennedy, stood the gray stone face of the Great Southern Hotel. When the wind was right, the square was perfumed with salty air of the nearby bay.

"Mr. Mayor, members of the County Council, Prime Minister, ambassadors," Kennedy opened. "If the day was clear enough, and if you went down to the bay, and you looked west, and your sight was good enough, you would see Boston, Massachusetts. And if you did, you would see down working on the docks there some Doughertys and Flahertys and Ryans and cousins of yours who have gone to Boston and made good.

"I wonder if you could perhaps let me know how many of you here have a relative in America, who you would admit to — if you would hold up your hand?"

Near the center of Galway, Kennedy is engulfed by the crowd.
Some witnesses say frustrated U.S. Secret Service agents were
a bit rough on people trying to touch Kennedy, while others say
the Irish police were adept at showing their toughness.

It would have been easier to count the hands not raised, as a great roar echoed around the square.

"I don't know what it is about you," Kennedy continued, "that causes me to think that nearly everybody in Boston comes from Galway. They are not shy about it, at all.

"I want to express — as we are about to leave here — to you of this country how much this visit has meant. It is strange that so many years could pass and so many generations pass and still some of us who came on this trip could come home and — here to Ireland — and feel ourselves at home and not feel ourselves in a strange country, but feel ourselves among neighbors, even though we are separated by generations, by time, and by thousands of miles.

"You send us home covered with gifts which we can barely carry, but most of all you send us home with the warmest memories of you and of your country.

"So I must say that though other days may not be so bright as we look toward the future, the brightest days will continue to be those in which we visited you here in Ireland.

"If you ever come to America, come to Washington and tell them, if they wonder who

In Galway's Eyre Square, Kennedy addresses a now-familiar scene, telling the Irish that if they come to Washington, "it will be 'céad míle fáilte.'" Alderman Patrick Ryan, Galway's lord mayor in his red robes, and the town clerk, L. Looney, sit in the front row.

you are at the gate, that you come from Galway. The word will be out and when you do, it will be '*céad míle fáilte*,' which means 'one hundred thousand welcomes!'

"Thank you and goodbye."

There was some chuckling at Kennedy's translation, not because of his pronunciation, but because here, Gaelic was still spoken.

The crowds in Galway pressed in on Kennedy. As he shook hands with people while standing in his limousine, his Secret Service detachment worked to make sure the overly enthusiastic didn't hold on too long. The car was moving while Kennedy was greeting his well-wishers. Kennedy seemed good-natured about the fuss, until a musician reached out and ran his hand through the president's hair. Kennedy's face looked angry as he shook the man off.

Randa Murphy didn't witness any unpleasantness. "There were all these minders in raincoats about," she said, referring to the Secret Service agents, but, she said, "the atmosphere in Galway seemed relaxed."

U.S. Army helicopter pilot Oscar Johnson filmed Kennedy with an eight-millimeter

Clearly in high spirits, Kennedy shares a moment with Galway's mayor, Alderman Patrick Ryan.

camera at a couple of the stops at the end of the trip. Being in uniform, the soldier had good access, and at points stood almost next to the president.

"I don't know how the [presidential] car got through the crowds," Johnson said, but Kennedy was "thrilled" with the boisterous reception from the Irish.

"He was thoroughly enjoying it," Johnson said.

Prime Minister Lemass remembered the Secret Service "quite roughly, quite roughly, knocked away hands who were tending to hold on too long."

The harried Americans were weary and bruised from the crowds. "Thank God they're friendly," said one agent.

♣ ♣ ♣ ♣

"It was an extraordinary visit for the whole of Ireland," one Irish woman remembered thirty-three years later. "I remember going to Galway and shaking hands with President Kennedy. I was, I think, determined to shake his hand in the crowd, and I achieved that. There was no photograph there to record it as somebody else had their photograph recorded. But I did it. I swear I did it. And I still remember it."

The tent on the South Lawn of the White House filled with laughter, and no one's guffaws were louder than those of President William Jefferson Clinton, who had been lucky enough to have his meeting with Kennedy photographed. The woman kidding him and recalling her experience in Galway was Mary Robinson, who, on this evening of June 13, 1996, was the president of Ireland.

♣ ♣ ♣ ♣

Kennedy was headed to Salt Hill, outside Galway, where his helicopter was waiting.

"What's this place, Salt Hill, that we're going to?" Kennedy asked the prime minister.

"It's a seaside resort," Lemass answered.

Even though it was late June and the sun was now shining, the morning was still cold. A north wind carried a bite.

"What people would bathe in the sea when . . ." Kennedy wondered aloud, then shivered. "Only the Spartans would do it."

Needless to say, Lemass didn't pass on Kennedy's observation, not wanting to hurt local tourism.

The crowds followed Kennedy to Salt Hill, crowding near his helicopter.

Kennedy grinned when he saw a sign that read: "Cheerio, Mr. Kennedy. Looking forward already to your visit during your next term."

In a cinematic moment, people waved their hats and kerchiefs to him as he lifted off. He waved from the window and shrank up into the sky, soaring out over Galway Bay.

♣ ♣ ♣ ♣

At one o'clock, the president arrived in Limerick.

The schedule had dictated the setting. Kennedy did not have time to motorcade through the city, where hulking King John's Castle brooded by the rushing shoals of the River Shannon and, across the river, the Treaty Stone stood guard. Instead, the presidential helicopter put down its distinguished passenger on the last furlong at Greenpark Racecourse, a compact horse track just south of the city center, where twenty thousand waited.

After alighting from the helicopter, with Lemass accompanying him, Kennedy yelled to his aides, O'Donnell and Powers.

"Kenny and Dave, come here!"

The puzzled pair pushed through the people to see what their chief wanted. He was standing beside an elderly man.

"Isn't he the image of Honey Fitz?" the president asked. "And his name is Fitzgerald!"

Two of Kennedy's closest aides, David F. Powers, in the hat and holding the camera, and Kenneth P. O'Donnell, step from the presidential helicopter in Limerick on June 29.

The official itinerary put Limerick down for fifteen minutes of fame. Ah, but now that the man himself was in their grasp, the people of Limerick were not about to let him slide away quickly. They had fought for him fair and square, and now they had him.

No one had battled harder for the Kennedy visit than Limerick Mayor Frances Condell, who by her own account did not take "No" meekly. Now, as she received the president, the fruits of all her persistence had been realized.

And Condell, the only woman during Kennedy's male-dominated trip to preside over any official proceedings, made the most of Limerick's moment. She greeted the president at the side of his helicopter and pretty much stayed glued to him. Limerick City Manager T.F. McDermott also walked with the mayor and the president as five city bands massed on the racecourse played the American national anthem.

Limerick, like the other cities Kennedy visited, had closed up most shops and businesses. The local *gardai* were reinforced by two hundred officers from Dublin. The crowd, too, was reinforced, by special trains and buses from cities and towns east and south of Limerick.

On the platform erected for the occasion in front of the judges' box at the track were all the top Limerick area officials and clergy.

After the Boherbuoy Brass and Reed Band played its rendition of "The Star-Spangled Banner," the freedom of the city, of course, was conferred on Kennedy, to the roars of the thousands packed into the racecourse stands and around the dais, decorated with an American flag fashioned from cornflowers and roses. The certificate was placed in a mahogany and silver box decorated with the arms of Limerick. Kennedy was the forty-second person since 1877 so honored by Limerick. Others included de Valera, Charles Stewart Parnell, and Andrew Carnegie the industrialist.

By one estimate, this celebration included some sixty known cousins of President Kennedy from the Limerick area, all Fitzgeralds from his mother's side. One of the oldest given a nice spot next to the platform was seventy-three-year-old Ned Fitzgerald, a third cousin. His grandfather was James Fitzgerald, brother of Thomas Fitzgerald, Kennedy's maternal great-grandfather.

The distinct smell of newly cut hay rode the chill wind blowing hard over the proceedings. The paddocks for the horses were directly behind the grandstands.

The mayor was resplendent in her official robe and cape.

"Mr. President, I wonder if it is possible for you to realize the great privilege and honor it is for me, on behalf of my fellow councilors, citizens and all those present here this afternoon, to welcome you to our City and County of Limerick," she began.

"Your unexpected but sincerely hoped for decision to come to Limerick was acclaimed with the widest jubilation and we thank you warmly, sir, for changing your plans at the last moment to permit us this privilege and the joy of meeting you and the other members of your family on our own soil.

"I am well aware that His Excellency, your ambassador, Mr. McCloskey, played a very important and effective part in your granting us this honor. I wish to thank him for his understanding and patient bearing with me in allowing me to use him as an ambassadorial pin-cushion, whom I kept on prodding to renew our request to the White House, that you come to visit us. Is it any wonder that the dear man eventually said in exasperation: 'Heaven protect me from a persistent woman.' I hope that your ambassador has forgiven me by this time and that you now understand with him, sir, that our enthusiasm to have you come to Limerick was set alight and fanned by a true Irish wind of affection and admiration blowing across the Atlantic to you, with the force of a great hereditary pride which we have in the leadership you are displaying and in your endeavors to accomplish the aims so dear to all Irish hearts, at home and abroad.

"While listening in awed admiration to your speeches in Germany on Wednesday last and later upon your arrival in Dublin, my mind was directed towards your threefold headings, which you gave as reasons for your work and visit to Europe.

"We in Ireland owe much to the threefold reasoning of another man, who returned to Ireland to give us a faith and a freedom of mind, for which you and I, sir, are proud to continue fighting and to practice in our lives.

"I refer, of course, to our Irish Saint Patrick and to the legend of the shamrock with its three leaves, growing from one stem.

"As I listened to you, Mr. President, I could not but interpret your reasoning to a modern ideal based on the symbol of the shamrock and our Christian belief; that you and your people with us see three good reasons for good living, for determined unity, and for working together towards world peace. Three good reasons springing from our common hereditary stem, which inspire us towards your aims and the aims of all free people, which we hope you will achieve, sir, as St. Patrick did in the name of God.

"In welcoming you here in this racecourse, Mr. President, I would like you to know that we of Limerick have a lovely city in there beyond these fields and trees — a city of which we are very proud, steeped as it is in history and antiquity, with its charter and its first mayor reaching back to the year 1197.

"It was from our docks, sir, that many emigrant ships set sail for your shores and from which point of departure our people became yours.

"That time of great exodus is over, thank God, and I'm sure you'll agree with me that you have enough of us over there to keep you happy and to assure you of our faithful support at all times.

"The day has come when the point of departure and arrival has transferred itself for us, some fifteen miles westward, and in keeping with modern times, to an airport. Limerick has benefited immeasurably by its close proximity to Shannon Airport, which, for the last eighteen years, has served as a major international airport, and as a strong connecting link between our old world and your new one.

"Because of our proximity to the airport, also, we have the pleasure of welcoming each year many of your fellow countrymen and our returning emigrants. Now with the setting up of the Industrial Estate at Shannon in which five American firms have established themselves, we have seen the introduction of a new type of American who is taking his place in our civic and social life, and who is bringing to our people the skills and techniques of industry.

"We welcome you, sir, on their behalf, as we welcome them on your behalf, and we trust that you will use your influence to send many more industrialists like them, not alone to Shannon, but to our city of Limerick. I assure you that we shall be very pleased to see a concentration of American industry in Limerick, and in its contiguous area — just to help us in this 'leveling up and not down' as you so aptly said in Germany.

"You see, Mr. President, we the women of Limerick City and County feel that we have a special claim on you! We claim the Fitzgerald in you, and are extremely proud of your heritage. Over there, you see a large number of your relatives and connections who have come to greet you — on the distaff side. As a matter of fact, there is only one Kennedy amongst them, Sean, who felt so strongly about you and America that he wrote an American history in which he forecast many years ago that you would become president of the United States. These good people have come to show our Limerick claim on you, and by their presence they prove that the Fitzgeralds are proud of their own Rose and her dynamic father, Honey Fitz, your reputable and colorful and most successful grandfather.

"But in talking so much of the Fitzgeralds and the Kennedys, we must not forget one, another woman, who is dear to our hearts — your lovely wife, Jacqueline. We shall be pleased if you will take back with you over the Atlantic warmest greetings, Irish prayers and thoughts from the mothers of Limerick City and County especially, to her whose gracious motherhood and wifely devotion and help to you, has endeared her to us all.

"You and your wife and family have become a symbol to us here in this country and an example of family life based on Irish heritage.

"We mothers, especially, sir, only excuse your not bringing your charming Jackie with you to Ireland for the excellent reasons that she has for staying at home. We women know that, however demanding your presidential commitments may be and the urgency for you to move on, we can only interpret part of that haste to your understandable longing to be back home with her again at this time, and we know that she, too, is counting the hours of your return again to her and your children.

"On behalf of my fellow councilors and citizens, I ask you, Mr. President, to accept the Honorary Freedom of our City of Limerick, in our full recognition of the great honor you have done us in coming to visit us, and in support of your distinguished leadership in aims vital, necessary, united and determined.

"May God Bless you and your family. May your work for Him, and of Him through you, have all the blessings that the prayers of the Irish people ask of Him for you."

Mayor Condell gave Kennedy a handmade, full-length Limerick lace christening gown, made by the nuns of Limerick's Good Shepherd Convent, for Mrs. Kennedy, and a piece of Waterford crystal and some porcelain. There also was a gold shamrock on a gold chain for Caroline, and a dog collar for a puppy the Irish would send her.

Amidst cheers, the president strode to the podium.

"Madam Mayor, clergy, members of the City Council, fellow citizens of Limerick," Kennedy began, "I want to express my thanks and also my admiration for the best speech that I have heard since I came to Europe, from your fine mayor.

"I asked your distinguished ambassador to the United States, Ambassador Kiernan — he has sort of an elfish look about him, but he is very, very good — I said, 'What is this county noted for?' and he said, 'It is noted for its beautiful women and its fast horses.' And I said, 'Well, you say that about every county.' And he said, 'No, this is true about this county.'

"I want to express my pleasure at seeing the Fitzgeralds. I wonder if they could stand up? One of them looks just like Grandpa, and that is a compliment.

"This is the last place I go, and then I am going to another country. . . ."

The crowd erupted in laughter, knowing England was the next stop.

". . . and then," Kennedy went on, "I am going to Italy, and then I am going back home to the United States."

Once again, Kennedy asked for a show of hands for those with relations in the United States.

". . . You would be proud of them," Kennedy said. "And they are proud of you. Even though a good many years have passed since most of them left, they still remain and retain the strongest sentiments of affection for this country. And I hope that this visit that we have been able to make on this occasion has reminded them not only of their past, but also that here in Ireland the word 'freedom,' the word 'independence,' the whole sentiment of a nation is perhaps stronger than it is almost any place in the world.

"I don't think that I have passed through a more impressive ceremony than the one I experienced yesterday in Dublin when I went with the prime minister to put a wreath on the graves of the men who died in 1916. What to some countries and some people words of 'freedom,' words of 'independence' . . . to see your president, who has played such a distinguished part, whose life is so tied up with the life of this island in this century — all this has made the past very real, and has made the present very hopeful.

"So I carry with me as I go the warmest sentiments of appreciation to all of you. This is a great country, with a great people, and I know that when I am back in Washington, while I will not see you, I will see you in my mind and feel all of your good wishes, as we all will, in our hearts.

Bidding farewell from Shannon Free Airport on June 29, Kennedy recites a poem and promises "I am going to come back and see old Shannon's face again."

"Last night somebody sang a song, the words of which I am sure you know, of 'Come back to Erin, Mavourneen, Mavourneen, come back aroun' to the land of thy birth. Come back with the shamrock in the springtime, Mavourneen.' This is not the land of my birth, but it is the land for which I hold the greatest affection, and I certainly will come back in the springtime. Thank you."

Kennedy had improvised a bit. He wasn't sure of the last lines of the poem. Neither were Lemass or others traveling with Kennedy's party. But he wanted to use it. So "he had to provide a bit of it himself," Lemass recalled.

St. John's Brass and Reed Band closed the official program with Ireland's national anthem.

The president walked down to the barriers to shake hands with the exuberant crowd. First, he met two more of his relations, Jim Hogan, ninety years old, of Glin, County Limerick, and Mrs. Celia Morgan, eighty, of Clounanna, Adare, County Limerick, both second cousins.

"How are you, Jack?" Hogan asked.

"I'm delighted to see you, and you are looking very well," the president told him.

Then, for twenty minutes Kennedy worked along the barriers. Once again, his security detail was nearly powerless trying to keep the people from engulfing the president. Yet Kennedy almost seemed to resent the intrusion of the security.

"Will you fellows step back?" he told his detail. "I'm doing all right."

But in the frenzy, some people were crushed against the barriers. Two children fainted in the close quarters.

Kennedy moved to his helicopter. As it rose, he waved through the windows to the crowd. The craft circled the racecourse once, then faded to a dot over the Cratloe Hills, bound for Shannon. Inside the helicopter, the president mused: "I wish I could stay here for another week, or another month."

Mayor Condell, determined to make the most of the day, roared off by police car to Shannon Airport for the departure ceremony. At times clocked at eighty miles per hour, the mayor made the seventeen-mile jaunt on the two-lane road in time. And the president was surprised to see her again.

"Did you have your own helicopter?" Kennedy kidded. "How nice of you to go to all this trouble."

♣ ♣ ♣ ♣

At Shannon Airport, where the estuary nearly lapped at the doors of the modest terminal and where men a few days before had swung scythes through the neighboring fields to give them a neat cut, the last gathering for Kennedy was almost intimate. About three thousand came to see him off.

The magic was not gone from the day, but the sheer overwhelming power of Kennedy's visit had lived up to and beyond every expectation. Ireland had turned itself inside out for JFK. That the president himself had gone all-out also was in no dispute. He had brought nearly every resource — and nearly every Irish-American in his government — to bear on this small island. The correspondent for the *Baltimore Sun,* William Knighton, Jr., was struck by that latter fact as he surveyed the array of American aircraft parked on the tarmac at Shannon: the presidential jet, two other government Boeing 707s, a chartered 707 for the press, a DC-7, a large cargo aircraft, four jet prop helicopters, and six smaller helicopters deployed to Ireland from various U.S. military units in Europe. It was evidence, he wrote, "that the Kennedy invasion of Ireland was the largest American airlift since the Communists shut down entry to West Berlin in 1948."

The presidential departure from Shannon was nearly a mirror-image of his arrival in Dublin: cannons boomed a twenty-one-gun salute; the Band of the Southern Command played the American anthem; and Kennedy inspected a hundred-man guard of honor, soldiers of the Twelfth Battalion Limerick and Clonmel.

On this final stop, Kennedy and his Irish hosts mingled. Education Minister Dr. Patrick Hillery was on the platform, along with an array of clergy and local civic officials.

The Clare County Council, through its chairman, Sen. Sean Brady, presented the president with a gift of old Irish silver, a claret jug. And Brady couldn't help but plug Shannon Airport, upon which hopes of economic prosperity in the region rested. (Indeed, Kennedy's sisters and sister-in-law were spotted taking advantage of the airport's duty-free shop before the president's arrival.)

Kennedy also received a gift not publicized until after he left: a bottle of holy water and clay from an Irish shrine to help his back. It was sent to the *Irish Independent* by an elderly lady in County Galway, and the newspaper passed it on to the presidential staff.

The president appeared somewhat wistful as he spoke to this, his last Irish audience. Dr. Hillery recalled the tone as "kind of plaintive."

"I want to express my thanks to the County Council, and this is where we all say good-bye," Kennedy said.

"I want to express our greatest thanks to the president of your country, your great president, to your prime minister, and to all the members of the government, and especially to all the people of Ireland who have taken us in.

"Ireland is an unusual place. What happened five hundred or a thousand years ago is yesterday, where we on the other side of the Atlantic three thousand miles away, we are next door. While there may be those removed by two or three generations from Ireland — they may have left a hundred years ago their people — and yet when I ask how many people may have relatives in America nearly everybody holds up their hands.

"So Ireland is a very special place. It has fulfilled in the past a very special role. It is in a very real sense the mother of a great many people, a great many millions of people, and in a sense a great many nations. And what gives me the greatest satisfaction and pride, being of Irish descent, is the realization that even today this very small island still sends thousands, literally thousands, of its sons and daughters to the ends of the globe to carry on an historic task which Ireland assumed fourteen hundred or fifteen hundred years ago.

"So this has been really the high point of our trip. Last night I sat next to one of the most extraordinary women, the wife of your president, who knows more about Ireland and Irish history. So I told her I was coming to Shannon, and she immediately quoted this poem, and I wrote down the words because I thought they were so beautiful:

> 'Tis it is the Shannon's brightly glancing stream,
> Brightly gleaming, silent in the morning beam,
> Oh, the sight entrancing,
> Thus returns from travels long,
> Years of exile, years of pain,
> To see old Shannon's face again,
> O'er the waters dancing.

"Well, I am going to come back and see old Shannon's face again, and I am taking, as I go back to America, all of you with me. Thank you."

The crowd had held its breath as Kennedy recited. Now it broke into a roar.

"A supremely Irish ending to his Irish adventure," declared Lord Longford.

It would be some years later when de Valera revealed that Kennedy had made errors in taking down the Gerald Griffin poem. Kennedy and the others on his helicopter "put their heads together, with the result they turned out something which wasn't the real poem at all." Lemass recalled that it was one word neither Kennedy nor anyone else on the helicopter on the way to Shannon could make out — from Kennedy's own scrawl of the night before — so they made up the word. In fact, as touching as Kennedy's version was, a lot of it was wrong. Griffin's original went like this:

> 'Tis the Shannon's stream, brightly glancing, brightly glancing!
> See, oh see the ruddy beam upon its waters dancing!
> Thus returned from travel vain, years of exile, years of pain,
> To see old Shannon's face again,
> Oh, the bliss entrancing.

The bump-and-run tour had given the gardai all they could handle, and Kennedy took a moment to speak with the assistant police commissioner, Michael Weymes, to praise the work of Irish law enforcement.

Dorothy Tubridy stopped Kennedy before he left.

"Are you glad you came?" she asked him.

"These were the three happiest days I've ever spent in my life," Kennedy answered.

A man yelled out: "It has been the greatest visit in our history!"

To which Kennedy answered: "It has been a great experience for me, too!"

It was obvious to all. George Meany, president of the AFL-CIO, whose ancestors had come from central Ireland, had been with Kennedy on the first day and watched him up close. "Oh, his mood was just as happy and just as delightful as could be. He just felt really at home. He had a rare sense of humor and he had the type of humor that the Irish understand. He was always poking a little fun at himself, which the Irish are very good at, and his visit there was, I am quite sure, one of the most pleasant days he ever spent because he felt right at home."

Kennedy walked to his jet as people called out to him, "God bless you."

Bunratty Castle's singers rendered "Danny Boy" one more time. And for all the exposure, all of his appearances across Eire, some people felt the party had hardly started. One sign held up at Shannon, which would have special poignancy five months later, borrowed the title from a sad Irish ballad: "Johnny, We Hardly Knew Ye."

"You are great people," the president was heard to say as he neared his plane. "You made me very happy here."

The president boarded his jet as a choir sang "Come Back to Erin." People in the crowd yelled "Come back, Jack!"

At 2:30 p.m., the great gleaming jet bearing John Fitzgerald Kennedy left Irish soil.

Lawrence O'Brien remembered seeing the president "deeply and visibly moved, as were we all."

"If there was a dry eye at the airport," O'Brien said, "I missed it."

seven

October 11–21, 1963:
Philadelphia, Chicago, Washington, New York, Boston

Sing the lords and ladies gay
   That are beaten into the clay
   Through seven heroic centuries;
Cast your mind on other days
   That we in coming days may be
   Still the indomitable Irishry.

William Butler Yeats
"Under Ben Bulben" (1939)

The indefatigable investigative columnist Drew Pearson was unmoved by Kennedy's Irish visit. In a column, he detailed how the White House had flown its fifty-member contingent of Irish-American staffers to Ireland at government expense. White Houses are notoriously alert to launching damage control over such stories. Not this time.

"That was one column that nobody in the White House gave a damn about," Kennedy's congressional liaison O'Brien huffed.

Indeed, Ireland's magic did not let go of Kennedy. He spoke of his Irish visit often, and even took to greeting people in the halls of the White House in Irish.

Immediately after his return from Europe, he took a Carrickmacross lace tablecloth and napkins given by Prime Minister and Mrs. Lemass and an antique silver dish ring from the de Valeras to Mrs. Kennedy, who was at the family home in Hyannisport, on Cape Cod.

"It truly brought a little bit of Ireland to the Cape and somewhat alleviated her disappointment in not being able to visit you and Mrs. de Valera also," Kennedy wrote the Irish president.

Kennedy played records over and over of the Irish groups that had provided the musical accompaniment to his tour.

And he watched the films of his days in Ireland. He took them to Hyannisport, screening them in the theater his father had built in the basement of one of the houses back when he was in the movie business in the 1930s. The first time Kennedy showed the trip, the first Friday evening he was back after Europe, he played to a full house of family and friends.

"The next night, after dinner, he said, 'What shall we do now? Anyone want to come back to my house to watch the films?'" Sen. Edward Kennedy recalled. "There were four or five people there."

The following night, President Kennedy asked who would join him for yet another encore.

"I said, 'I will,'" remembered the senator, who was thirty-one at the time. "And it was my brother and myself in there."

By then, the president "knew the films," Ted Kennedy said. "He'd say, 'Watch so-and-so tapping her foot. . . . Watch this, watch that.' . . . He lived it, he enjoyed it."

Kennedy indeed may have surprised himself by his reaction to Ireland this time. But he was not that surprised by the Irish reaction to him, said the president's sister, Jean Kennedy Smith.

"I think he had a great deal of empathy as a person," she said. "He understood it right away. He knew history very well. . . . And you couldn't help but feel it with the Irish. . . . It's really hard to explain, it was so emotional. They loved you and you loved them, and it didn't have to be said."

The joys of Ireland were tempered by great sadness in early August. The birth of the Kennedys' third child, so anticipated by the Irish as well as Americans, came nearly two months early. But little Patrick Bouvier Kennedy, his lungs underdeveloped, died after only thirty-nine hours of life.

As Ireland's effect on Kennedy was palpable, so, too, was Kennedy's impact on Eire.

In Ireland, the presidential journey would be assessed, dissected, and, above all, fondly recalled, for decades into the future.

The Irish government, in the afterglow of Kennedy's tour, gave their guest a boffo review.

"In essence, it can be said President Kennedy 'stole the show,'" a Department of External Affairs memo said. "Had he been schooled in advance by professional publicists employed by Irish interests he could not possibly have 'identified himself' more thoroughly or more favorably with Ireland and the Irish."

"Some people believe that what did most to restore the self-confidence of Ireland," wrote Walter Bryan, "was the emotion-charged visit of President Kennedy in 1963, probably the happiest and most hopeful event in Irish history since his ancestor defeated the Norsemen at Clontarf in 1014. A woman journalist, thinking of the time it had taken for the free air of America to produce a president from the poor Irish, described him as 'the Irishman of the year 2000.'"

Other commentators depicted Kennedy as nothing less than the healer of the Irish spirit, beaten down and degraded for so many centuries.

"The Irish rose up to greet him in a massive, vibrating demonstration that was thrilling to behold. He afforded them a singular opportunity to express openly their inner conviction that they were the equals of any race on earth including their classic antagonists, the English," John Philip Cohane maintained. "He soothed and nurtured a national psyche which has taken a nasty beating for many long, drab years.

"This was in large measure the key to Kennedy's enormous popularity in Ireland. He was the only Irish-American who successfully bridged the gap in their hearts, not just because he was the president of the United States but because they saw in him a fellow Irishman who could move gracefully, affably, and naturally in all circles, in terms of politics, diplomacy, wealth and society. He had pole-vaulted in one generation right over the heads of the English."

Kennedy cemented an identity for Ireland, according to a political correspondent for the

Sunday Independent: "What has he brought back to us? He brought the realization that Ireland has at last reached true nationhood; that we have at last fulfilled our destiny and taken our place amongst the nations of the earth."

"By his coming," agreed Dr. Hillery, "the stature of Ireland was raised."

Whatever doubts he had about Kennedy's willingness to work on Northern Ireland or the nature of Kennedy's Irishness, Ambassador Kiernan was absolutely certain the president had made history in Ireland. "I think that his coming back to Ireland was a closing of a chapter that began with the Famine. It was triumphant in that way," he said. "It was the first year by coincidence since the Famine that the population of Ireland showed an increase. It was the first year when emigration turned into an inward flow of immigration. These are simply historical coincidences, but I think he appeared to the people as an ending to the Famine, as a triumph out of the Famine. The Famine, although it happened a hundred years ago, remained in the consciousness of the people. The Famine and the evictions following the Famine on such a huge scale, reducing the population from nine million to four million, somehow remained, although for that reason wasn't spoken of. But at the back of people's minds was a feeling of failure. Famine spelled failure. And the entire government of the country [after] the Famine had been a government by non-Irish. This again indicates failure. And here was a success come at top level. Here was a fellow who came from Famine stock on both paternal and maternal sides and who had reached the very top in the United States. That was felt throughout the country. I think in that sense you could say he wasn't coming as the king, he was coming as an ending of a bad epoch, a bad century."

"It is tempting to see Kennedy's Irish visit as the end of an era," wrote Fergal Tobin, "the final apotheosis of that traditional Ireland which had looked to America as the land of opportunity where Irish energy could prosper in a manner impossible at home."

Kennedy, Tobin contended, "spoke to the Irish people in traditional terms," reminding his listeners that Ireland had come through centuries of oppression with its loyalty to faith and nation intact. "This was the authentic self-image of post-Famine Ireland, a nation in eternal and tenacious communion with its past," Tobin wrote. And yet, he added, "Kennedy spoke to an Ireland that was passing away: the inert, defeated country which never ceased to contemplate its own miseries and keep warm its old resentments. But the image he employed was one that went very deep in the Irish psyche, and which was impervious to the effects of modernization. For what Kennedy had stated was a definition of nationality. . . . It was unhistorical, as all such definitions are, but it had great emotional power and popular appeal, for this was how the Irish nation saw itself in history."

The American president also was aid and comfort to Lemass and his party, suggested historian Dermot Keogh.

"JFK personified the brash, self-image of the new Fianna Fail: he was young and handsome; he was wealthy and almost self-made; he was a conservative social reformer who favored free enterprise; but, above all, he was a successful Irish-American politician who had outmaneuvered the WASP opposition in the United States and had made it to the White House. Kennedy was proof that the Irish were made of the 'right stuff.'"

From the viewpoint of opposition Fine Gael, Kennedy's effect on Ireland was equally remarkable.

Sen. Maurice Manning, a Fine Gael leader reflecting on the trip in 2001, said Ireland before June 1963 "mattered very little and attracted little attention" from Kennedy.

"We were economically weak, on the fringe of Europe, outside of NATO, with little self-confidence, inward-looking and with no great sense of self-belief," was Manning's analysis.

"And then the magic happened," he said. Ireland discovered it could organize itself for so great an occasion as a presidential visit. The Irish also revealed to themselves that, despite decades of deprivation and hardships, they were, indeed "a demonstrative people, capable of great enthusiasm and emotion, given the reason and opportunity," Manning said. Ireland learned the power of the shared experience through television, too.

"Most of all, perhaps, the visit engendered a sense of national pride," the Fine Gael leader said. "It was not owned by Fianna Fail, or Fine Gael, or Labour. It was not owned by one church or other, by one county or one city. It was an event in which all could take pride and in part, in a way as yet only incipient, it gave a new meaning to what it meant to be Irish."

"John F. Kennedy," Manning said, "showed us a new face of ourselves — what we might be. . . . No wonder the young politicians studied him so carefully. He was the future — what they wanted to be."

Former SDLP leader John Hume, one of the architects of the 1998 Good Friday Agreement on Northern Ireland, was twenty-six in 1963. Kennedy, he said, "made a huge impact on Ireland."

"As young people, we had no doubt that President Kennedy's visit reflected in depth his pride in his Irish roots. And he gave a great sense of self-confidence to the people of Ireland, North and South," Hume said.

Irish journalist Tim Pat Coogan detected positive cultural influences of Kennedy's trip on a nation where some books and movies still were banned, and where the Catholic archbishop Dr. McQuaid warned parishioners that it was a mortal sin to attend Protestant Trinity College without his permission. Kennedy's visit was a factor in "liberalizing the climate of opinion in Ireland," Coogan asserted three years after the president's tour.

"The reader outside Ireland may wonder why I single out Kennedy's visit," the journalist wrote. "It had a peculiarly Irish effect which is hard to explain. For the few days he was in the country it was possible to engage wholeheartedly, without cynicism or dissension, in honoring a man who was not only an Irish hero but also a politician. For too long in the island one man's admiration for a political figure has been another man's hatred. I trust I

181

shall be excused a little sentiment when I say that it meant something inexpressibly moving to an Irishman to stand beside President Kennedy in the grounds of Aras an Uachtarain the day he planted the tree. This man's great-grandfather left Ireland during the Famine. The great-grandson of him was now president of the United States. The [Aras] used to be the Vice-Regal Lodge, the center of Dublin's high social life under the British. After independence it eventually became the home of the president of Ireland. And here now was this descendant of stricken peasants planting a tree hard by one planted by Queen Victoria when she came to Ireland as the Famine was ending. A wind blew from Dallas and the tree died. But Kennedy's memory is strong: more steadfast than any tree could be; more enduring than the vicissitudes of parties or states. He helped to solder past and present together, and suddenly to make politics something which gave a future meaning to the present."

The events of June 1963 also complemented the concerted effort since the late 1950s under Lemass and his foreign minister, Aiken, to end Ireland's international isolation and move the nation decidedly into "westernism," historian F.S.L. Lyons pointed out. "The American orientation which this implied was greatly reinforced by the triumphant visit of President Kennedy to Ireland in the summer of 1963, and the bond of sympathy between the two countries which he then established or renewed was not to be broken even by his assassination a few months later."

Kennedy's very presence in the White House had necessitated an adjustment in Ireland's stance towards the world, historian Ronan Fanning argued. ". . . Harping on neutrality," he said, "struck a somewhat incongruous chord when John Fitzgerald Kennedy became the first American Catholic and the first Irish-American with whom Irish Catholics could identify to become the president of the United States. Kennedy's official visit to Ireland in the summer of 1963 had a stunning impact. The later day Hero/Playboy of the Western World and the apotheosis of the returned Yank who had made good, Kennedy personified the wider ambitions of a new Ireland in which anything was possible."

Indeed, Kennedy's stature in Europe may have furthered American foreign policy interests on the continent, the president's hometown paper, the *Boston Globe*, editorialized: "Mr. Kennedy's visit to his ancestral Ireland identifies him somewhat with the peoples of Europe. The president's very youth gives his commitment 'to stay . . . as long as our presence is desired' (as Kennedy promised on his arrival in Bonn) much greater authority for the long-term future than doubts raised by the far older statesman who heads the Republic of France."

The extensive world exposure Kennedy won for Ireland could not be underestimated, the *Connacht Tribune* in Galway said. For all the historical symbolism of Kennedy's visit, it also could spark real economic benefits, "material gain" in the form of tourists, the newspaper said.

The Irish Tourist Association certainly agreed. The impact of Kennedy's visit on tourism from the United States was "incalculable," the association concluded by season's end.

And the meaning of Kennedy's return to Ireland could not be understated for Irish-Americans, according to Richard Finnegan, director of Irish studies at Stonehill College in Easton, Massachusetts.

"Its significance has a sort of deeper, more wave-like effect," he said. "He goes [to Ireland], and it's a moment at which, if you want to symbolically do so, you can identify the transformation of the Irish-American into those who are going to emerge as not only extraordinarily well-assimilated, but into positions of power and wealth . . . with religious, artistic, and other significant roles."

Kennedy, Finnegan said, "represents the first wave that results in the American renaissance off of the explosion of Irish culture, the global explosion of Irish culture that has occurred" in recent decades.

Sen. Edward Kennedy, whose personal and familial involvement in Irish affairs spans the decades since 1963, views his brother's visit as "a real validation for the Irish." It was a signal, the senator said, "that one of their own could achieve the position of the highest office in the world." Like Dr. Hillery and others, Sen. Kennedy sees June 1963 as a moment when Ireland attained a new stature in the international community. And, seen from the other side of the Atlantic, President Kennedy's tour through Ireland was "a triumph" for Irish Americans, the senator believes. "For the American Irish to see one of their own overcome prejudice and real discrimination was really an historic breakthrough. . . . It announced to the world that they were worthy, they had achieved the American dream."

Significantly, it quickly became clear that a trip that had started primarily as a mere sentimental visit for Kennedy to the home country was transforming the relationship between the United States and Ireland. No further proof was needed than Prime Minister Lemass's trip to America, arranged and carried out only months after Kennedy had returned to Washington.

This was to be no routine state visit. Lemass was the first Irish head of state to visit the United States, and Kennedy was determined to repay in kind his reception in Ireland.

". . . The president wanted to put on a great show for him because he had been entertained so royally when he had been in Ireland," recalled Assistant Treasury Secretary James A. Reed, a friend of Kennedy's dating back to their days as PT boat skippers in World War II. ". . . He was particularly anxious to have a very festive time for the prime minister."

The itinerary for Lemass covered Philadelphia, Chicago, Washington, New York, and Boston. ". . . I told him that the schedule was fit only for a veteran campaigner," Kennedy wrote Ireland's president of his warning to Lemass, "but that I was sure he would survive it as I survived my visit to Ireland." The tour was not for mere honors and sightseeing, but to give Lemass a chance to tell Ireland's economic story, to promote that nation's exports and, it was hoped, draw more American investment to Ireland.

"Prime Minister Lemass is the chief architect of the 'New Look' in Ireland," an internal State Department briefing paper summarized. "As a result of his initiative and vision, the Irish have embarked on a new course which is designed to invigorate the Irish economy, to alter its traditional insular and parochial outlook, and to recognize that Ireland's destiny must be realized within a larger European context. Introspective policies, which in the past have been dominated by excessive preoccupation with the partition question, are being replaced by outward and forward-looking policies calculated to put Ireland into the main stream of international developments of this century. At the same time, conscious efforts are being made to maintain the charm of old Ireland. . . . Expanded foreign investment along with modernization of the Irish economy and increased tourism are the principal objectives of Lemass's new seven-year economic expansion program. . . ."

Kennedy lent Lemass Air Force One, the presidential jet and a great symbol of prestige, to ensure his comfort and to send a not-so-subtle message that this international guest had the absolute endorsement of the White House. "No one does that. . . . They don't do that kind of stuff," Sen. Edward Kennedy said, chuckling at the memory of what he called this "personal" gesture from his brother to the leader of Ireland.

Lemass and his wife arrived October 11 in Philadelphia, where they visited Ambassador and Mrs. McCloskey. At a dinner given in his honor by Philadelphia Mayor James Tate, Lemass noted that in America, "there is not a state where an Irishman walks as a stranger." The prime minister received an honorary law degree from Villanova University, and the key to the city of Philadelphia.

On October 13, Lemass and his party, including External Affairs Minister Aiken, flew to Chicago. Mayor Richard J. Daley conferred on the prime minister honorary citizenship of the city, whose main streets Lemass traveled were decorated with harps on the lampposts. Addressing business leaders at the Chicago Club, Lemass called Kennedy's visit of the previous June "an historic occasion for us which marked the fulfillment of many of our hopes and aspirations."

"Although we are, as President Kennedy pointed out . . . the first of the small nations to obtain our independence in the twentieth century, we are not seeking financial aid but are trying to build up our economy by our own efforts and mainly with our own capital and resources," the prime minister said. "All we ask of our friends is that they should not overlook the opportunities which Ireland may offer to them for expansion — expansion which would be profitable to themselves and of immeasurable assistance to us."

In Washington on October 15, Lemass received the full diplomatic treatment: from Air Force One, to helicopter transportation direct to the Ellipse adjoining the White House, to an official welcome on the White House's South Lawn amidst blaring trumpets and booming guns.

Kennedy presided, with evident relish, at the welcoming ceremony. Afterwards, the two leaders then reproduced in America one of the scenes from Ireland: a motorcade. This one wound through Washington, to the cheers of some eighty thousand people, Kennedy and Lemass both standing and waving. Lemass knew that Kennedy was trying to make the reception for the Irish leader as impressive as possible.

"He was, I think, a little bit worried that I wouldn't get in Washington anything like the same turnout of people along the street for the ceremony there that he got in Dublin, and no doubt this would have been so," Lemasss later remembered. But he somehow became privy

Kennedy has a little fun with the golf clubs he is giving the Irish prime minister, Sean Lemass, during Lemass's visit to Washington in October 1963. A grinning Lemass, in the center of the picture, watches to see if the president takes a divot out of the carpet. Irish External Affairs Minister Frank Aiken is behind Kennedy. U.S. Ambassador Matthew McCloskey, far right, seems less amused.

to Kennedy's efforts to pump up the size of the crowd. ". . . He apparently gave orders that all the Civil Service staffs in Washington were to take the morning off on condition that they be there [for the motorcade]," Lemass recalled, laughing.

Lemass was hosted at a glittering Department of State luncheon by Secretary Rusk, who was unveiling for the first time some $100,000 in American antiques and art that had been acquired to furnish the diplomatic reception rooms.

That night, Kennedy feted the Irish leader at a state dinner for 102 in the White House. With Jacqueline Kennedy out of the country, the president's sister Jean Kennedy Smith was the hostess. Around the tables were Supreme Court Chief Justice and Mrs. Earl Warren; Secretary of State Rusk; Undersecretary of Commerce and Mrs. Franklin D. Roosevelt, Jr., son of the late president; Sen. and Mrs. Hubert H. Humphrey; and the president's brothers, Attorney General Robert F. Kennedy, with his wife, Ethel, and Sen. Edward Kennedy and his wife, Joan. The senator and his wife were attending their first state dinner.

After expansive speeches and toasts from both the president and Lemass, the Bagpipe Band of the United States Air Force entered the room, skirling familiar pieces from Ireland. Then the pipers premiered a new marching song, "President Kennedy Welcomes the Prime Minister of Ireland," composed just for the event.

The following day, Lemass mirrored Kennedy's visit to Arbour Hill, laying a wreath at the Tomb of the Unknown Soldier in Arlington National Cemetery. He also addressed the National Press Club and met on Capitol Hill with House Speaker John W. McCormack and the chairman of the Senate Foreign Relations Committee, Sen. J.W. Fulbright of Arkansas. Lemass hosted a reception for Kennedy at one of Washington's finest hotels, the Mayflower, was given a medal of honor by Georgetown University, and dined with the directors of the American-Irish Foundation. The *Washington Post* that day gave a lot of space to Lemass' arrival the previous day, right next to a story about Kennedy's intentions to keep Vice President Lyndon B. Johnson on the ticket in 1964, and plans to try to make some political inroads in the South, particularly in Texas, where Kennedy would travel in November.

It was at the press club luncheon that the subject that was not publicly spoken of by Kennedy in Ireland was raised by Lemass in America, and at some length: partition.

"While the reunification of the Irish people is seen by us as a matter for Irishmen in Ireland, partition is, of course, a political arrangement and its termination must involve the British government by which it was devised," Lemass said. "What we would like to see happening now would be a clear statement by British political leaders that there would be no British interest in maintaining partition when Irishmen want to get rid of it. That has not yet been said."

The British, Lemass argued, had accepted the "wind of change blowing through their former colonial possessions in Africa and Asia, and this has encouraged us in hoping that a similar attitude of goodwill and enlightened self-interest will ensure their cooperation in the elimination of the one outstanding political problem arising between our nearest neighbor and ourselves, and thus to clear away the last obstacle to the closest and most friendly relations between us."

Partition, Lemass told the reporters, "is never absent from our minds or from our hearts."

This was front-page news back in Dublin, and Terence O'Neill up in Belfast felt Lemass was discarding all the "civil exchanges" and talk of "cooperation" between the two in recent months.

"'Cooperation' certainly does not stem from derogatory speeches in another country," Northern Ireland's minister said. "It is notable that when President Kennedy came to Dublin he was a model of circumspection. No mention of Northern Ireland came from his lips. Yet, now on a return visit, we have Mr. Lemass in an address to the press in Washington calling on Britain to end partition."

It is intriguing that Lemass would take this stance, in this city, at this time. Could he have told Kennedy ahead of time what he was going to say? Quite possibly. Could Kennedy have assented to this aggressive move as a means of prompting some movement in London on Northern Ireland? Perhaps. It could be argued strongly that the prime minister of Ireland would not, on a highly visible state visit to the closest ally of the United Kingdom, unilaterally pound away on the need for action from Whitehall without the prior knowledge of his American host. The evidence has yet to surface.

The moment may have been propitious, too, because Britain was hours away from a new prime minister. Macmillan, with whom Kennedy enjoyed a relationship as close as that between Franklin D. Roosevelt and Winston Churchill, was about to step down. (Conservative Sir Alec Douglas-Home would become the new prime minister.)

On October 17, after their private talks, Kennedy and Lemass issued a joint statement, noting that they discussed improving Ireland's economic links with its European neighbors, and hopes for more American investment in, and trade with, Ireland. Northern Ireland was not even indirectly referred to.

Kennedy's generosity to Ireland did not end with the state dinner for the prime minister and his whirlwind tour of the Irish diaspora in America. He sent Lemass home with another gift for de Valera: this time, a reproduction of the sword Gen. George Washington wore during most of the American Revolution. In a letter accompanying the gift, Kennedy explained that Washington's will provided that each of his nephews should receive a sword after he died. The will also provided that "these swords are accompanied with an injunction not to unsheathe them for the purpose of shedding blood, except it be for self-defense or in defense of their country and its rights; and in the latter case to keep them unsheathed and prefer falling with them in their hands to the relinquishment thereof."

"I think the words of General Washington reflect a sense of values which both Irishmen and Americans share in common," Kennedy wrote.

As a measure of Kennedy's personal regard for the prime minister, Lemass was given a custom-made set of golf clubs. Kennedy had cabled Dublin for Lemass's measurements and had detailed an American Embassy staffer to watch the Irish leader play to pick up any subtleties the equipment should allow for.

Lemass went on to New York. Mayor Robert Wagner gave the Irish leader the key to the city. Then Lemass delivered an address to the General Assembly of the United Nations. He expressed his hope that the spread of nuclear arms could be halted. And again, for the second time in two days, Lemass called on Britain to take a step on ending the partition of Ireland.

In the evening, Lemass dined with a gathering of the American financial world's who's who, hosted by J. Peter Grace, president of W.R. Grace, one of the largest companies in the United States. Here, once again, Lemass made an appeal to the bankers and industrialists to give Ireland a serious look for investment.

On October 18, Lemass journeyed to Boston, where he addressed the Advertising Club of Greater Boston. The following day he was back in New York, visiting an Irish goods display at a department store, checking on the progress of the Irish pavilion at the upcoming 1964 World's Fair, and enjoying the horses at Aqueduct, where he awarded a Waterford glass trophy to the winner of the Irish Progress, the day's sixth race.

The prime minister spent his final day, a Sunday, back in Boston. He attended a special Mass celebrated by Cardinal Richard Cushing, met with Senator Kennedy, and made two speeches, one at Boston College and one to a joint meeting of Boston's Irish societies.

Lemass arrived back in Dublin with his first prize: a Boston company had agreed to lease fifty thousand square feet of factory space in Shannon. And more deals were to come from American companies in the following weeks: W.R. Grace announced a partnership with Urney Chocolates Ltd. of Dublin to boost exports to England and North America; Olin Mathieson Corp. unveiled a plan to build a new pharmaceutical plant near Dublin; and Becton Dickinson & Co. said it would construct a new factory in Drogheda to make sterile and disposable syringes.

While American business was showing initiative, obviously as an outgrowth of Lemass's visit at the invitation of Kennedy, the American president's longer-term intentions in Ireland weren't entirely clear, and he never had a chance to articulate them in a public forum. But evidence abounds that he was contemplating initiatives to assist the Irish economy.

The formation of the Irish-American Foundation was intended as such a step. The foundation was announced by Ireland's Government Information Bureau the same day Kennedy left Ireland. De Valera had proposed such an institution years before. The idea was to set up an exchange of students, teachers, and experts in various fields between Ireland and the United States.

The groundwork for the foundation had been carefully laid the previous year, when the

Irish had met with the U.S. Internal Revenue Service to go over the proper method of making the organization tax-exempt. In a St. Patrick's Day speech in 1963 before the Charitable Irish Society of Boston, Ireland's Ambassador Kiernan had talked up the foundation. He envisioned an organization with a $5 million budget. Once Kennedy's trip to Ireland was set, Kiernan pushed the idea of announcing the foundation during the trip, with the president and de Valera serving as co-chairmen.

Hibernia, a Catholic journal in Ireland, took up the call as Kennedy was about to arrive in Ireland.

"The foundation would promote the long term welfare of the Irish people by the development of their potential in education, science, technology and culture," the journal said. "Such a body to be effective should be completely autonomous. Church and State in Ireland could and should subscribe to its initial endowment and encourage individuals and groups to assist its work in the years ahead.

"It would provide an immediate means," *Hibernia* added, "by which the Irish in the United States and throughout the world could contribute to the social, economic and cultural development of the homeland."

And so the foundation was announced, albeit in a low-key way, as Kennedy's visit ended. As Kiernan recalled it, Kennedy himself drafted the communique about the foundation while flying in his helicopter from Dublin to Galway. And, in October, even as the foundation still was getting organized, Kennedy had it on his mind. After the meeting with Lemass, the president took Kiernan aside as the prime minister and his party were leaving, asking him to "keep me fully informed" about the progress of the foundation.

The U.S. Department of State, meanwhile, was pressuring Irish officials about what they wanted from the American government.

"The State Department were asking me," Kiernan revealed later, ". . . what were we going to — what proposal were we going to put? And we couldn't believe it. We didn't come for any proposal. . . . That became a grievance with them. It honestly did, so much a grievance that I was pressing my own government, 'For God's sake, can't you think of . . . anything?'"

Kennedy came up with the idea that the United States and Ireland should engage in joint research on fish and the potential for expanded development of commercial fishing. As a former House and Senate member from Massachusetts, where fishing is a major industry, Kennedy probably knew more about the subject than did any other occupant of the White House. The American government already was conducting research in the North Atlantic on fish and plankton. The idea was to help develop Irish fisheries. Talks, in fact, already had been underway at a sub-cabinet level between Dublin and Washington.

Kennedy, according to Lemass, wanted to show "his desire to help us if there was any way in which we needed help."

By 1966, the United States had, in fact, conducted a survey of Irish fishing resources and the potential for commercial development, which Lemass said proved "quite useful to us."

In retrospect, the new American business ventures, the boost in tourism from the United States, the exchange of students and academics, and the modest fishing study all were different paths to the same goal of aiding Ireland's economic progress.

William V. Shannon, who helped to write the speeches Kennedy gave in Ireland and who later was President Jimmy Carter's ambassador to Ireland, believed U.S.-Irish relations were on the brink of major change. In his second term, Shannon quoted Kennedy as saying, he would "do big things for Ireland."

After his visit to Ireland, "he felt a tremendous connection," said the president's sister Jean Kennedy Smith. She said she heard her brother speak of plans for Ireland, too, but said he was not specific. Sen. Edward Kennedy, too, is "convinced he would have continued that interest [in Ireland] in a constructive way as president."

On the other hand, Theodore C. Sorensen didn't hear about any "big things for Ireland" in a second term.

"I'm not certain what, specifically, concretely, that would have meant," he said. "Ireland was not on the list of the neediest cases."

Kennedy's future plans for dealing with Northern Ireland were not clear. It seems reasonable to assume there might have been an American effort on the problem of partition in a second Kennedy term.

In the days after Kennedy's departure from Ireland, some were struck by the lack of resentment in Belfast to a trip that had excluded all Northern Irish leaders sympathetic to the Unionist cause. On the other hand, there was disappointment that Lemass and O'Neill had given Kennedy no opportunity to at least broach the subject of Northern Ireland.

"In fact, both prime ministers in Ireland stuck to the old guns of convention," said the *Irish Times*. "By doing so they probably spiked President Kennedy's guns as far as giving him room to make a statesmanlike speech on politics in Ireland, a pronouncement that might have amounted to nothing more than counseling closer co-operations between North and South."

Hopes in Ireland remained high that such a pronouncement and more were coming. Dublin's *Sunday Independent* would later say: "Gradually his influence would have been more and more directed to trying to bring about a peaceful solution of a very difficult problem."

By his visit to Ireland and by giving Lemass an American forum in which to make explicit declarations on Northern Ireland, Kennedy, the thinking went, had laid the foundation for deeper American engagement in the partition issue. He was ready for the next step. "It was generally accepted in Dublin after the visit that, had he not been assassinated, Kennedy would have given priority to the Irish issue," wrote Tim Pat Coogan.

Stonehill College's Finnegan said there may have been a subtle, long-term effect Kennedy had on the later peace process in Northern Ireland.

"You can't say something Kennedy did or said directly impacted the peace process in 1998, but you can say the ability of the Americans to be confidently assertive, that they could say, 'Something should be done about this' — that would be" a lasting effect of the Irish-American president's 1963 visit, Finnegan said.

Sen. Edward Kennedy, who himself became a key figure in the peace process in Northern Ireland, insisted that resolving the partition matter was very important to his brother and "would have had a central place in his mind" later in his presidency. "I'm convinced," the senator said, "that this would have been something he would have been involved in," despite "so much on that plate, with Berlin . . . the Russians, Laos, and what was happening on civil rights in the South. . . . There is no question in my mind."

And the critical importance of the new relationship Kennedy established with Ireland cannot be overstated, according to Senator Kennedy. The president's going to Ireland " created a link . . . with the South," the senator said. "Historically, everything that had to do with Northern Ireland went through London. . . . You couldn't even blow your nose unless it went through London.

"Suddenly, the U.S. had a special relationship through Ireland, not through London. The idea of going directly to Dublin, of establishing a relationship there . . . it was the underpinning that made the rest possible," years in the future.

Ireland, indeed, had an advantage with Kennedy in the White House. It went beyond the intellectual and the political: this president loved Ireland.

On the night of the state dinner for Lemass, Kennedy extended the evening far past the conclusion of the usual formalities. The president did not want the celebratory mood to end. He invited a select group to the upstairs family quarters of the White House for a more intimate party. Lemass and his wife were joined by the president's brother Edward Kennedy and his wife, Joan, the actor Gene Kelly, James A. Reed, Dorothy Tubridy, and a few others. And up to the quarters the bagpipers came.

Reed treasured the night with his friend the president as "one of the most enjoyable I had ever spent with him. . . . It was a very nostalgic evening."

Ted Kennedy sang. Kelly danced and sang. The ballads and the jigs went into the early part of the new day.

"Oh, it was magical," Tubridy said. "I cried through most it, to tell you the truth — the Irish, you know."

At one point, Reed looked over at the president.

Kennedy, he remembered, "was just overcome with it all."

"You know, the Irish have their very happy songs and they also have their very sad and plaintive melodies, and they played some of the favorite songs of the president — 'The Boys of Wexford' . . . and a couple of others," Reed related. "During the course of their singing these songs, the president had the sweetest and saddest kind of look on his face. He was over standing by himself, leaning against the doorway there, and just sort of transported into a world of imagination, apparently. But he had a wonderful evening — it was a splendid time."

President Kennedy signs the Limited Nuclear Test Ban Treaty at the White House on Oct. 7, 1963. Vice President Lyndon B. Johnson stands at far right. Among those in the ceremonial group are Secretary of State Dean Rusk and then-Minnesota Senator, later Johnson's vice president, Hubert H. Humphrey, both standing in the second row under the painting.

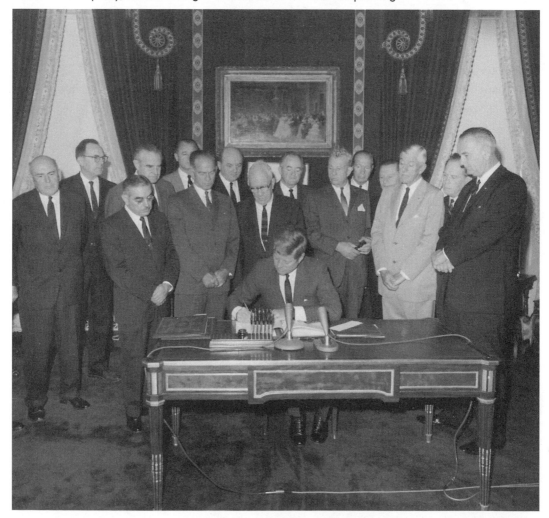

epilogue

November 22, 1963

Mr. Casey, freeing his arms from his holders,
suddenly bowed his head on his hands with a sob of pain.
"Poor Parnell!" he cried loudly. "My dead king!"
He sobbed loudly and bitterly.

James Joyce
Portrait of the Artist as a Young Man *(1916)*

A t **Mary Ryan's home** in Dunganstown, the radio was on. She and her daughter Josephine were listening to a program when it was interrupted with news that could not be absorbed at first. Their guest of five months before had been shot at. Then, he had died.

"It was terrible," Josephine recalled of the night of Friday, November 22, 1963. "It was really unbelievable."

Her sister, Mary Ann, collapsed at the news and was confined to bed at the hospital in Dublin where she worked.

Father William Mernagh, of Ballykelly, rushed to the home to be with the Ryans.

The silence of the farmyard was broken only by the muffled sound of the women crying in the house.

In the days after the assassination, people came to call on Mary Ryan and her daughter in Dunganstown. The first of thousands of letters began arriving. Then total strangers were coming to the door. It was a bit much for the Kennedy cousins, but, quite obviously, understandable.

Little by little, the house and yard in Dunganstown changed from a point of interest to a shrine. Carloads of visitors came down the road to see where President Kennedy had toasted with a cup of tea all those who had gone and all those who had stayed. The carloads were there at breakfast, and they were there late into the night.

New Ross on November 22 canceled events around town immediately. People drew their blinds. Women cried on the street while men apologized they were too shocked to weep.

Andrew Minihan, man of many and colorful words, had just three: "I am stunned."

In Wexford, a student's mother ran into the Loreto Convent with the news.

Mother Superior Clement directed everyone into the chapel, where the nuns and the children prayed the rosary for the fallen president.

"It is so difficult to even think that he is dead," Mother Clement said.

Frances Condell, who had been re-elected lord mayor of Limerick two days after Kennedy had visited her city and then left Ireland, could barely speak to reporters after hearing the news from Dallas.

"I am absolutely shattered," she said, then broke down.

Dorothy Tubridy and her nine-year-old daughter, Aine, sat before the television, stunned.

"Ireland, the entire island, was devastated, devastated," Tubridy said. "I felt I'd lost a family member."

She got a call through to the home of her friends Robert and Ethel Kennedy. She did not speak to the president's brother. But she spoke a little to Ethel.

"We did not talk much, because she was very upset, but she showed the great fortitude of the Kennedy family in time of tragedy — she spoke of the full, wonderful life he had had," Tubridy said.

President de Valera had been sitting in a room with a television set. He could see some of what was on the screen by turning his head to the side, to take advantage of what peripheral vision he still had. An American drama had been on. And then it was interrupted by RTE announcer Charles Mitchel, who "looked pale-faced even in black and white," as he told viewers President Kennedy had been badly wounded.

"And then there was a delay. And later on we were told that he was dead," de Valera remembered. Mitchel delivered this news in a shaking voice. "I was dumfounded," de Valera said.

That evening, de Valera spoke on the radio and television to the people of Ireland, to offer what solace he could.

In the streets of Dublin, people huddled around the windows of television stores, watching the grim news in silence and tears.

Ireland, wrote Wesley Boyd of the *Irish Times,* "mourned him with a personal grief that no other leader of the world could command. . . . For all the roar of the traffic, the cries of the newsboys and the murmuring of the crowds, there was a quietness in the air."

There would be no soccer matches and no hockey games. Also canceled were the ceremony marking External Affairs Minister Aiken's forty years in the Dail, the commemoration of the founding of the Irish Volunteers, and a scheduled lecture about Michael Collins, the Irish patriot who was himself cut down in his prime by an assassin. Instead, special religious services spread from Friday night all through the weekend. On buildings all over Ireland, and in Northern Ireland, flags sank to half-mast.

The Irish government shut down. "We had never done anything like this before on the occasion of the death of a head of state — not even a pope," said Dr. Nicolas G. O Nuaillain, secretary of the Department of the Taoiseach.

"You Americans had another president a few minutes after Kennedy was shot," a man in County Kerry told a writer. "But, God rest his soul, we lost the man this country's been waiting for over hundreds of years. He made us proud. Who knows how long it will take us to see his like again?"

The official messages of sympathy poured out of Ireland to Washington, to Jacqueline

At the request of Jacqueline Kennedy, the Irish Army Cadets, rifles on their shoulders, participate in a final tribute to Kennedy at his funeral on a hillside at Arlington National Cemetery, across the Potomac River from Washington, on Nov. 25, 1963.

Kennedy, to Robert Kennedy, and to the new president, Lyndon Baines Johnson. De Valera, Lemass, Aiken, members of the Parliament, mayors and clergy, all conveyed their sorrow and prayers.

"I find it hard to express adequately my feelings at this time . . . ," admitted Alderman Sean Moore, the lord mayor of Dublin.

"America's loss is Ireland's too," wrote Sen. T.L. Mullin, general secretary of Fianna Fail.

"In the end," the *Sunday Press* in Dublin observed in a front-page editorial, "we remember him as he moved among us in those few summer days — the golden boy who was at once the President of the United States, distinguished and honored, and also one of our own, a young man glad to be at home with his own folk. We shall not soon forget those gracious speeches and a thousand intimations of pride in his shared heritage. Nor ignore the conviction, courage and love that lay behind them."

On the Saturday night after Kennedy's killing, Jacqueline Kennedy made it known Ireland would play an honored role in the funeral.

Amidst her shock and grief in the hours after the assassination, Mrs. Kennedy somehow had the presence of mind to begin thinking about how to conduct her murdered husband's burial. The conversation turned to the president's trip to Ireland.

"How I envied you being in Ireland with him," the first lady told Dave Powers and Ken O'Donnell. "He said it was the most enjoyable experience of his whole life."

The president had talked to her and others many times about the Arbour Hill ceremony and the Irish cadets' drill.

"I must have those Irish cadets at his funeral," Mrs. Kennedy said.

And so, at Dublin Airport on Sunday, November 24, many of the Irish officials who had gathered only five months before for the joyous arrival of John Fitzgerald Kennedy met once again, this time in somber mood to see de Valera off to America — his first visit there in fifteen years — for the funeral of the president of the United States. External Affairs Minister Aiken boarded the Aer Lingus jet, too, along with American Ambassador McCloskey; the Army chief of staff, Lt. Gen. Sean McKeown; de Valera's sons, Maj. Vivion de Valera and Dr. Eamonn de Valera; New Ross Urban District Council Chairman Andrew Minihan; and the twenty-six cadets from the Irish Army who would stand as a guard of honor at Kennedy's graveside. Bidding farewell to de Valera and his party were Prime Minister Lemass, members of the cabinet, the clergy, and Dublin's lord mayor. At a refueling stop in Shannon, the place where Kennedy promised he would return but now never would, de Valera met with local officials, including Limerick Lord Mayor Frances Condell.

Mary Ann Ryan, daughter of Mrs. Ryan of Dunganstown, accepted a White House invitation to attend the funeral as the representative of the president's family in Ireland. Pan American Airways diverted its London-to-New York flight to Shannon to pick up President

Kennedy's cousin.

Back in Dublin, Lemass thought of a package he had put in the mail, addressed to President Kennedy's sister Eunice Shriver. Mrs. Shriver had asked Lemass for help with a Christmas present she wanted to give her brother. She needed a recording of his favorite song, and Lemass had located it and sent it on its way. It had gone out on the morning of November 22.

The song, of course, was "The Boys of Wexford," whose verses end with the lines the president was fond of quoting:

> We are the Boys of Wexford, who fought with heart and hand,
> To burst in twain the galling chain and free our native land.

☘ ☘ ☘ ☘

The day after the drums and prayers and processions and final rites were concluded, Malcolm Kilduff found himself back at his desk in the White House press office. His phone rang. It was a Secret Service officer from the guard booth at the White House gate.

"There's a man here who wants to see you by the name of Minihan," the officer told Kilduff.

"He's bald and has a reddish beard?" Kilduff queried.

"Yes, he does."

Andrew Minihan walked through the gates of the White House and was directed to Kilduff's office. The two who had sparred with each other and plotted out every moment of John Fitzgerald Kennedy's visit to New Ross greeted each other warmly.

Minihan saw Pierre Salinger, too, remembering with tears in his eyes the president's joyous tour through Eire. It was the one time during his presidency, Salinger said, when he saw Kennedy totally relaxed and happy. Salinger was so glad Kennedy had had that happiness before being struck down.

Kilduff and Minihan were planning again. But this time, what they wanted to do needed no approvals from anyone. They walked down the White House driveway, past the Secret Service officers, and out through the gates.

The men strolled north in the slanted November light, sure they would find the right kind of place where they could sit for a while over drinks and talk of Ireland and three-and-a-half days of speeches, of music, of dancing, of laughing and public hugs and surprise kisses, of ceilis in tiny gray towns that went on for days, of crushing motorcades and squealing teens and matrons, of hands that waved ceaselessly, of voices that yelled louder than at the Curragh, of a change in the spirit, in history, that would endure . . . and, of course, what it meant to have met, to have known this man named Kennedy, forever an American, yes, but forever, too, a boy of Wexford.

appendix

The Kennedys
and Fitzgeralds in Ireland

There is no luck under heaven for the Gael except
the wind that blows his ship away from Ireland.

Irish proverb

But for the turns of fate and history, President Kennedy might have come home to an Irish castle.

For his family, especially on the Fitzgerald side, prospered in Ireland for centuries.

The Fitzgeralds were Welsh-Norman, with origins in Italy. There, in eleventh century Florence, the family name was Gherardini. A young fellow named Otho, son of Gerardo Gherardini, set in motion the genealogy we are concerned with, leaving his little town for Normandy in France. In his new surroundings, Otho became a landowner. And in that time when the world was a much smaller place, he gained the attention and favor of King Edward of France. Otho's son, Walter, signed up with William the Conqueror in the Norman conquest of England in 1066. Now it was Walter's turn to be honored, with the lordship of Windsor. He also was made constable of the castle in Windsor. In time, Walter married the daughter of the Prince of North Wales, Gladys.

The family closeness to the crown extended into the next generation, when Gladys's and Walter's son, Gerald, was made constable of Pembroke Castle in South Wales by King Henry I. Clearly following his parents' example, Gerald married the daughter of the Prince of South Wales, Nesta.

By all accounts, Gerald was the power in South Wales, a Celtic land now firmly under control of the Normans.

And now Ireland enters the story.

In 1166, King Dermot MacMurrough of Leinster sought help in his return to the throne from England's King Henry II. Dermot had become embroiled in what, to the casual observer of this part of Irish history, was constant and bloody clan warfare among numerous kingdoms. One is tempted to say that Ireland was too small for so many kings. Dermot's fall was Henry's chance. The English king had had designs on Ireland for some time, and to aid Dermot he raised troops from Wales. Among those who volunteered were Maurice and William FitzGerald, sons of Gerald. This had become the Norman custom, to add "Fitz," which means "son of," to the father's Christian name. And thus we see the first appearance of the Fitzgerald name.

Remarkably, the Gherardini-FitzGerald line, who would also be known through history as the Geraldines, had migrated, in the short space of a little more than a century, from Italy, to France, to England and now, where roots would take hold for centuries to come, to Ireland. But the opening of this familial transplantation was rugged, to say the least.

The FitzGeralds (and, for simplicity, we will henceforth drop the middle capital "G") had signed on for duty with Richard FitzGilbert, also known as Strongbow, in the Anglo-Norman assault on Ireland. At least one commentator considered the Fitzgeralds an impressive lot: "Had events brought the Geraldines and their race to Ireland in times better suited to their genius for conquest we cannot doubt that they would have founded an independent Norman monarchy in Ireland."

While the Irish were undoubtedly accomplished fighters, they proved less than a match for the technology employed by the Norman invaders, bound in chain mail, protected by iron helmets, and adept in the use of the crossbow. The Irish weren't politically suited to oppose the Normans, either. Unlike in England, where there was a modicum of unification, Ireland was a collection of disjointed kingdoms with no tradition of working in concert nor an inclination to give large alliances a try.

The Norman invasion was conducted in stages, first by Dermot himself in 1167, then by a larger force in 1169. The following year, Maurice Fitzgerald and more Normans landed at Waterford and conquered the town. Within a month, Dublin was taken, too, and was destined to become the seat from which England would hold sway over Ireland for 750 years. The art of conquest in those days, as in ours, was a bloody enterprise, and many unarmed Dubliners, including women and children, perished in the Norman onslaught. In rapid succession, challenges to the Norman occupiers from the Norsemen, former residents of Dublin, and from a force of united Irishmen were repelled.

The Normans nominally ruled Ireland for England, but in truth it was more for the land they could conquer and hold, and it took many decades for the Crown to solidify control. By the beginning of the thirteenth century, the Fitzgeralds were prominent in County Limerick, County Cork, and County Offaly. The family essentially had two branches: those in the south and southwest became known as the Desmond Fitzgeralds, while those in the central part of the island were the Kildare Fitzgeralds. Successive English kings, Edward II and Edward III, recognized, albeit reluctantly, it appears, the power of the Fitzgeralds, granting the titles of Earl of Kildare and then Earl of Desmond. There were sixteen Earls of Desmond between 1329 and 1601, and twenty Earls of Kildare between 1316 and 1766.

As might seem inevitable, marriage among the Normans and the Irish was commonplace, despite strong efforts from England to discourage it. The Fitzgeralds gradually adopted Irish manners and speech and, most important, a tendency to question authority from London.

It would require more space than we have here to retell many hundreds of years of Fitzgerald history, but some key events should be noted.

Gerald Fitzgerald, the eighth Earl of Kildare, proved a particularly prickly subject of Henry VII at the end of the fifteenth century and the opening of the sixteenth. The earl

The old Kennedy lands along the Barrow River in Dunganstown, as seen from one of the helicopters on the day the president visited, June 27, 1963. Mary Ryan's home is amidst the trees almost in the lower-center of the picture.

repeatedly opposed the king and backed would-be replacements, but, amazingly, the Irishman's failed plots were pardoned by his sovereign. At last, accusations of treason landed the earl in the Tower of London. With this Fitzgerald absent from Ireland, however, there was disorder. The king sought a speedy trial, bringing the earl before him. Asked about charges that he had burned the cathedral in Cashel, the earl readily admitted to it.

"But," Fitzgerald continued, "I would not have done it but that I thought the bishop was inside it."

The earl revealed that he had intended to build a more magnificent edifice.

The bishop of Meath, one of Fitzgerald's accusers, uttered a denunciation for the ages: "Why, all Ireland cannot rule this man."

King Henry had heard enough. "Then," he proclaimed, "this man shall rule all Ireland."

The earl was later assassinated in Ireland, an act that was avenged by the son, Garrett Oge. But the vengeance, against the O'Moores and, collaterally, the domain of the O'Carrolls, allied at the time with the O'Moores and the Butlers, set in motion the decline of the influence of the Fitzgeralds. Garrett was jailed for a time by Cardinal Wolsey, but cleared by Henry VIII, his former playmate at court. More plotting by Wolsey brought the earl back to London and prison again. This time, a false report of the earl's execution reached the Irish leader's son, Thomas. In a rage, the young son revolted against the king. Garrett reportedly died of grief upon hearing of his heir's impetuous move. Thomas eventually was arrested and, in 1537, beheaded.

The Earls of Desmond suffered misfortunes, too. None was worse than that of Thomas, seventh earl, whose casual advice to King Edward IV would come back to kill him. Edward, who ruled from 1461 to 1470, revealed to Thomas he intended to marry Elizabeth Woodville. Thomas was against the match and told Edward so. Disregarding the advice of his friend, Edward went ahead with the marriage.

Much later, in a heated argument with his wife, the king disclosed Thomas's opposition to the union. The earl's initial instincts proved tragically well-tuned. The king's wife faked an execution warrant against Thomas, and it was carried out. When the deceit was uncovered, Elizabeth was forced to live out her days in a convent.

The Desmond Fitzgeralds suffered further setbacks from internecine and incessant clan warfare. Garrett, a later Earl of Desmond, was pushed into war against England. In 1582, deserted by his troops and betrayed by fellow Irishmen, he was captured and beheaded.

A direct descendant of the Kildare line, Lord Edward Fitzgerald, made a remarkable journey across the political spectrum in his brief life between 1763 and 1798. A soldier for England at the end of the American Revolution, he later served in the Irish Parliament, arranged for the construction of, and lived in, Leinster House — later the seat of the Dail — and became a convert to rebellion against the Crown.

In 1798, he was an integral figure in a planned revolt. It would attract many to his banner, including some Kennedys, as we shall see. But, like all the Irish revolts to the start of the twentieth century, this one failed. Fitzgerald was wounded, captured, and died of his injuries in prison. He remains a much-celebrated figure in Irish lore.

But the Kennedys, too, stake a claim on Ireland's history, in the person of Brian Boru.

His name is familiar to the Irish from school-age onward, but is but a vague reference for the vast majority of Americans and, indeed, among Irish-Americans, if he is known at all. Boru is viewed among many, but not all, Irish historians as the first to try to unify Eire.

Brian Boru was King of Munster, and by the start of the eleventh century laid claim to Ireland from Limerick to Cork and to the territory all the way to Dublin. He was not without opposition, and in 1014, the King of Leinster allied with the Vikings holding Dublin to challenge Boru's authority. The inevitable clash came on April 23, 1014, in a seaside battle of some forty thousand men at Contarf, outside Dublin. The Vikings and Leinster's king were vanquished, but Boru lost his life. The seventy-three-year-old leader was left almost unguarded in his tent and was slain by the Viking Brodir, whom Brian killed as he succumbed to his own wounds. While his victory is credited with ending Viking influence in Ireland, Boru's death ended any semblance of unity on the island.

Brian Boru was the son of a man named Kennedy, or, in Gaelic, Cinneide, which means "a nation." Munster's great king had two brothers, Mahon and Duncan. Duncan, honoring his father, named a son Kennedy, and it is from this line that the future president of the United States came. The family name, O'Kennedy, derives from the use of the Irish "O" to show one was either a grandson or, more generally, a male heir of someone named Kennedy. And, as we saw with Fitzgerald, the use of hereditary surnames had become widespread by Brian Boru's time — indeed, some historians credit him with helping to spread the practice.

The O'Kennedys at first were based in Glen Ora, in the eastern part of County Clare, and later moved across the Shannon River to Ormond in County Tipperary. The O'Kennedys were the rulers of Ormond when the Normans, including the Geraldines, invaded Ireland in the twelfth century. The Norman inroads set up continuing conflict between the O'Kennedys and a family that would be known as the Butlers. In time, the O'Kennedys would become allied with the Geraldines, the Fitzgeralds.

"The O'Kennedy-Fitzgerald rapport was more than an accident of history, for it was not based solely on their having a common enemy," writes John F. Brennan. "The O'Kennedys were thoroughly Irish, the Fitzgeralds were Welsh (Celtic)-Norman and constantly moved toward being identified as Irish. The Butlers were French-Anglo-Norman in background, loyal almost always to the Crown, English in their interests."

King John of England "gave" the O'Kennedy territory to the Butlers in 1185. But the Butlers had to fight the O'Kennedys quite regularly in often vain attempts to assert authority. After 150 years, the O'Kennedys and the Butlers in 1336 signed a treaty, scrawled in tiny script on a scroll smaller than a handkerchief. More than six hundred years later, the accord,

The 1336 treaty between the Earl of Ormonde and the O'Kenedys, presented to Kennedy by Prime Minister Lemass during the president's visit to Ireland. Written in Latin, the pact between the warring parties failed to hold.

as previously mentioned, was given to John Fitzgerald Kennedy as a gift of the Irish government during his return to Ireland. It now hangs on public view at the John Fitzgerald Kennedy Library in Boston.

The treaty says: "This indenture testifies that a final agreement has been made between the noble Lord James le Buteller, Earl of Ormonde, on the one part and O'Kenedy Clangillekevynboy on the other part, concerning all burnings, spoils, homicides and other transgressions whatever done in the past up to the day of making these presents. Furthermore the said Lord James grants to the said O'Kenedy and those of his nation thirteen carucates of land in Meinarge and one carucate of land in Clomolyn, the afore-mentioned O'Kenedy and his people paying to the said Lord James and his heir twenty pounds per annum for eleven carucates and they are to have three carucates without payment."

There were penalties for violating the pact.

"It is likewise agreed that if any of the said Earl's men, English or Irish, slay the afore-mentioned O'Kenedy or any of his men by treachery, the body of the traitor shall be handed over for the body of the slain if he can in any way be found, and if the lord with whom he was or to whose sept he belonged cannot be found, compensation shall be levied and paid to the kindred of the slain two-fold, and one payment to the lord, and he shall have no peace from the lord forever without the consent of O'Kenedy and his kindred, and the same justice shall be done to the lord and his men on the part of the said O'Kenedy and his men."

Ten years after they had talked peace, the O'Kennedys and the Butlers warred again. Donal O'Kennedy briefly reclaimed the title of King of Ormond, only to be captured and hanged by Butler allies. For good measure, the humiliation of the O'Kennedys was capped by the public desecration of Donal's body, which was dragged by horses through the town of Thurles. The spectacle had little impact on the Butlers' foes, who returned to arms again and again. Ultimately, the O'Kennedys prevailed. At the close of the 1300s, the O'Kennedys were forced to pledge their fealty to the Crown in what was known as the "submissions," but in so doing, won recognition of their rights to their territories.

The relative peace, however, held only for so long. In the mid-1500s, O'Kennedy alliances with the brief and futile Fitzgerald rebellion proved costly, forcing new promises of loyalty to England. Ireland and England were then under the rule of King Henry VIII, who considered opposition treason, punishable by death and forfeit of all lands to the Crown.

The Reformation wreaked more havoc in Ireland, as those who opposed conversion from Catholicism to the new Protestant faith were dispossessed of land and, often, their lives. The O'Kennedys at first were shielded from persecution because of close ties they had developed with their old enemies, the Butlers, who were in favor in London. The Kennedys also were powerful. In the Nine Years' War at the end of the sixteenth century, the O'Kennedys at one point fielded five hundred foot soldiers and thirty horsemen, the largest single force among any of the lords in Munster. They owned eleven castles in the seventeenth century. But when the O'Kennedys joined in open rebellion they suffered the fates of many of their countrymen.

The persecutions of the Irish extended from Queen Elizabeth's reign (1558–1603) through the English Civil War (1641-49) and into the 1700s. O'Kennedys who resisted were executed, their lands given to English overlords.

It is unclear when the Kennedys who would produce a president moved into County Wexford.

"We don't know exactly," Mary Ryan apologized in 1963. The family had kept no Bible recording who was born and died when and where, she explained. No priests in the family, though, James Kennedy was clear. "We weren't good enough," he joked.

The Kennedys in Dunganstown at first were tenants, like most Irish. The land was owned by an English family, the Tottenhams, who were significant property owners in the area. Their eighteenth century manor house in New Ross would later be known as the Royal Hotel.

In Lord Fitzgerald's rebellion of 1798, two Kennedys from Dunganstown, Patrick and John, signed on. Nearby New Ross was the scene of one of the short-lived triumphs of the uprising. But 19-year-old John died in the fight. Twenty-year-old Patrick escaped in a boat on the River Barrow.

It was this Patrick Kennedy who had a son of the same name, born in 1823. The younger Patrick would emigrate to the United States in 1847 and plant the roots for a family that would become a political force a century later.

In the years before the Famine, life for most Irish was lived in wretched conditions. What farmers could produce went almost entirely to the landlords. Only the potato — "lumpers," once thought fit only for animals — stood between the desperate farmer and disaster. "To see Ireland happy," French traveler Gustave de Beaumont wrote in the 1830s, "you must carefully select your point of view, look for some narrow, isolated spot, and shut your eyes to all the objects that surround it; but wretched Ireland, on the contrary, bursts upon your view everywhere. Misery, naked and famishing, that misery which is vagrant, idle and mendicant covers the entire country; it shows itself everywhere, and at every hour of the day; it is the first thing you see when you land on the Irish coast, and from that moment it ceases not to be present to your view."

Yet even in the blush of President Kennedy's visit, some Irish wondered why Patrick Kennedy chose to leave for America.

"The Kennedys," one Wexford denizen sniffed, "weren't poor by ordinary standards then. In the 1830s they owned a farm of 27 acres. By the 1860s they owned 60 acres. And that, as you know perfectly well, is quite a bit of land in Ireland."

It is more likely the Kennedys were still tenants in the 1830s and 1840s. Rents rose in relatively well-off County Wexford as farms were stricken by the potato blight and famine elsewhere. And young Patrick Kennedy, being a younger son, had little prospect of being left much property.

The Kennedys who stayed did seem to prosper. One sign of that are the graves at Whitechurch near Dunganstown. Edward Keane, a genealogist at the National Library of Ireland, pointed out at the time of President Kennedy's visit that Irish without any means had plain headstones that were laid flat on the ground. The Kennedys had ornamented headstones that stood upright, an indication the family was able to hire a craftsman to do a job that would also show they enjoyed, in Keane's view, "financial superiority."

Eventually, they owned one hundred acres of the main farm and an additional thirty-five acres by the River Barrow. The family on the original farm were known as the "Kennedys above," while their kin on the other farm were the "Kennedys below."

The farms passed from father to son until there was no Kennedy among the Kennedys above, so it went to a nephew, Mike Ryan, who married Mary Ryan, who had been on the lower farm. When Mike died, Mary and her daughters (an only son died in 1957) kept the farm above going. James Kennedy was the owner of the lower farm in 1963.

Between 1849 and 1856, twenty-nine ships are recorded in the leather-bound registry of vessels in the office of the New Ross Harbor Commission as having sailed from the quay, in a town that once was a larger port than Dublin. Most of the ships were bound for Quebec, but some went to New York, New Orleans, and Savannah.

In 1963, New Ross had embraced the 458-ton *Dunbrody* as Patrick Kennedy's ship. New Ross admitted there was no solid evidence that Patrick Kennedy sailed on the vessel, but officials were fairly certain. Jack Shannon, proprietor of the New Ross Motor and Engineering Co., was the proud custodian of what remained of the vessel: its wheel, which hung in his office. The wheel had been owned by the previous proprietor, Ignatius Williams, whose great-grandfather, Capt. William Williams, was a skipper on the *Dunbrody*.

Research much later showed the vessel in which Patrick Kennedy spent six weeks crossing the Atlantic was the *Washington Irving*.

In any case, Patrick Kennedy would have paid about eighteen dollars for the arduous journey. That bought him some twelve square feet of living space belowdecks in steerage — a stuffy, unhealthy place of disease and, sometimes, death. Patrick worked as a cooper in Boston, but died poor, of cholera, fourteen years after landing in his new country.

One of Patrick's children was Patrick Joseph Kennedy, who showed shrewd business sense, first buying taverns, then importing liquor. His son, Joseph Patrick Kennedy, President Kennedy's father, would prove even more successful in business.

The Fitzgeralds were on the move, too. Thomas Fitzgerald, born at Loughgur, Bruff, County Limerick, arrived in Boston on November 6, 1850. His mother, Ellen Fitzgerald, had preceded him to the United States, as did a younger brother, James, and three sisters.

Thomas Fitzgerald, a peddler, married Rosanna Cox. One of their children was

John Francis Fitzgerald, later to be known throughout Boston and New England politics as "Honey Fitz." The future Boston mayor married Mary Josephine Hannon. Their daughter, Rose, would marry Joseph Patrick Kennedy, and they would be the parents of nine, including John Fitzgerald Kennedy.

Honey Fitz made a pilgrimage to Ireland in 1938, visiting Loughgur and Adare. It actually was his second trip. According to one story, Honey Fitz was stunned to find, while visiting distant relatives, a photo of his brother, a priest, on the family wall. He took a taxi from Bruff to the old family homestead, which was nothing but piles of stones and foundations. Relatives had knocked down the old place around the turn of the twentieth century and moved nearby. Denis Conway, the taxi driver who took Honey Fitz to Loughgur, didn't know who his rider was until they had been in conversation for a while. The former mayor of Boston walked the last quarter-mile to the homestead site and gazed out at the lake. On his return trip, Honey Fitz filled in a few more blanks for Conway, revealing that his daughter Rose was married to Joseph Kennedy, then the U.S. ambassador to the Court of St. James's.

The emigration from Ireland was family lore in the Kennedy and Fitzgerald families in America. And John Fitzgerald Kennedy was profoundly influenced by what he heard. Immigration was such an intense interest that he authored a book about it entitled *A Nation of Immigrants*. In it, the Irish experience, as well it should, figures prominently.

The men, women, and children from Dublin and Cork and Donegal, from Dunfanaghy and Quin and Birr, made up a new surge of settlers in America. And, Kennedy pointed out, their presence in their adopted country created a new kind of social tension.

By the middle of the nineteenth century, just after the potato famine receded, the Irish were forty-four percent of the foreign-born in the United States. Between 1820 and 1920, four and a quarter million Irish went to America — a million just in the five years after the outbreak of the Famine in 1845.

Many of the Irish were illiterate, poor, of rural background and skills. Some spoke only Gaelic. The vast majority were Catholic.

"The Irish," Kennedy wrote, "were the first to endure the scorn and discrimination later to be inflicted, to some degree at least, on each successive wave of immigrants by already settled 'Americans.' . . . The Irish are perhaps the only people in our history with the distinction of having a political party, the Know-Nothings, formed against them."

But the Irish persevered. "Gradually, rung by rung, the Irish climbed up the economic and social ladder," Kennedy related, detailing how sons and daughters of Eire gravitated to politics and government, to law and education. And to business. The Irish found the "areas in which they could demonstrate their abilities of self-expression, of administration and organization," wrote Kennedy, who could have added that such was the general upward trajectory of the Kennedys and the Fitzgeralds.

The Kennedy coat of arms, with the green wax seal of the Chief Herald of Ireland, was presented to the president in 1961. The three helmets symbolize the three septs within the O'Kennedy clan. The upraised hand holding arrows and surrounded by olive branches is a variation on the theme from the coat of arms of the United States. Note that unlike many coats of arms, Kennedy's carries no motto. The Irish government considered that a personal choice that was left to Kennedy to select.

Notes

Oral histories, which this book liberally mined, were transcribed by and are available at the John Fitzgerald Kennedy Library in Boston. They are indicated in the following notes as OH.

Interviews by the author of various participants in the events of June 1963 are indicated as such.

Introduction

"This is the part that he really looks forward to: Benjamin C. Bradlee, *Conversations with Kennedy* (New York: W.W. Norton & Co., 1975), p. 192.

"I want to thank you": The exchange of letters is published by the United States, in *Public Papers of the Presidents of the United States: John F. Kennedy. Containing the Public Messages, Speeches, and Statements of the President. Jan. 1 to Nov. 22, 1963.* Washington, D.C.: Government Printing Office, 1964.

"We Irish are the greatest wandering people: Author interview with John Hume.

"Here was one who personified: *Tipperary Star,* June 29, 1963.

"Mr. Kennedy has returned to Ireland: *Evening Herald* (Dublin), June 28, 1963.

"The great-grandson of the famine emigrant: *Irish Independent,* June 26, 1963.

Patrick O'Donovan of the *London Observer:* Published in *Boston Globe,* June 26, 1963, and *Washington Post and Times-Herald,* June 30, 1963.

"a union of hearts": *Cork Examiner,* June 27, 1963.

while Ireland had contributed troops to the United Nations' peacekeeping: Ireland joined the United Nations in 1955.

after a prayer, the president crossed himself: *Los Angeles Times,* June 29, 1963.

"I imagine: Arthur M. Schlesinger, Jr., A *Thousand Days: John F. Kennedy in the White House* (Boston: Houghton Mifflin Co., 1965), p. 885.

"He was very happy there: Author interview with Eunice Kennedy Shriver.

His brother's days in Ireland, Sen. Edward Kennedy: Author interview with Sen. Edward Kennedy.

The *Kerryman* complained of "just one irritation persisting: *Kerryman* (Tralee), July 6, 1963.

"It was the first time: Donald S. Connery, *The Irish* (New York: Simon & Schuster, 1968), p. 32.

Among the most condescending assessments: *National Observer,* July 1, 1963.

"The aftermath of such intoxicated: Fintan O'Toole, "What We Think of America," *Granta* 77, Spring 2002, pp. 61-64.

Crosby S. Noyes: *Washington Evening Star,* June 28, 1963.

"He and the crowds: quoted in Donald S. Connery, *The Irish*, pp. 32-33.

"the social and psychological highpoint: Sean McMahon, *A Short History of Ireland* (Dublin: Mercier Press, 1996), p. 196.

In July of 1999: *Limerick Leader,* July 24, 1999.

In 2001, the *Sunday Mirror* in Dublin asked readers: *Sunday Mirror,* March 11, 2001.

"to give public expression": Text of remarks in Eire/Ireland: *Weekly Bulletin of the Department of External Affairs*, no. 640, Dec. 2, 1963.

One: June 26, 1963: Dublin Airport and Dublin

"I am of Ireland": Published in *1000 Years of Irish Poetry: The Gaelic and Anglo-Irish Poets from Pagan Times to the Present,* Kathleen Hoagland, ed. (New York: Grosset & Dunlap / The Universal Library, 1962), p. 605.

framed with a rainbow: *San Francisco Examiner,* June 27, 1963.

"WELCOME HOME" was the three-inch-high banner: *Evening Herald* (Dublin), June 26, 1963.

Air Force One punched through a crosswind: Arrival details from various sources, including *Boston Globe,* June 27, 1963; *New York Journal-American,* June 26, 1963; *New York World-Telegram & Sun,* June 26, 1963; *New York Daily News,* June 27, 1963; *New York Herald-Tribune,* June 27, 1963; *New York Times,* June 27, 1963; *Washington Post and Times-Herald,* June 27, 1963; *Cork Examiner,* June 27, 1963; *Irish Independent,* June 27, 1963; *Irish Press,* June 27, 1963; *Irish Times,* June 27, 1963.

"There's silence. . . . it's totally quiet": Author interview with Theodore C. Sorensen.

"Maybe we got our schedules: Ibid.

"President Kennedy had achieved mythic: Ibid.

"the transition from freedom fighter: Morley Ayearst, *The Republic of Ireland: Its Government and Politics* (New York: New York University Press/London: University of London Press, 1970), p. 177.

"the main agent for bringing Ireland to the fore: Tim Pat Coogan, *Ireland Since the Rising* (London: Pall Mall Press, 1966), p. 123.

A journalist once complained: Author interview with Dr. Patrick Hillery.

McCloskey had jumped up and applauded: Author interview with Hillery.

its fuselage was decorated with tissue-paper shamrocks: Author interview with Jean Price Lewis.

"He was very excited at this trip": Author interview with Jean Kennedy Smith.

Dorothy Tubridy thought: Tubridy OH, Aug. 8, 1966, p. 22.

"The more fuss: Evelyn Lincoln, *My Twelve Years with John F. Kennedy* (New York: David McKay Co., 1965), p. 345.

in truth de Valera frequently carried the umbrella: *Chicago Daily News,* June 28, 1963.

De Valera opened in Gaelic: *A Memory of John Fitzgerald Kennedy. Visit to Ireland, 26th-29th June,* 1963, Sean F. Lemass, foreword (Dublin: Wood Printing Works, 1964).

Kennedy, his eyes fixed: *New York Mirror,* June 27, 1963.

President Kennedy then spoke: *Public Papers (1963),* pp. 531-42. Informal comments are taken from the various sources noted.

Lemass's cabinet and local officials: Besides McQuaid and Hillery, prominent Irish officials included the Protestant archibishop of Dublin, Most Rev. Dr. George Otto Simms; the Apostolic Nuncio, Most Rev. Dr. Sensi; the Chief Justice, Cearbhall O Dalaigh; the *Ceann Comhairle* (the speaker of the Dail), Patrick Hogan; the *Cathaoirleach* of the Senate, Liam O Buachala; Finance Minister Dr. James Ryan; Agriculture Minister Patrick Smith; Transport and Power Minister Erskine Childers; Industry and Commerce Minister John Lynch (who would succeed Lemass as prime minister in 1966 and serve seven years); Local Government Minister Neil Blaney; Social Welfare Minister Kevin Boland; Minister for Lands and the Gaeltacht Micheal O Morain; Posts and Telegraphs Minister Michael Hilliard; Defence Minister Gerald Bartley; Justice Minister Charles Haughey (also a future prime minister); Attorney General Aindrias O Caoimh; James Dillon, leader of the main opposition party, Fine Gael; and Brendan Corish, leader of the Labour party.

"Are these the guys that kept you: Author interview with Hillery.

"our lord mayor of two days' standing": *Irish Independent,* June 27, 1963.

"What happened to the other man?": Ibid.

People would speak about: Tubridy, who was involved in business on both sides of the Atlantic, makes this point clearly in Tubridy OH, pp. 19-21.

"probably did more: Tony Gray, *The Irish Answer* (Boston and Toronto: Little, Brown & Co., 1966), p. 377.

An Irish aristocrat told: *London Sunday Times,* June 30, 1963.

"But the Irish: Mark Bence-Jones, *The Remarkable Irish: Chronicle of a Land, a Culture, a Mystique* (New York: David McKay Co., 1966), p. 125.

". . . While his first and last loyalty must be: *Irish Times,* June 26, 1963.

Kennedy, the *Irish Independent* in Dublin editorialized: *Irish Independent,* June 26, 1963.

"In the ceremonial confrontation of two presidents": *Irish Press,* June 26, 1963.

"For him," the commentator said, "his Irish visit: Ibid.

Under the leadership of Lemass: See "President's European Trip, June 1963. Ireland. (Background Paper)," June 17, 1963, in Papers of President John Fitzgerald Kennedy:

National Security Files, box 239. See also Eire/Ireland, Department of External Affairs, *Facts about Ireland* (1963), pp. 68-73; *Irish Press,* May 13, 1963; *Washington Sunday Star,* June 23, 1963; *Irish Times,* June 26, 1963; *Boston Globe,* June 26 and 30, 1963; and *Boston Herald,* June 28, 1963.

The number of hotel rooms: *Irish Press,* May 23, 1963.

The Kennedy visit itself was viewed as an economic boon: *Irish Times,* June 26, 1963.

Irish International Airlines, or Aer Lingus: *Esquire,* April 1963.

from the gate of a thatched-roof cottage: *Irish Independent,* June 27, 1963.

"a little bit disappointed myself: Kiernan OH, Aug. 5, 1966, p. 3.

Iron and steel mogul Fred Kennedy: *New York Mirror,* June 27, 1963.

"No partition for the Congo: *Chicago Tribune,* June 27, 1963; *New York Times,* June 27, 1963.

Said another: "Undivided Ireland welcomes: *New York Herald-Tribune,* June 27, 1963.

Many of the souvenirs: *Newsweek,* July 8, 1963, p. 35.

In record stores: *Boston Globe,* June 26, 1963; *New York Times,* June 26, 1963.

O'Beirne and Fitzgibbon: *Boston Evening Globe,* June 27, 1963.

"It was unbelievable how thundering it was": Author interview with Lenore Donnelly.

"You would have thought that everybody in that bus: Author interview with Pauline Fluet.

(the latter sold out across Ireland: *Baltimore Sun,* June 23, 1963.

In Dublin pubs, heated discussions: *Washington Daily News,* June 26, 1963.

"I bet," a red-haired officer said: *New York Mirror,* June 27, 1963.

In fact, officials had been reporting a flood across the border: *Irish Independent,* June 26, 1963.

"Isn't he just wonderful?": *New York Herald-Tribune,* June 27, 1963.

The top of the great pillar: *Toledo Blade,* June 27, 1963.

"a Guinness leakage": *London Sunday Times,* June 30, 1963.

Riding through the packed streets: De Valera OH, Sept. 15, 1966, p. 4.

but "there was no time: De Valera OH, p. 8.

Marching at a respectful distance: *Cork Examiner,* June 27, 1963; *San Francisco Examiner,* June 27, 1963.

Every hotel within five square miles: *Irish Independent,* June 26, 1963.

A few intrepid souls somehow had climbed: *Irish Times,* June 27, 1963.

"I'm glad we gave him such a welcome": *Irish Times,* June 27, 1963.

"Now that I've really seen the president in person": Ibid.

"I will not be sorry when the Kennedy visit is over": Ibid.

As he stepped from the limousine, he threw the coat: *Irish Independent*, June 27, 1963.

"What did you think of the procession?" Kiernan OH, p. 22.

formed a wedge: *Kansas City Star*, June 27, 1963; *Louisville Courier-Journal*, June 27, 1963.

"What do you think of it?": Kenneth P. O'Donnell and David F. Powers, with Joe McCarthy, *"Johnny, We Hardly Knew Ye": Memories of John Fitzgerald Kennedy* (Boston and Toronto: Little, Brown & Co., 1972), p. 362.

"A triumphal procession": De Valera OH, p. 3.

a plane called Talking Bird: *Los Angeles Times*, June 24, 1963.

Kennedy was never more than two minutes: *New York Mirror*, June 23, 1963.

Press arrangements for Kennedy's visit: *Irish Independent*, June 24, 1963; *Irish Times*, June 24, 1963; *Irish Press*, June 25, 1963. One of the green valises is owned by the author.

As a swamped official in the Irish foreign office: *Associated Press*, Sept. 24, 1979.

"This is a most serious challenge: *Irish Press*, June 14, 1963.

Government officials had worried for some time: *Irish Times*, June 11 and 14, 1963.

And here he sat in a place of supreme irony: *Sunday Independent* (Dublin), June 23, 1963.

munched on a chicken sandwich: Editors of *Look: JFK Memorial Book*, (New York: Cowles Magazines & Broadcasting, 1964).

His welcome, he told them, had been "fantastic": *Irish Press*, June 28, 1963.

"The reception was totally overwhelming": Author interview with Smith.

Two: I want to go to Ireland

"created great excitement" in Ireland: Author interview with Hillery.

In early 1962, Kennedy's first ambassador to Dublin: Aide-memoire, Embassy of Ireland, Washington, D.C., March 29, 1962. Papers of President John Fitzgerald Kennedy: National Security Files, box 188.

At a June 9, 1962, dinner in Washington's Mayflower: *Public Papers* (1962), pp. 469-70.

In July 1962: *Boston Evening Globe,* July 16, 1962.

the new U.S. Embassy, then under construction: The ground was broken for the new embassy on July 1, 1962.

"There was no discussion of an actual visit: Department of State transcript of Rusk press conference. Papers of President John Fitzgerald Kennedy: National Security Files, box 188.

That U.S.-Irish relations were warming: Aiken OH, pp. 17-23.

On the last day of 1962: Telegram, McCloskey to Rusk, Jan. 18, 1963. Papers of President

John Fitzgerald Kennedy: National Security Files, box 188.

The June European trip: Kenneth P. O'Donnell and David F. Powers, *"Johnny, We Hardly Knew Ye,"* pp. 358-9.

"The trip had a more personal, sentimental: Author interview with Sorensen.

England's Lord Longford: Lord Longford (Frank Pakenham), *Kennedy* (London: Weidenfeld & Nicolson, 1976), p. 150.

On March 15, Ireland's ambassador presented: Kiernan OH, p. 6.

Kiernan cabled Dublin that Kennedy "wanted a proper: Lemass Cabinet Papers, quoted in *Irish Times,* Jan. 3, 1994.

President de Valera wasted no time: Papers of President John Fitzgerald Kennedy: Presidential Office Files: Correspondence Files, box 119a.

Word of an Irish: For events leading up to, and including, the announcement, see *Boston Globe,* April 7, 1963; *Boston Traveler,* April 16, 1963; *Boston Evening Globe,* April 20, 1963.

Reporter Eoin O'Mahony: *Sunday Review* (Dublin), April 7, 1963.

Indeed, in Dublin that morning: *Irish Times,* April 16, 1963.

"He called up," Mrs. Shriver recalled: Author interview with Shriver.

It was some time during the early days of planning: Tubridy OH, p. 24.

One of eleven children, Tubridy grew up in a household: Author interview with Dorothy Tubridy.

". . . I tried to explain this to him: Tubridy OH, pp. 24-25; author interview with Tubridy.

"I want you to be the first to know: Tubridy OH, p. 24.

"I felt that he should see more of the country: Ibid., p. 25.

"Yes, yes. Perhaps I should: Ibid., p. 30.

In Ireland, de Valera's office released: *Sunday Review* (Dublin), April 21, 1963; *Irish Times,* April 22, 1963.

"Welcome, J.F.K.!": *Sunday Independent* (Dublin), April 21, 1963.

"Jack in June": *Sunday Review* (Dublin), April 21, 1963.

enthusiasm about the trip "amazing": *Louisville Courier-Journal,* April 21, 1963; *Washington Post and Times-Herald,* April 21, 1963; *Boston Evening Globe,* April 22, 1963.

Kennedy's visit also would mark a new chapter: *Irish Times,* April 23, 1963.

Tubridy, back in Dublin: JFK letter to Tubridy, April 23, 1963. Papers of President John Fitzgerald Kennedy: Presidential Office Files: Correspondence Files, box 119a.

On May 2, Dublin's lord mayor: *Irish Press,* May 3, 1963; *Irish Times,* May 3, 1963; *Sunday Independent* (Dublin), May 5, 1963; *Boston Globe,* May 7, 1963.

As a measure of the Irish esteem: *Boston Evening Globe,* May 8, 1963; *Boston Globe,* May 29, 1963.

"It's gone to my brother," Kennedy told: Kiernan OH, p. 15.

headed up a twenty-four person White House advance team in Dublin: *Louisville Courier-Journal,* May 6, 1963; *Irish Press,* May 7, 1963; *Irish Times,* May 7-8, 1963; *Christian Science Monitor,* May 7, 1963.

"This will be the greatest day: *Irish Press,* May 7, 1963.

"I hope when he comes: Ibid.

O'Donnell witnessed a blow-up: Kenneth P. O'Donnell and David F. Powers, *"Johnny, We Hardly Knew Ye,"* p. 362.

Salinger went out of his way: *Irish Times,* May 8, 1963.

the limit in sickening idolatry: *Sunday Review* (Dublin), May 12, 1963.

the Irish "had no idea what was involved: Author interview with Malcolm Kilduff.

On May 18, the outline of the official itinerary: *Sunday Independent* (Dublin), May 19, 1963; *Boston Sunday Globe,* May 19, 1963.

Dublin, where Kennedy would stay: *Louisville Courier-Journal,* May 16, 20-24, 28, 1963.

"tremendous political difficulty" for Irish leaders: Kiernan OH, p. 7.

But Salinger later would demur: *Boston Globe,* May 24, 1963.

"They're hijacking the president": *Boston Sunday Globe,* May 27, 1963.

Initially, Limerick was not: *Chicago Daily News,* June 3, 1963.

By the end of May, city officials: *Irish Independent,* June 1, 1963; *Irish Press,* June 1, 1963.

Skibbereen did not make: *Boston Globe,* May 29, 1963.

"There is no question of politics": *Irish Press,* May 2, 1963.

American commercial interests had a toe-hold in the North: *Irish Times,* June 18, 1963.

"I would not like to see him coming": *Irish Press,* May 1, 1963.

The United Ireland Association in London: Ibid., May 2, 1963.

The Association of Old I.R.A.: Ibid.

The president also had received some protests: Ibid., May 3, 1963.

"uninspiring reading": *Irish Times,* May 3, 1963.

Unbeknownst to Kennedy, some Nationalist members: May 3, 1963, letter and an undated letter from the unnamed secretary of the Nationalists to the unnamed private secretary to Aiken, contained in Eire/Ireland, Department of Foreign Affairs (formerly Department of External Affairs), Protocol Files, 434/682, file 22; also *History Ireland,* vol. 1, no. 4, winter 1993, p. 41.

"Thank you very much for your warm invitation: *Irish Times,* May 6, 1963.

A spokesman for O'Neill sought to put: *Irish Press*, May 6, 1963; *Irish Times,* May 6, 1963.

"I think the prime minister was foolish: *Irish Press*, May 6, 1963.

"For President Kennedy to go to the partitioned: *Sunday Independent* (Dublin), May 5, 1963.

"JFK Declines Invite to North": *Irish Press,* May 5, 1963.

From Stormont Castle in Belfast, O'Neill: Letters of JFK and O'Neill, in Papers of President John Fitzgerald Kennedy: Presidential Office Files: Correspondence Files, box 119a.

Northern Ireland's ties to the White House: *From Here to the White House* (Belfast: Northern Ireland Tourist Board, McCaw, Stevenson & Orr, printers, 1983).

"I tried to show some statesmanship: *Irish Times,* May 16, 1963.

"Later perhaps: *Sunday Review* (Dublin), May 19, 1963.

Only the "nationally-minded opposition" were invited: *Sunday Independent* (Dublin), June 30, 1963. The Lemass Cabinet Papers, opened to the public and the press in 1993, revealed even some Nationalist politicians initially were left off the invitation lists. One, Northern Ireland MP Gerry Fitt, had to call Lemass to request invitations to two Dublin receptions for Kennedy. Fitt and his wife were included. See *Irish Times,* Jan. 3, 1994. Lemass met O'Neill in a history-making trip to the North on Jan. 14, 1965.

The whole matter "did seem inept": *Irish Times,* May 17, 1963.

In the House of Commons on May 21: Ibid., May 22, 1963.

He agreed to participate in a program: Reprinted in *Irish Press,* May 20, 1963; also see *Sunday Review,* May 19, 1963.

The biggest change in plans: *Irish Times,* May 20, 1963.

whether the welcoming carpet: *Irish Independent,* June 10, 1963; *Irish Press,* June 10, 1963.

Cork and Wexford, meanwhile: *Irish Times,* June 10, 1963.

On May 27, about two-thirds of the forty-five members: *Irish Times,* May 28, 1963.

that the small city of Ennis: Ibid., May 30, 1963.

The leaders of New Ross, meanwhile, were a bit peeved: See, for example, *The People* (Wexford), June 15, 1963.

On June 12, an American government Convair: *Irish Press,* June 13, 1963.

The next day, four U.S. Army: *Irish Times,* June 14, 1963.

This was Johnson's first visit: Author interview with Johnson.

Limerick's lord mayor was at the ready: *Irish Press,* June 15, 1963; *Irish Times,* June 15, 1963.

How long would the visit to Cork be?: *Irish Independent,* June 15, 1963.

Five days after her talk with Salinger: *Irish Times,* June 20-22, 1963.

officials in County Clare were unwilling to allow Condell: *Irish Independent,* June 22, 1963.

"We are trying to put a month's work: *Irish Times,* June 25, 1963.

Kilduff revealed four decades later: Author interview with Kilduff.

"Oh, the Irish all wanted to go to Ireland": Author interview with Donnelly.

On June 17, Ambassador Kiernan dropped by: *Irish Independent,* June 18, 1963; *Irish Press,* June 18, 1963; *Irish Times,* June 18, 1963.

The president had dived into his homework: Kenneth P. O'Donnell and David F. Powers, *"Johnny, We Hardly Knew Ye,"* p. 359.

"I guarantee," Salinger boasted to an Irish journalist: *Irish Times,* June 26, 1963.

"We're adhering rigidly to the schedule": *London Sunday Times,* June 23, 1963.

On June 18, an American flag: *Irish Press,* June 18, 1963.

"I'm sure," resident Sean Doyle declared: *London Sunday Times,* June 23, 1963.

"If it is not too late": *Irish Press,* June 20, 1963.

Tensions in the Irish government: *Irish Times,* June 13, 1963; *Irish Independent,* June 14, 1963; *Irish Independent,* June 19, 1963; *Irish Press,* June 19, 1963; *Irish Times,* June 19, 1963; *Irish Independent,* June 20-21, 1963.

Two days later, tempers flared again: *Irish Independent,* June 21, 1963; *Irish Times,* June 21, 1963.

Efforts to gauge the importance: *Washington Sunday Star,* June 23, 1963.

"The Ireland leg: Ibid.

"Germany was business: *Time,* July 5, 1963.

The *National Observer* called the venture: *National Observer,* June 24, 1963.

"Cancel that trip": *New York Times,* June 5, 1963.

The Republicans, including Arizona's Sen. Barry Goldwater: *Washington Post and Times-Herald,* June 17, 1963.

"Americans were still a little uncertain: Author interview with Jerald F. terHorst.

He told Eamonn Andrews: *Irish Independent,* June 6, 1963.

"What he can do is to re-establish the presidency: *Minneapolis Tribune,* June 28, 1963.

The olive branch he offered the Soviets: For this reasoning, obviously leaked by administration sources, see *Washington Post and Times-Herald,* June 16, 1963.

McGeorge Bundy was concerned enough: Confidential White House memorandum, dated June 14, 1963, from Thomas C. Sorensen, USIA deputy director, to Bundy, with Murrow attachment. Papers of President John Fitzgerald Kennedy: Presidential Office Files: Trip Files, box 108.

trying to put some substance on the Ireland portion: *Philadelphia Sunday Bulletin,* June 23, 1963.

Skeptical reporters who didn't believe: *National Observer,* June 24, 1963.

Three: June 27, 1963: New Ross, Dunganstown, Wexford, and Dublin

"JFK Wows 'Em in Eire": *Washington Daily News,* June 27, 1963.

The *Irish Independent* greeted Kennedy in proper Irish: *Irish Independent,* June 27, 1963.

Sybil Connolly, the Irish designer: Rose Fitzgerald Kennedy, *Times to Remember* (Garden City, N.Y.: Doubleday & Co., 1974), p. 439.

Prime Minister Lemass, arriving a half hour late: *New York Herald-Tribune,* June 28, 1963; *New York Journal-American,* June 27, 1963.

". . . As he came down the stairs: Lemass OH, Aug. 8, 1966, p. 10.

Kennedy started off congratulating: The details of this meeting were written down by U.S. officials in a memorandum of conversation, which, as many such international contacts are, was classified as "secret" for some years. It is contained in Papers of President John Fitzgerald Kennedy: National Security Files, box 240.

enacting a general sales tax: Up until the vote, taxes were imposed only on tobacco, beer, spirits, and oils. That revenue, Lemass and his allies maintained, was insufficient to the budget demands of modernizing Ireland.

It is not recorded whether the two men chuckled: *Boston Evening Globe,* June 26, 1963; *Washington Post and Times-Herald,* June 26, 1963; *Irish Independent,* June 26 and 28, 1963; *Irish Press,* June 26, 1963; *Irish Times,* June 26, 1963.

The defeat of Ireland's application in 1961 to the European Economic Community: Ireland applied again in 1967 and was rejected. Six years later, Ireland and Great Britain at last were admitted to the EEC.

Earlier in the year, External Affairs Minister Aiken suggested: Secret background paper, "President's European Trip, June 1963, Ireland," Department of State, dated June 17, 1963, from Papers of President John Fitzgerald Kennedy: National Security Files, box 239.

Ireland had been assisting American efforts to keep Soviet offensive weapons: Ibid.

The two leaders briefly accommodated the photographers: *Newsday,* June 27, 1963.

"ending emigration, unemployment and partition": *Irish Independent,* June 28, 1963.

Kennedy's talk with Lemass "was the highlight of the visit" for Dublin: *History Ireland,* vol. 1, no. 4, winter 1993, p. 39.

"They didn't want the press bringing it up": Author interview with Malcolm Kilduff.

"We had a heck of a time trying to find out anything: Author interview with terHorst.

Tom Wicker, a *New York Times* reporter covering the trip: Author interview with Wicker.

A Labour party member of the Dail: *Irish Independent,* July 3, 1963; *Irish Press,* July 3, 1963.

Kennedy was impatient to get on to Dunganstown: Kenneth P. O'Donnell and David F. Powers, *"Johnny, We Hardly Knew Ye,"* p. 362.

The Irish, like most Americans, had never seen such an arrival: *The People* (Wexford), June 29, 1963.

The debris was, in fact, cow patties: Author interview with Kilduff..

Kilduff's previous encounter with Andrew Minihan: Ibid.

A Dublin military school band: *New York Times,* June 28, 1963.

Donovan issued the formal welcome: *Evening Herald* (Dublin), June 27, 1963; *Irish Independent,* June 28, 1963.

"Now I don't want any singing: John H. Davis, *The Kennedys: Dynasty and Disaster, 1848-1983* (New York: McGraw-Hill, 1984), p. 384.

Asked by the nun directing the children: Kenneth P. O'Donnell and David F. Powers, *"Johnny, We Hardly Knew Ye,"* p. 363.

"He had a lousy voice for singing": Author interview with terHorst.

Officials tried in vain to truncate: *Newark Evening News,* June 28, 1963.

Eunice Shriver thought the whole reception: Author interview with Shriver.

The four-man pool of reporters: *Dallas Morning News,* June 29, 1963.

The president requested "Grainvaile": *Chicago Tribune,* June 28, 1963.

The Loc Garman brass band played a new piece: *Chicago Tribune,* June 23, 1963.

"the most unforgettable character: *Pierre Salinger, With Kennedy* (Garden City, N.Y.: Doubleday & Co., 1966), p. 171.

Minihan, from Skibbereen in County Cork: *Cork Examiner,* June 27, 1963.

the best small-town politician: Author interview with Eoin Minihan.

Indeed, there were reports of resentment: *Wall Street Journal,* June 25, 1963.

"I could use a dozen more men: *Chicago's American,* June 23, 1963; *Washington Sunday Star,* June 23, 1963.

Fifty cents could fetch: *Newsweek,* July 1, 1963.

"Just listen to the bloody thunder": *Chicago Daily News*, June 24, 1963; *New York Post*, June 25, 1963.

Minihan applied what he knew: Author interview with Eoin Minihan.

Joked one citizen who knew Minihan well: *Chicago Daily News*, June 26, 1963.

Or tried to speak: *Irish Press*, June 28, 1963; *Irish Times*, June 28, 1963; *Boston Globe*, June 28, 1963; *New York Times*, June 28, 1963.

an anonymous phone call in Wexford threatening Kennedy: *Baltimore Sun*, June 28, 1963.

"They're all police out there": Davis, *The Kennedys*, p. 384.

"Can ye hear me now?" Minihan bellowed: *Dallas Morning News*, June 28, 1963.

"Mr. President," Minihan pushed on: *Irish Independent*, June 28, 1963; *Irish Press*, June 28, 1963; *Wexford Free Press*, June 28, 1963; *Baltimore Sun*, June 28, 1963; *Chicago Sun-Times*, June 28, 1963.

Minihan has personal present: *Chicago Daily News*, June 27, 1963; *Evening Press (Dublin)*, June 27, 1963; *Irish Independent*, June 27 and 28, 1963.

Minihan tried to keep control: *Boston Evening Globe*, June 27, 1963.

When the men's chorus sang "Boolavogue": *Evening Herald* (Dublin), June 27, 1963.

it was clear Kennedy was "perfectly happy: Minihan OH, pp. 6, 8.

"It's a great thing to see a man like you: *Newsday*, June 27, 1963.

Duke later protested that he did have Irish blood: *New York Times*, June 28, 1963; *Washington Post and Times-Herald*, June 28, 1963.

presented Kennedy with a fourteen-inch-high Waterford decanter: *The People* (Wexford), June 29, 1963.

"The light of the day shines through: *Irish Independent*, June 28, 1963; *Washington Evening Star*, June 28, 1963.

Local officials had been told by the American Embassy: Minihan OH, p. 5.

"Mayor," he told Minihan, "we go this way": Ibid.

Minihan pleaded with his countrymen: *Washington Evening Star*, June 28, 1963.

One man didn't heed: *Irish Times*, June 28, 1963.

John V. Kelly was asked: *New York World-Telegram & Sun*, June 27, 1963; *Washington Daily News*, June 27, 1963.

"He was charmed at the reception: *Irish Times*, June 28, 1963.

A century before, the "town" in Dunganstown: *New York Herald-Tribune*, June 23, 1963.

Tommy Lennon, fifteen, helped: *New York Journal-American*, June 30, 1963.

The security at the farm: *Washington Daily News*, June 27, 1963.

she had a television antenna: *New York Journal-American*, June 27, 1963.

The closest telephone was four miles: *Irish Independent,* June 7, 1963; *Boston Globe,* June 28, 1963.

For more routine communications: *Irish Press,* June 20, 1963.

Cousin James Kennedy, meanwhile, decided the old pillars: *New York Sunday News,* June 23, 1963.

("How about putting some concrete in front: JFK letter to McCloskey, July 11, 1963, Papers of President John Fitzgerald Kennedy: Presidential Office Files: General Correspondence, box 24.

James Kennedy was concerned: *Boston Evening Globe,* June 27, 1963.

"I can tell you one thing: Jackie wouldn't live here: *Evening Herald* (Dublin), June 22, 1963; *Kansas City Star,* June 23, 1963.

Most of the men wore ties: *New York Mirror,* June 28, 1963; *Philadelphia Inquirer and Public Ledger,* June 28, 1963.

"You were tots then": *New York World-Telegram & Sun,* June 27, 1963.

"If only Mike Ryan had lived to see: *New York Journal-American,* June 27, 1963; *Boston Record-American,* June 28, 1963; *San Francisco Examiner,* June 28, 1963.

"We have much more opportunity to do good work: *Chicago Daily News,* June 26, 1963.

The yard got rather crowded: *Dallas Morning News,* June 29, 1963.

"It was kind of a joke among the press: Author interview with Wicker.

"The fire feels good: Kenneth P. O'Donnell and David F. Powers, *"Johnny, We Hardly Knew Ye,"* p. 364.

the American cousin was able to pass off the elixir: Ibid.

"Have this placed in the hospital room: *Philadelphia Inquirer and Public Ledger,* June 28, 1963.

Josephine and her family were tense: Grennan OH, p. 4.

"The president told me that I looked just like a sister": *Irish Press,* June 28, 1963.

Kennedy also inquired about the man: Ibid., pp. 5-6.

Someone went to fetch Burrell: Editors of *Look: JFK Memorial Book; Evening Press* (Dublin), June 27, 1963.

Burrell nonchalantly replied: Kenneth P. O'Donnell and David F. Powers, *"Johnny, We Hardly Knew Ye,"* p. 364.

Josephine revealed: *Boston Globe,* June 28, 1963.

Mrs. Ryan was heard to tell: *New York Daily News,* June 28, 1963.

The widow later slyly advised: *New York Herald-Tribune,* June 28, 1963.

The Irish Kennedys were numerous: *Irish Independent,* June 28, 1963; *Irish Times,* June 28, 1963; *The People* (Wexford), June 29, 1963.

"I remember going into the house there: Author interview with Shriver.

"You know you are next to the pope": *Evening Herald* (Dublin), June 27, 1963.

the government had ignored her earlier requests: *Detroit News*, June 23, 1963.

Curiously, President Kennedy never went into the hut: *Los Angeles Times*, June 28, 1963.

"Did you catch this one, Jim?": *New York World-Telegram & Sun*, June 27, 1963; *Boston Record-American*, June 28, 1963; *Irish Independent*, June 28, 1963; *Irish Press*, June 28, 1963; *Irish Times*, June 28, 1963.

Surveying the plenty before him: *Boston Record-American*, June 28, 1963; *New York Post*, June 28, 1963.

"Don't cut yourself!" yelled a White House cameraman: *Boston Record-American*, June 28, 1963.

"You've cut yourself": *Chicago Tribune*, June 28, 1963.

"I'm definitely cutting myself up": *Irish Times*, June 28, 1963.

One young girl: *Los Angeles Times*, June 28, 1963.

But another cousin: *Boston Globe*, June 28, 1963; *Des Moines Register*, June 28, 1963; *Los Angeles Times*, June 28, 1963; *Evening Bulletin* (Philadelphia), June 28, 1963.

"Mr. Aiken wants me to leave all this beautiful brown bread": *Evening Herald* (Dublin), June 27, 1963; *Irish Independent*, June 28, 1963.

"I'm afraid we must go": *Irish Times*, June 28, 1963.

"'Don't go?'" Kennedy repeated: *Irish Times*, June 28, 1963.

"Why not partake of all this hospitality: *Irish Times*, June 28, 1963.

Mary Ryan scolded her nation's foreign minister: Kenneth P. O'Donnell and David F. Powers, *"Johnny, We Hardly Knew Ye,"* p. 364.

"I've got to go," Kennedy apologized: *Irish Independent*, June 28, 1963.

the tree was in the ground: *Boston Herald*, June 28, 1963.

"Cousin Mary, the next time I come: Goddard Lieberson, ed., *John Fitzgerald Kennedy . . . As We Remember Him* (New York: Atheneum, 1965), p. 205.

"He said they were dying to come: *Dublin Evening Press*, June 29, 1963.

A little boy grabbed the president: *Irish Times*, June 28, 1963.

"This is one of the most remarkable tea parties: *Washington Post and Times-Herald*, June 28, 1963.

"stared in wide-eyed astonishment": Kenneth P. O'Donnell and David F. Powers, *"Johnny, We Hardly Knew Ye,"* p. 364.

"We were all very excited: Josephine Grennan OH, Aug. 7, 1966, p. 2.

"No, he wasn't president: Ibid., p. 6.

"Mr. Kennedy's team," he wrote: *Los Angeles Times,* June 28, 1963.

Richard Wilson: *Minneapolis Sunday Tribune,* June 23, 1963.

George Kentera: *Newark Sunday News,* June 30, 1963.

Prime Minister Lemass, while sure politics "wasn't very much: Lemass OH, p. 14.

De Valera was representative of that Irish perspective: De Valera OH, p. 7.

Nor global doings, insisted the *Carlow Nationalist: Carlow Nationalist,* June 28, 1963.

Ringing the wreath were miniatures: *Cork Examiner,* June 28, 1963.

The local economy was sagging: *Wexford Free Press,* June 14, 1963.

Byrne proceeded with the official: *Atlanta Journal,* June 27, 1963; *Cork Examiner,* June 28, 1963; *Dublin Evening Press,* June 27, 1963; *Irish Independent,* June 28, 1963; *Irish Times,* June 28, 1963; *Wexford Free Press,* June 28, 1963.

The resolution, adopted on May 27: *Wexford Free Press,* June 21, 1963; *Evening Press* (Dublin), June 27, 1963.

Kennedy stepped up to sign the roll of freemen: *Irish Press,* June 28, 1963.

The pride of the moment: *Newsweek,* July 8, 1963, p. 35; *New York Daily News,* June 28, 1963; *New York Times,* June 28, 1963.

"this great man who had to take a risk: *Wexford Free Press,* June 28, 1963.

"The members of Wexford County Council extend to you: *Cork Examiner,* June 28, 1963; *Irish Press,* June 28, 1963; *Wexford Free Press,* June 28, 1963.

a voice yelled out "Welcome Home!": *Irish Independent,* June 28, 1963.

A single Irish tenor sang "The Soldier's Song": *New York Times,* June 30, 1963.

"This is one of the greatest moments of my life": *Irish Press,* June 28, 1963.

"The president signed autographs: *Boston Evening Globe,* June 27, 1963; *New York Mirror,* June 28, 1963; *Philadelphia Inquirer and Public Ledger,* June 28, 1963.

Mother Superior Clement had a political answer: *Boston Record-American,* June 28, 1963.

"Never before in this country": *Washington Post and Times-Herald,* June 28, 1963.

De Valera pleaded with the throng: Mark Bence-Jones, *The Remarkable Irish,* p. 125.

"I had planned to wear a lovely: *Irish Press,* June 28, 1963.

"What a store of knowledge: Ibid.

"It was very wet, so the people: De Valera OH, p. 3.

Women were pushed out of their high-heeled shoes: *Kansas City Star,* June 28, 1963; *Toledo Blade,* June 28, 1963.

An embarrassed attendee declared: *Chicago Tribune,* June 28, 1963.

"At Buckingham Palace": *Kansas City Star,* June 28, 1963; *Newark Evening News,* June 28, 1963.

"If half these people stayed home": *Kansas City Star,* June 28, 1963; *Newark Evening News,* June 28, 1963.

"I'll have a Power's Gold Label": *Evening Press* (Dublin), June 28, 1963.

"No eruption of mass orgasmic excitement: Thomas J. O'Hanlon, *The Irish: Sinners, Saints, Gamblers, Gentry, Priests, Maoists, Rebels, Tories, Orangemen, Dippers, Heroes, Villains and Other Proud Natives of the Fabled Isle* (New York: Harper & Row, 1975), p. 13.

"Top society in Ireland did not behave well": Author interview with Hillery.

"Mr. Kennedy," the aging Irish leader said: *Irish Times,* June 28, 1963.

"Now let's see the expert: Ibid.

Lord Longford, de Valera's old friend, witnessed: Longford, Kennedy, pp. 151-52.

Pierre Salinger, cigar in hand: *Irish Times,* June 28, 1963.

Henry Cabot Lodge, Jr.: *Washington Daily News,* June 28, 1963; *Irish Times,* June 28, 1963.

"Sometimes he gives one and sometimes he does not": *Irish Independent,* June 28, 1963.

"We really leaned on Salinger": Author interview with terHorst.

The press took solace in Dublin's eating: Author interview with Wicker.

Kennedy discovered it didn't pay to be last in line: Author interview with Donnelly.

There weren't many blue flowers: *Irish Times,* June 26, 1963.

M. Pierre Rolland: *Irish Times,* June 28, 1963.

The Minihans came up from New Ross: Author interview with Eoin Minihan.

it was difficult to find that many suits of white tie and tails: *New York Post,* June 23, 1963.

"one of the gravest crises in Hibernian sartorial history": *Irish Times,* June 24, 1963.

a very conspicuous Secret Service agent: *Evening Press* (Dublin), June 29, 1963.

Jean Price Lewis, who worked in the White House's congressional: Author interview with Lewis.

Lenny Donnelly was enticed: Author interview with Donnelly.

At evening's end, outside Iveagh House: *Boston Record-American,* June 28, 1963; *Washington Daily News,* June 28, 1963.

One young lady made a sprint: *Boston Record-American,* June 28, 1963.

"hospitality verging on assault: Joseph Roddy in *JFK Memorial Book,* editors of *Look.*

Four: June 28, 1963: Cork and Dublin

Our weapons were the weapons: Leon Uris, *Trinity: A Novel of Ireland* (Garden City, N.Y.: Doubleday & Co., 1976), p. 431.

Lenny Donnelly and her colleagues laughed: Author interview with Donnelly.

his limousine was out of commission: *Evening Herald* (Dublin), June 28, 1963; *Irish Independent,* June 29, 1963.

customary morning deliveries by the milkmen: *Cork Examiner,* June 28, 1963.

Skibbereen played a part after all: *Evening Herald* (Dublin), June 28, 1963.

Kennedy delighted in the signs people waved: Kenneth P. O'Donnell and David F. Powers, *"Johnny, We Hardly Knew Ye,"* p. 365.

major faiths of the city: They were the Most Rev. Dr. Cornelius Lucey, bishop of Cork; Most Rev. John Ahern, bishop of Cloyne; Right Rev. Dr. Perdue, bishop of Cork, Cloyne, and Ross; and Max Buddiel, representing the Jewish community. H. St. J. Atkins, president of University College, Cork, also stood with city officials.

"Everybody in Kerry, Tipperary, Kilkenny, and Wexford: Ibid.

the audience stomped the floor: *Irish Independent,* June 29, 1963; *Baltimore Sun,* June 29, 1963; *New York Herald-Tribune,* June 29, 1963.

Kennedy was introduced to four distant cousins: *Evening Herald* (Dublin), June 28, 1963; Irish Press, June 29, 1963.

The Fitzgeralds then unfolded a copy: *Sunday Independent* (Dublin), May 26, 1963.

"in token of our pride that this descendant: *Evening Press* (Dublin), June 28, 1963; *New York Times,* June 29, 1963.

Lord Mayor Casey made the presentation: *Evening Press* (Dublin), June 28, 1963; *Irish Independent,* June 29, 1963; *Irish Press,* June 29, 1963; *Irish Times,* June 29, 1963; *London Times,* June 29, 1963; *New York Times,* June 29, 1963; *Washington Post and Times-Herald,* June 29, 1963.

The president had a surprise: Lawrence F. O'Brien, *No Final Victories: A Life in Politics from John F. Kennedy to Watergate* (Garden City, N.Y.: Doubleday & Co., 1974), p. 153.

Kennedy tripped over something: *Kansas City Star,* June 28, 1963.

Their enthusiasm was impossible to contain: *Detroit News,* June 28, 1963; *Louisville Courier-Journal,* June 28, 1963; *Philadelphia Inquirer and Public Ledger,* June 29, 1963; *Boston Globe,* June 29, 1963; *Irish Independent,* June 29, 1963.

The president was not alarmed: *Philadelphia Inquirer and Public Ledger,* June 29, 1963.

People kept grabbing at his outstretched hands: *Boston Evening Globe,* June 28, 1963;

Boston Globe, June 29, 1963; *Los Angeles Times,* June 29, 1963; *New York Daily News,* June 29, 1963; *New York Journal-American,* June 28, 1963; *New York Mirror,* June 29, 1963; *New York Post,* June 28, 1963; *New York Times,* June 29, 1963; *New York World-Telegram & Sun,* June 28, 1963; *Evening Bulletin* (Philadelphia), June 28, 1963; *Philadelphia Inquirer and Public Ledger,* June 29, 1963; *Chicago Tribune,* June 29, 1963; *Washington Post and Times-Herald,* June 29, 1963.

Secret Service agent Jerry Blaine: News accounts did not identify the agent, but he was identified in author's interview with Donnelly.

The president laughed off the incident: *Evening Press* (Dublin), June 28, 1963; *Newark Evening News,* June 28, 1963; *Des Moines Register,* June 29, 1963.

"It was very frenetic": Author interview with terHorst.

the enthusiasm nearly turned tragic: *Los Angeles Times,* June 29, 1963; *Philadelphia Inquirer and Public Ledger,* June 29, 1963; *Washington Post and Times-Herald,* June 29, 1963; *Irish Press,* June 29, 1963; *Irish Times,* June 29, 1963.

In the melee: Author interview with Fluet.

"We were fighting through the crowd: Author interview with Donnelly.

"They had a heck of a time: Author interview with terHorst.

Even so, it took fifteen minutes: *Boston Record-American,* June 29, 1963.

"Gee," said another worried White House press: *Irish Times,* June 29, 1963.

Connor Coughlan came from Mallow: *Evening Herald* (Dublin), June 28, 1963.

President Kennedy "was very good about it": *Chicago Sun-Times,* June 30, 1963; see also *Sunday Review* (Dublin), June 23, 1963.

"The Irish dances were wonderful": *Chicago Sun-Times,* June 30, 1963.

"the Order of St. John: *Irish Times,* June 29, 1963.

"I'm sure the president would have come to see you: *Chicago Sun-Times,* June 30, 1963.

"Come quick and we can see ourselves: Quoted by Tubridy in *Irish Independent,* Nov. 25, 1963.

The women from Bunratty Castle's nightly medieval gatherings: Kenneth P. O'Donnell and David F. Powers, *"Johnny, We Hardly Knew Ye,"* p. 365; Irish Press, June 29, 1963.

"We were absolutely thrilled": *Irish Press,* June 29, 1963.

attended to almost constantly by a hovering aide: *St. Louis Post-Dispatch,* June 28, 1963.

It was in the notorious provost's prison here in 1798: For an account, see Thomas Pakenham, *The Year of Liberty: The Great Irish Rebellion of 1798* (Englewood Cliffs, N.J.:Prentice-Hall, 1970).

"The fact that he: Lemass OH.

The Irish army band played Chopin's "Funeral March": *New York Times,* June 29, 1963.

And he requested for a film of the ceremony: Kenneth P. O'Donnell and David F. Powers, *"Johnny, We Hardly Knew Ye,"* p. 366.

"It's a pity he couldn't wave: Aiken OH, p. 4.

Lemass, sitting with: Lemass OH, pp. 7-8.

The presence of O'Kelly and Cosgrave: See, for example, *Washington Post and Times-Herald,* June 29, 1963.

He stopped behind Cosgrave's chair: *Evening Press* (Dublin), June 29, 1963.

the first speech in a parliamentary session to be televised: *Sunday Independent* (Dublin), June 9, 1963.

the wire mesh that protected: *New York Herald-Tribune,* June 29, 1963. The Dail is now shielded from the gallery by bulletproof glass, and regular proceedings are televised daily.

Hogan greeted Kennedy: In addition to the Kennedy text from *Public Papers* (1963), this account includes material from Joint Sitting of Dail Eireann and Seanad Eireann on the Occasion of the Visit of John Fitzgerald Kennedy, President of the United States of America, Friday, June 28th, 1963 (Dublin: The Stationery Office, 1963).

One of the American leader's trouser legs: Author interview with Hillery.

"The thirteenth day of [December], 1862: In his address, Kennedy actually erroneously said "September" and mistakenly identified Fredericksburg as being in Maryland rather than Virginia. The *New York Times,* recording the address over the ABC Radio Network, transcribed the speech, error and all. See *New York Times,* June 29, 1963. For a note on the errors, see *New York Times,* June 29, 1963, *Washington Post and Times-Herald*, June 29, 1963, and *Time,* July 5, 1963.

the words of one of the great orators of the English language: Sorensen states in his book that Kennedy was being diplomatic by not attributing the quotation to David Lloyd George, prime minister of England.

Kenneth O'Donnell was stopped by an Irish woman: Kenneth P. O'Donnell and David F. Powers, *"Johnny, We Hardly Knew Ye,"* pp. 366-67.

"To most residents of this independent-minded republic: *Dallas Morning News,* June 29, 1963.

The White House position, enumerated in internal communications: June 7, 1963, secret White House memorandum for Bundy. Papers of President John Fitzgerald Kennedy: Presidential Office Files: Trip Files, box 108.

"We'll settle the matter of Ireland: *Washington Sunday Star,* June 23, 1963.

Violence on both sides claimed eighteen lives: Fintan O'Toole, *The Irish Times Book of the Century* (Dublin: Gill & Macmillan, 1999), pp. 208-11.

"Irridentism — the movement for recovery: *Washington Post and Times-Herald,* June 29, 1963.

the Irish population figures combined North and South: *Washington Post* and *Times-Herald,* June 29, 1963.

tried to "heal the breach between us": Donald S. Connery, *The Irish,* p. 262.

A group called the Border Protest Committee: *Evening Herald* (Dublin), June 27, 1963; *Irish Independent,* June 28, 1963; *Irish Times,* June 28, 1963.

Belfast's Nationalist newspaper, the *Irish News*: Quoted in *New York Times,* June 30, 1963.

"The visit of an American president with roots in Ireland: *Detroit Free Press,* June 28, 1963; and *Miami Herald,* June 28, 1963.

"I would like to have seen him be a bit more active: Aiken OH, pp. 29-30.

In the view of opposition leaders in Fine Gael: Remarks of Sen. Maurice Manning, "The Kennedy Visit" (New Ross, Ireland, July 21, 2001).

"I said, of course, that I'd never troubled him: For this recollection and the subsequent talk with Kennedy about Northern Ireland, see Kiernan OH, pp. 8-9.

In a "personal and secret" cable to Hugh McCann: Lemass Cabinet Papers, quoted in *Irish Times,* Jan. 3, 1994.

Kennedy did spend some time with Prime Minister Lemass: See the White House memorandum on the June 27, 1963, private meeting between Kennedy and Lemass in the Papers of President John Fitzgerald Kennedy: National Security Files, box 240; for Lemass's private notes, see the Lemass Cabinet Papers, quoted in *Irish Times,* Jan. 3, 1994.

(Taking the matter of partition to the United Nations: Author interview with Hillery.

The president, Lemass later remembered, offered no solutions: Lemass OH, p. 11.

Lemass had hoped that Kennedy might be helpful: *History Ireland,* vol. 1, no. 4, winter 1993, p. 40.

columnist W.A. Newman: *Irish Press,* June 29, 1963.

At a different time, the Irish ambassador: Kiernan OH, pp. 8-9.

obviously felt this medieval-style headgear: *Boston Herald,* June 29, 1963.

Dr. Michael Tierney, vice-chancellor: *Cork Examiner,* June 29, 1963; *Irish Press,* June 29, 1963; *Irish Times,* June 29, 1963.

"Is this the real John F. Kennedy?": Kenneth P. O'Donnell and David F. Powers, *"Johnny, We Hardly Knew Ye,"* p. 367.

The presentation was made in Latin by Dr. D.E.W. Wormell: *Irish Press,* June 29, 1963.

"Now summoned to the highest office: *Irish Times,* June 29, 1963.

Kennedy joined a long list of distinguished visitors: *Boston Herald,* June 28, 1963.

"To us," the lord mayor said, "you are the personification: *A Memory of John Fitzgerald Kennedy,* p. 21; *Irish Times,* June 29, 1963.

"It is doubtful if any single address: *Midland Tribune* (Birr), July 6, 1963.

"pointed the way to a role of growing influence: *Cork Examiner,* June 29, 1963.

But de Valera felt warmly: Lemass OH, pp. 5-6.

Prime Minister Lemass later marveled: The sentence, however, is published in the government's official proceedings, Joint Sitting of Dail Eireann and Seanad Eireann.

"He said, 'You cannot have a strong culture: Author interview with Shriver.

"But there were many times: Kenneth P. O'Donnell and David F. Powers, *"Johnny, We Hardly Knew Ye,"* p. 368.

"If you are weak in your dealings with the British: Ibid.

"Here lies an Englishman and a good man": Ibid.

"He was very taken with her": Author interview with Shriver.

She was nearly sixty when she launched: Mary Murray Delaney, *Of Irish Ways* (Minneapolis: Dillon Press, 1973), p. 263.

"They got on very well together: De Valera OH, p. 6.

"Oh, he seemed to be interested: Ibid., p. 7.

in fact felt that Kennedy's constant queries had, perhaps, a personal purpose: Kiernan OH, p. 21.

they wanted to visit a pub: *Evening Press* (Dublin), June 29, 1963; *Sunday Review* (Dublin), June 30, 1963.

a man rushed out: *Boston Record-American,* June 28, 1963.

"You're one of them, aren't you?": Author interview with terHorst.

asking the pilot to circle low: Editors of *Look, JFK Memorial Book.*

Five: . . . A flow of nostalgia and sentiment

When I went to those great cities: Published in *The Genius of the Irish Theater,* Sylvan Barnet, Morton Berman and William Burto, eds. (New York: New American Library, 1960), p. 42.

Seventeen days after the German invasion: There has been some confusion about the number of trips Kennedy took to Ireland before 1963. In Maurice N. Hennessy's book, *I'll Come Back in the Springtime: John F. Kennedy and the Irish* (New York: Ives

Washburn, 1966), pp. 27-28, the manager of Dublin Airport is quoted as remembering the entire Kennedy family flying to Ireland in 1938, when Ambassador Kennedy was awarded an honorary degree by National University. The airport official said the ambassador had hired a de Havilland 86, one of three planes owned by Ireland's national airline, to bring his wife and nine children from London. Other records do not support that memory. I am inclined to believe this incident may have occurred a decade later, in 1949, when Mrs. Kennedy and many of her children (John F. Kennedy by then was thirty-two) visited Ireland. Newspaper accounts of the ambassador's quick, one-day trip to Ireland in 1938 states he was accompanied by Joseph P. Kennedy, Jr., his oldest son, and a John B. Kennedy, who was a writer friend but no relation. There is no mention of second son John F. Kennedy. In addition, the extensive picture coverage of the ambassador's visit also shows that only Joseph P., Jr., was with his father. See *New York Times,* July 8-9, 1938; *Irish Press,* July 6-9, 1938; and *Irish Times,* July 7-9, 1938.

Only days before hostilities broke out: Amanda Smith, ed., *Hostage to Fortune: The Letters of Joseph P. Kennedy,* (New York: Viking, 2001), p. 360.

referred to himself as "the Irishman": Paul B. Fay, Jr., *The Pleasure of His Company* (New York, Evanston and London: Harper & Row, 1966), p. 146.

talked about Ireland "at times": Author interview with Shriver.

"Any time Honey Fitz would come down: Ibid.

"And he was very Irish in his personality": Author interview with Smith.

Sen. Edward Kennedy remembered Honey Fitz: Author interview with Sen. Kennedy.

"Jack delighted in his Irish heritage": Rose Fitzgerald Kennedy, *Times to Remember,* p. 438.

Gray had a rather dim view: John F. Kennedy, *Prelude to Leadership: The European Diary of John F. Kennedy, Summer 1945* (Washington, D.C.: Regnery Publishing, 1995), pp. 25-26.

Gray was in that group: John A. Murphy, *Ireland in the Twentieth Century* (Dublin: Gill & Macmillan, 1975), p. 105.

Later, in the 1950s, Gray would be even harsher: See William A. Carson, *Ulster and the Irish Republic* (Belfast: William W. Cleland, 1956), pp. i-ix.

In a separate travel diary entry: Amanda Smith, ed., *Hostage to Fortune,* p. 621.

It is not entirely clear: Arthur Mitchell, *JFK and His Irish Heritage* (Dublin: Moytura Press, 1993), p. 111.

In a piece he wrote for Hearst: *New York Journal-American,* July 29, 1945.

On this trip, Kennedy stayed: details are from James MacGregor Burns, *John Kennedy: A Political Profile* (New York: Harcourt, Brace & Co., 1960), pp. 3-4; Editors of *Look: JFK Memorial Book;* Kenneth P. O'Donnell and David F. Powers, *"Johnny, We Hardly*

Knew Ye," pp. 361-62; and Arthur Mitchell, *JFK and His Irish Heritage,* pp. 30-33 and 112-13.

Linsmore Castle: Details about Lismore Castle come from John FitzMaurice Mills, *The Noble Dwellings of Ireland* (New York: Thames & Hudson, 1987), pp. 154-59.

The congressman acquired a green, softcover guidebook: See *Irish Tourist Directory, Comprising Hotels, Boarding Houses, Restaurants, Garages and Other Businesses in the Irish Free State* (Dublin: Irish Tourist Association), in the collection of the Florida International Museum, St. Petersburg, Fla.

That is the way James Kennedy remembered it: His recollections and those of Mary Ryan are briefly detailed in *New York Sunday News,* June 23, 1963.

"He didn't look well at all": *New York Times,* June 23, 1963.

"Begod, and he was shook-looking": *New York Times,* June 23, 1963.

But he also was battling Addison's disease: For details see Doris Kearns Goodwin, *The Fitzgeralds and the Kennedys: An American Saga* (New York: Simon & Schuster, 1987), pp. 734-35.

Whichever way he went first: *Boston Sunday Globe,* April 7, 1963.

"Did they have a bathroom?": Joan and Clay Balir, Jr., *The Search for J.F.K.* (New York: Berkley Publishing /G.P. Putnam's Sons, 1976), p. 559.

Kennedy visited the *Irish Press*: See Mark O'Brien, *De Valera, Fianna Fail and the Irish Press: The Truth in the News?* (Dublin and Portland, Ore.: Irish Academic Press, 2001), pp. 80, 99.

refreshment at John Mulligan's on Poolbeg Street: *Irish Times,* June 15, 1963. Some of the account of his visit in this story is muddled and certain details appear to have been confused with later visits. For example, the report states that Kennedy met Sean Lemass on his 1947 trip. Lemass, in his oral history for the Kennedy Library, recalled meeting Kennedy in 1953 "just to shake hands." Whether that was in Washington Lemass does not say, but the Massachusetts senator made no trip to Ireland in 1953. See Lemass OH, p. 1.

Rep. John E. Fogarty recalled: Fogarty OH, April 14, 1965, pp. 2-4.

The couple had lunch with: Cosgrave OH, pp. 1-2.

That afternoon, Kennedy spoke: Arthur Mitchell, *JFK and His Irish Heritage,* pp. 40-41; *Irish Independent,* Oct. 1, 1955.

"He was very friendly, matter-of-fact: For this and the subsequent descriptions of Kennedy, see Cosgrave OH, p. 4.

"He was rooted there forever": John F. Kennedy, *Prelude to Leadership,* p. xl.

"The turning point did come on his visit: Kiernan OH, p. 21.

"comes out in moments of stress or strain: Ibid., p. 20.

Prime Minister Lemass, on the other hand, had an entirely different sense: Lemass OH, pp. 4-5.

Only Irish Need Apply: Author interview with Donnelly.

Once, in May 1963, Kennedy teased his wife: Benjamin C. Bradlee, *Conversations with Kennedy,* p. 190.

"We have felt this way toward him from the beginning": *Milwaukee Journal,* June 24, 1963.

"We had celebrations at exactly the same hour: Minihan OH, p. 2.

"the interest was always there": Author interview with Sorensen.

Sen. Edward Kennedy remembered his brother reading Irish history: Author interview with Sen. Kennedy.

"I used my Irish seal on a letter today: Theodore C. Sorensen, *Kennedy* (New York: Harper & Row, 1965), p. 582.

"Now look here," he remembered answering: De Valera OH, p. 5.

Six: June 29, 1963: Galway, Limerick, and Shannon Airport

I have put away sorrow: Published in *The Genius of the Irish Theater,* Sylvan Barnet et al., eds., p. 192.

"How do you think the people of Ireland would like me: Quoted by Tubridy in *Irish Independent,* Nov. 25, 1963.

Kennedy went to the embassy's dining room: *New York Journal-American,* June 30, 1963; *Washington Evening Star,* June 29, 1963; *Washington Post and Times-Herald,* June 30, 1963.

"President Kennedy's visit here has given joy: *Evening Press* (Dublin), June 29, 1963.

Before boarding the helicopter: Evelyn Lincoln, *My Twelve Years with John F. Kennedy,* p. 346.

that spill the day before in Cork was, indeed, bothering him: *Cleveland Plain Dealer,* June 29, 1963; *Evening Press* (Dublin), June 29, 1963.

Kennedy told the small gathering: *Evening Herald* (Dublin), June 29, 1963.

He had forgotten to say goodbye: *Evening Herald* (Dublin), June 29, 1963; *Atlanta Journal,* June 29, 1963; *Chicago's American,* June 29, 1963.

Dorothy Tubridy and Kennedy's sisters waited in the drawing room: Author interview with Tubridy.

"You can't get away from the American Legion: Kenneth P. O'Donnell and David F. Powers, *"Johnny, We Hardly Knew Ye,"* p. 369.

Out in Galway Bay, fishing trawlers: *New York Mirror,* June 30, 1963.

As he reached Forster House, the residence of the mayor: *Connacht Tribune* (Galway), July 6, 1963.

The president approached: *New York Times,* June 30, 1963.

Women appeared to outnumber the men: *Chicago's American,* June 29, 1963.

McCloskey also were there: Among others, Ireland's minister of defense, G. Bartley; the Catholic bishop of Galway, the Rev. Dr. Brown; the Catholic archibishop of Tuam, the Most Rev. Dr. Walsh, and his protestant counterpart, the Most Rev. Dr. Butler, all shook hands with Kennedy.

In Gaelic, the lord mayor: *New York Mirror,* June 30, 1963.

"We are honored today that John Fitzgerald Kennedy has accepted: A *Memory of John F. Kennedy,* pp. 27-28.

"He went on and on": Author interview with Randa Murphy.

"The reading of a long address in Irish: *Connacht Tribune* (Galway), July 6, 1963.

until a musician reached out and ran his hand through the president's hair: *Irish Times,* July 1, 1963.

Randa Murphy didn't witness: Randa Murphy e-mail to author.

"I don't know how the [presidential] car: Author interview with Johnson.

Prime Minister Lemass remembered the Secret Service: Lemass OH, p. 16.

"Thank God they're friendly": *Irish Times,* July 1, 1963.

"It was an extraordinary visit: From "Remarks by President Clinton and President Robinson of Ireland in Exchange of Toasts," the White House, Washington, D.C., June 13, 1996.

The crowds followed Kennedy to Salt Hill: *Chicago Tribune,* June 30, 1963.

Kennedy grinned when he saw a sign: *Connacht Tribune* (Galway), July 6, 1963.

at Greenpark Racecourse, a few minutes' drive south of the city center: The racecourse was later abandoned for a newer facility farther out of town. The old site is still there, the grandstands dilapidated, the track overgrown, visited now only by neighbors walking their dogs and surrounded on all sides by housing and businesses.

"Isn't he the image of Honey Fitz?": Kenneth P. O'Donnell and David F. Powers, *"Johnny, We Hardly Knew Ye,"* p. 370.

Limerick, like the other cities: *Cork Examiner,* June 27, 1963; *Limerick Leader,* June 29, 1963.

area officials and clergy: Among the officials present were T.M. O'Connor, Limerick County manager; Denis Naughton, chairman of the Limerick County Council; J.C. Barrett, chairman of the Limerick Health Authority; Cork's Lord Mayor Casey and

City Manager Walter McEvilly; Sen. Sean Brady, chairman of the Clare County Council; J. Boland, Clare County manager; J.P. Flynn, Tipperary County manager; Most. Rev. Dr. Henry Murphy, Catholic bishop of Limerick; Right Rev. Dr. Robert Wyse-Jackson, the Church of Ireland's bishop of Limerick, Ardfert and Aghadoe; and Rt. Rev. Dr. Dom Dowdall, Lord Abbot of Glenstal.

this celebration included some sixty known cousins: *Limerick Leader,* June 29, 1963; *Cork Examiner,* July 1, 1963.

The distinct smell of newly cut hay: *Toledo Blade,* June 30, 1963.

"Mr. President, I wonder if it is possible for you: The lord mayor's address comes from two sources, *Evening Press* (Dublin), June 29, 1963, and *A Memory of John Fitzgerald Kennedy,* pp. 28-29.

Kennedy had improvised: Lemass OH, p. 8.

"How are you, Jack?": *Evening Press* (Dublin), June 29, 1963.

"Will you fellows step back?": *Evening Press* (Dublin), June 29, 1963.

Mayor Condell, determined to make the most: *Irish Times,* July 1, 1963; Kiernan OH, p. 7.

The correspondent for the *Baltimore Sun: Baltimore Sun,* June 30, 1963.

The presidential departure from Shannon: Details from various sources, including *Cork Examiner,* July 1, 1963.

and local civic officials: They included the Most Rev. Dr. Joseph Rodgers, bishop of Killaloe; Right Rev. Dr. Stannistreet, bishop of Killaloe and Clonfert; Joseph Boland, Clare County manager; D.P. Honan, chairman of the Ennis Urban District Council; Barry Howard, chairman of the KilRush Urban District Council; Martin Mungovan, chairman of the Kilkee Town Commissioners; and Brendan O'Regan, chairman of the Airport Development Company at Shannon.

a bottle of holy water and clay: *Irish Independent,* June 29, 1963; *Philadelphia Inquirer and Public Ledger,* June 30, 1963.

Dr. Hillery recalled the tone as "kind of plaintive": Author interview with Hillery.

A supremely Irish ending: Lord Longford, *Kennedy,* p. 155.

(It would be some years later when de Valera revealed: De Valera OH, p. 6; Lemass OH, p. 7; and *Irish Press,* July 1, 1963. The *Press* generously reported on the previous Saturday's departure and recitation without mentioning the errors, substituting the faithful version for Kennedy's creative alternative. For Kennedy's version, see Public Papers (1963), p. x.

The bump-and-run tour had given the gardai: *Irish Press,* July 1, 1963.

Dorothy Tubridy stopped Kennedy: Tubridy OH, p. 25.

A man yelled out: "It has been the greatest: *Philadelphia Evening Bulletin,* June 29, 1963.

"Oh, his mood was just as happy: George Meany OH, July 16 and Aug. 18, 1964, p. 40.

Kennedy walked to his jet: *Washington Daily News,* June 29, 1963; *Irish Press,*
   July 1, 1963.

the president boarded his jet: Lawrence F. O'Brien, *No Final Victories,* p. 153.

Seven: October 11-21, 1963: Philadelphia, Chicago, Washington, New York, Boston

"That was one column: *Washington Post and Times-Herald,* July 2, 1963;
   Lawrence F. O'Brien, *No Final Victories,* pp. 154-55.

"It truly brought a little bit of Ireland: Letter from President Kennedy to Lemass, July 22,
   1963, and letter from President Kennedy to de Valera, July 25, 1963, in Eire/Ireland,
   Department of Foreign Affairs (formerly Department of External Affairs), Protocol
   Files, 434/682, file 26.

screening them in the theater his father had built: Author interview with Shriver.

"The next night, after dinner, he said: Author interview with Sen. Kennedy.

But he was not that surprised by the Irish reaction: Author interview with Smith.

"In essence, it can be said President Kennedy 'stole the show'": From a document titled
   "Press, radio and television coverage of President Kennedy's visit to Ireland," July 12,
   1963, Department of External Affairs, contained in Eire/Ireland, Department of Foreign Affairs (formerly Department of External Affairs), Protocol Files, 434/682, file 1.

"Some people believe that what did most: Walter Bryan, *The Improbable Irish* (New York:
   Taplinger Publishing Co., 1969), p. 212.

"The Irish rose up to greet him: John Philip Cohane, *The Indestructible Irish* (New York:
   Meredith Press, 1969), pp. 12-13.

"What has he brought back to us?: *Sunday Independent* (Dublin), June 30, 1963.

"By his coming," agreed Dr. Hillery: Author interview with Hillery.

"I think that his coming back to Ireland was a closing: Kiernan OH, p. 23.

"It is tempting to see Kennedy's Irish visit: Fergal Tobin, *The Best of Decades:
   Ireland in the 1960s* (Dublin: Gill & Macmillan, 1984), pp. 91-94.

"JFK personified the brash: Dermot Keogh, *Twentieth-Century Ireland: Nation and State*
   (Dublin: Gill & Macmillan, 1994), p. 252.

From the viewpoint of opposition Fine Gael: Manning, "The Kennedy Visit"

Kennedy, he said, "made a huge impact: Author interview with Hume.

a factor in "liberalizing the climate of opinion: Tim Pat Coogan, *Ireland Since the Rising,*
   p. 181.

"The reader outside Ireland may wonder why I single out: Ibid., p. 182.

"The American orientation which this implied: F.S.L. Lyons, *Ireland Since the Famine* (London: Fontana Press, 1985), p. 596.

". . . Harping on neutrality," he said: Ronan Fanning, *Independent Ireland* (Dublin: Helicon, 1983), p. 203.

"Mr. Kennedy's visit to his ancestral Ireland identifies him: *Boston Globe*, June 24, 1963.

"material gain" in the form of tourists: *Connacht Tribune* (Galway), July 6, 1963.

tourism from the United States was "incalculable": *Irish Press*, Oct. 16, 1963.

"Its significance has a sort of deeper: Author interview with Finnegan.

"a real validation for the Irish": Author interview with Sen. Kennedy.

". . . The president wanted to put on a great show: James A. Reed OH, June 16, 1964, p. 74.

". . . told him that the schedule: Letter from JFK to de Valera, Oct. 15, 1963, Papers of President John Fitzgerald Kennedy: Presidential Office Files: General Correspondence, box 24.

"Prime Minister Lemass is the chief architect: From "Visit of Prime Minister Lemass, October 15-16, 1963, Scope Paper," Department of State, dated Oct. 7, 1963, from Papers of President John Fitzgerald Kennedy: Presidential Office Files: Country Files, box 119a.

"No one does that . . . They don't do: Author interview with Sen. Kennedy.

Lemass and his wife arrived October 11 in Philadelphia: *Irish Press*, Oct. 12, 1963; *Irish Times*, Oct. 14, 1963.

On October 13, Lemass and his party: *Irish Press*, Oct. 14-15, 1963; *Irish Times*, Oct. 15, 1963.

In Washington on October 15: *Irish Press*, Oct. 16, 1963; *Irish Times*, Oct. 16, 1963; *Washington Post and Times-Herald*, Oct. 15-16, 1963.

"He was, I think, a little bit worried: Lemass OH, p. 10.

The following day, Lemass mirrored: *Irish Press*, Oct. 17, 1963; *Irish Times*, Oct. 17, 1963; *Washington Post and Times-Herald*, Oct. 17, 1963.

The British, Lemass argued, had accepted the "wind of change: *Irish Press*, Oct. 17, 1963; *Irish Times*, Oct. 17, 1963; *Washington Post and Times-Herald*, Oct. 17, 1963.

O'Neill up in Belfast felt Lemass was discarding: *Irish Press*, Oct. 18, 1963; *Irish Times*, Oct. 18, 1963.

On October 17, after their private talks: The statement is published in *Public Papers* (1963), p. 788.

Northern Ireland was not even indirectly referred to: It should be noted that the remarks

Lemass made on partition were excerpted in Eire/Ireland: Weekly Bulletin of the

Department of External Affairs, Government of Ireland, Dublin. No. 637, Oct. 28, 1963, p. 6.

"I think the words of General Washington: Oct. 15, 1963, letter from JFK to de Valera, in Papers of President John Fitzgerald Kennedy: Presidential Office Files: General Correspondence, box 24.

Lemass was given a custom-made set of golf clubs: *Irish Press,* Oct. 16, 1963.

Lemass went on to New York: *Irish Press,* Oct. 18, 1963; *Irish Times,* Oct. 18, 1963.

On October 18, Lemass journeyed to Boston: *Irish Press,* Oct. 19 and 21, 1963; *Irish Times,* Oct. 19 and 21, 1963.

Lemass arrived back in Dublin with his first prize: *Irish Press,* Oct. 22, 1963; *Irish Times,* Oct. 22, 1963.

more deals were to come from American companies: Eire/Ireland: Weekly Bulletin of the Department of External Affairs, Government of Ireland, Dublin. No. 639, Nov. 18, 1963, p. 4.

De Valera had proposed such an institution: *Irish Times,* June 28, 1963; *Washington Post and Times-Herald,* June 30, 1963; *Boston Globe,* July 4, 1963.

In a St. Patrick's Day speech: *Sunday Independent* (Dublin), June 30, 1963.

Hibernia, a Catholic journal in Ireland: Quoted in *Irish Times,* June 14, 1963, and *New York Journal-American,* June 30, 1963.

Kennedy himself drafted the communique about the foundation: *Irish Independent,* Nov. 25, 1963.

The U.S. Department of State, meanwhile, was pressuring Irish officials: Kiernan OH, pp. 10-11.

Kennedy, according to Lemass, wanted to show "his desire to help: Lemass OH, pp. 11-12. Also *Irish Press,* Oct. 12, 1963.

William V. Shannon: Quoted in Tim Pat Coogan, *Eamon de Valera: The Man Who Was Ireland* (New York: HarperCollins, 1993), p. 681.

After his visit to Ireland, "he felt a tremendous: Author interviews with Smith, Sen. Kennedy.

didn't hear about any "big things: Author interview with Sorensen.

"In fact, both prime ministers in Ireland: *Irish Times,* July 2, 1963.

"Gradually his influence would have been more and more: *Sunday Independent* (Dublin), Nov. 24, 1963.

"It was generally accepted in Dublin: Tim Pat Coogan, *The Troubles: Ireland's Ordeal 1966-1996 and the Search for Peace* (Boulder, Colo.: Roberts Rinehart, 1996), p. 344.

"You can't say something Kennedy did: Author interview with Finnegan.

Sen. Edward Kennedy, who himself became a key figure in the peace: Author interview with Sen. Kennedy.

Reed treasured the night: Reed OH, pp. 74-75.

"Oh, it was magical": Author interview with Tubridy.

Epilogue: November 22, 1963

At Mary Ryan's home in Dunganstown: Grennan OH, p. 6.

Her sister, Mary Ann, collapsed: *Irish Press,* Nov. 23, 1963; *Sunday Independent* (Dublin), Nov. 24, 1963.

The silence of farmyard was broken: *Irish Press,* Nov. 23, 1963.

people came to call on Mary Ryan: Grennan OH, p. 7.

New Ross on November 22 canceled events: *Irish Times,* Nov. 23, 1963.

In Wexford, a student's mother: *Irish Press,* Nov. 23, 1963.

"I am absolutely shattered": *Sunday Independent* (Dublin), Nov. 24, 1963.

"Ireland, the entire island, was devastated: Author interview with Tubridy.

"We did not talk much, because she was very upset: *Irish Press,* Nov. 23, 1963.

who "looked pale-faced even in black and white": Hugh Oram, *The Newspaper Book: A History of Newspapers in Ireland, 1649-1983* (Dublin: MO Books, 1983), p. 293.

"And then there was a delay: De Valera OH, pp. 5-6.

Mitchel delivered this news in a shaking voice: *Irish Press,* Nov. 23, 1963.

"mourned him with a personal grief: *Irish Times, Nov. 23, 1963.*

"We had never done anything like this before: Ibid., Jan. 3, 1994.

"You Americans had another president: Editors of *Look: JFK Memorial Book.*

"I find it hard to express adequately: *Irish Times,* Nov. 23, 1963.

"America's loss is Ireland's too": Ibid.

"In the end," the *Sunday Press* in Dublin observed: *Sunday Press,* Nov. 24, 1963.

Amidst her shock and grief: Kenneth P. O'Donnell and David F. Powers, *"Johnny, We Hardly Knew Ye,"* p. 40.

And so, at Dublin Airport on Sunday: *Irish Press,* Nov. 24, 1963.

Mary Ann Ryan, daughter of: Ibid., Nov. 25, 1963.

Lemass thought of a package: Lemass OH, p. 6.

"There's a man here who wants to see you: Author interview with Kilduff.

Appendix: The Kennedys and Fitzgeralds in Ireland

The Fitzgeralds were Welsh-Norman: This is discussed in John F. Brennan, *The Evolution of Everyman: Ancestral Heritage of John F. Kennedy* (Dundalk, Ireland: Dundalgan Press, 1968). I am indebted to this work for its painstaking research into both the Fitzgeralds and Kennedys. See also extensive background on the families in *The Midland Tribune* (Birr), June 22, 1963.

This had become the Norman custom: An invaluable source for how names evolved is Edward MacLysaght, *Irish Families: Their Names, Arms and Origins* (New York: Crown, 1972, originally published Dublin: Hodges Figgis & Co., 1957). For Fitzgerald, see pp. 142-3; for O'Kennedy, p. 198.

"Had events brought the Geraldines: Edmund Curtis, *A History of Ireland* (London: Methuen & Co. 1942, fourth edition, rev.), p. 48.

The Irish weren't politically suited: A point well made in Karl S. Bottigheime, *Ireland and the Irish: A Short History* (New York: Columbia University Press, 1982), pp. 52-53.

"But," Fitzgerald continued, "I would not have done it: John F. Brennan, *The Evolution of Everyman,* pp. 58-59.

the domain of the O'Carrolls: The author notes that his ancestors were another powerful neighboring clan of the O'Kennedys and the Fitzgeralds, and seem to have found reason to fight them both at various times. For the reasons why, and for much on the O'Kennedys, Fitzgeralds, and many other Irish families, see the John Gleeson, *History of the Ely O'Carroll Territory* or *Ancient Ormond* (Kilkenny, Ireland: Roberts' Books, 1982).

The inevitable clash came on April 23, 1014: For a particularly engaging account, see *Milwaukee Journal,* June 25, 1963.

"The O'Kennedy-Fitzgerald rapport: John F. Brennan, *The Evolution of Everyman,* pp. 117-18.

The treaty says: *A Memory of John Fitzgerald Kennedy,* p. 25.

In the Nine Years' War at the end of the sixteenth century: *The Irish Press,* June 28, 1963.

They owned eleven castles: John Gleeson, *History of the Ely O'Carroll Territory,* p. 279.

"We don't know exactly," Mary Ryan apologized: *New York Sunday News,* June 23, 1963.

two Kennedys from Dunganstown: *Boston Evening Globe,* June 25, 1963.

"To see Ireland happy": Quoted in *Irish Times,* June 25, 1963.

Yet even in the blush of President Kennedy's visit: *London Sunday Times,* June 30, 1963.

It is more likely the Kennedys were still tenants: *New York Times,* June 23, 1963.

The Kennedys who stayed did seem to prosper: *New York Sunday News,* June 23, 1963.

One sign of that are the graves: *Evening Press* (Dublin), June 26, 1963.

Between 1849 and 1856, twenty-nine ships: *Boston Evening Globe,* June 27, 1963.

Jack Shannon, proprietor of the New Ross Motor: *Irish Press,* May 11, 1963.

The Fitzgeralds were on the move: *Boston Globe,* May 29, 1963; *Philadelphia Inquirer and Public Ledger,* June 27, 1963; Doris Kearns Goodwin, *The Fitzgeralds and the Kennedys: An American Saga* (New York: Simon & Schuster, 1987), pp. 3-10.

Honey Fitz made a pilgrimage: *Limerick Leader,* June 29, 1963.

the Irish were forty-four percent of the foreign-born: *John F. Kennedy, A Nation of Immigrants* (New York: Harper & Row, 1964), p. 17. In truth, John Kennedy wrote the book twice, first as a short work in 1958, then, as a considerably revised book, unfinished at the time of his assassination in 1963 but brought out the following year.

"The Irish," Kennedy wrote, "were the first: Ibid., p. 18.

"Gradually, rung by rung: Ibid.

"areas in which they could demonstrate: Ibid., p. 51.

Sources

Oral Histories

The oral history interviews in the John Fitzgerald Kennedy Library in Boston proved extremely helpful. Those consulted and/or quoted from in this book include

Aiken, Frank (1898-1983). Irish minister of external affairs, 1957-69.

Cosgrave, Liam (1920-). Irish minister of external affairs, 1954-57; president of Fine Gael; prime minister of Ireland, 1973-77.

Cushing, Richard (1895-1970). Roman Catholic archbishop of Boston, 1944-70; close Kennedy family friend.

De Valera, Eamon (1882-1975). President of Ireland, 1959-73.

Fogarty, John E. (1913-1967). Member of the U.S. House of Representatives, Rhode Island, 1945-67; close political ally of John F. Kennedy.

Fraser, Hugh (1918-1984). British under secretary of state for the colonies, 1960-62; British secretary of state for air, 1962-64; Kennedy family friend.

Grennan, Josephine. Irish cousin of John F. Kennedy.

Kiernan, Thomas J. (1897-1967). Irish ambassador to the United States, 1961-64.

Lemass, Sean (1899-1971). Prime minister of Ireland, 1959-66.

McCormack, John W. (1891-1980). Member of the U.S. House of Representatives from Massachusetts, 1928-71, and Speaker of the House, 1962-71.

Meany, George (1894-1980). President, American Federation of Labor–Congress of Industrial Organization (AFL-CIO), 1955-79.

Minihan, Andrew (1911-89). Member of the New Ross Urban District Council, 1955-75; member of the New Ross Harbor Board, 1948-89.

Reed, James A. (1919-). Special assistant to the U.S. attorney general, 1961; assistant secretary of the treasury, 1961-65.

Tubridy, Dorothy. Public relations executive for Waterford Crystal and Irish friend of the Kennedy family.

Tyler, William (1910-). Assistant secretary of state for European and Canadian affairs, 1962-65.

Interviews

Donnelly, Lenore "Lenny". Administrative assistant to David F. Powers, special assistant to the president, in the Kennedy administration. Nov. 17, 2002.

Finnegan, Richard. Director of Irish Studies, Stonehill College, Easton, Mass., and author. Jan. 14, 2003.

Fluet, Pauline. Administrative assistant to Kenneth P. O'Donnell, special assistant to the president, in the Kennedy administration. Dec. 29, 2002.

Hillery, Dr. Patrick. Ireland's former minister of education; also former minister of industry and commerce, former minister for foreign affairs, and former president of Ireland. April 5, 2003.

Hume, John. Nobel Peace Prize laureate. Founder and former leader of the Social Democratic and Labor Party in Northern Ireland. April 14, 2003.

Johnson, Oscar. Former U.S. Army helicopter pilot. March 30, 2003.

Kennedy, Sen. Edward M. President Kennedy's brother. United States senator from Massachusetts since 1962. April 16, 2003.

Kilduff, Malcolm. White House assistant press secretary in the Kennedy administration. Nov. 13 and 18, 2002.

Lewis, Jean Price. Assistant, White House congressional relations office, in the Kennedy administration. Dec. 28, 2002.

Minihan, Eoin. Son of the late Andrew Minihan. Former member of the New Ross Urban District Council, a director of the John F. Kennedy Trust in New Ross, and managing director of Steele and Co. Ltd., New Ross. Jan. 17, 2003.

Murphy, Randa. Proprietor, Magowna House, Inch, County Clare, Ireland. Nov. 30, 2002.

Salinger, Pierre. Former White House press secretary in the Kennedy administration. Former U.S. senator from California, former journalist, and author. Dec. 31, 2002.

Shriver, Eunice Kennedy. President Kennedy's sister. Founder and honorary chairman, Special Olympics. Dec. 5, 2002.

Smith, Jean Kennedy. President Kennedy's sister and former U.S. ambassador to Ireland. Founder and member of the board of trustees, VSA arts, formerly known as Very Special Arts. March 3, 2003.

terHorst, Jerald F. Former reporter for the *Detroit News,* White House press secretary to President Gerald R. Ford, and author. Dec. 23, 2002.

Sorensen, Theodore C. White House special counsel in the Kennedy administration. New York City attorney and author. Nov. 20, 2002.

Tubridy, Dorothy. Former public relations executive for Waterford Crystal and Irish friend of the Kennedy family. Dec. 29, 2002.

Wicker, Tom. Former reporter for the *New York Times,* and author. Jan. 9, 2003.

Papers of President John Fitzgerald Kennedy

The following files at the John Fitzgerald Kennedy Library in Boston were consulted and, in some cases, quoted for this book:

Presidential Office Files: Trip Files, box 108.

Presidential Office Files: Country Files, box 119a.

Presidential Office Files: General Correspondence, box 24.

National Security Files: boxes 118 (general), 239, and 240; briefing book for Sean Lemass visit.

Newspapers and Magazines in the United States

Atlanta Journal

Baltimore Sun

Boston Evening Globe

Boston Globe

Boston Herald

Boston Record-American

Boston Traveler

Boston Sunday Advertiser

Buffalo Evening News

Chicago Daily News

Chicago's American

Chicago Sun-Times

Chicago Tribune

Christian Science Monitor

Cleveland Plain Dealer

Dallas Morning News

Des Moines Register

Detroit Free Press

Detroit News

Hartford Courant

Kansas City Star

Kansas City Times

Los Angeles Times

Louisville Courier-Journal

Miami Herald

Milwaukee Journal

Minneapolis Tribune

Newark Evening News

National Observer

Newsday

New York Daily News

New York Herald-Tribune

New York Journal-American

New York Mirror

New York Post

New York Times

New York World-Telegram and Sun

Philadelphia Evening Bulletin

Philadelphia Inquirer and Public Ledger

Rochester Democrat and Chronicle

Sacramento Union

St. Louis Globe-Democrat

St. Louis Post-Dispatch

San Francisco Chronicle

San Francisco Examiner

Seattle Times

Toledo Blade

Wall Street Journal

Washington Daily News

Washington Evening Star

Washington Post and Times-Herald

Congressional Quarterly

Esquire

Granta

Holiday

Life

Look

Newsweek

Time

U.S. News & World Report

Newspapers and Magazines in Ireland

Carlow Nationalist

Tipperary Star (Clonmel)

Cork Examiner

Evening Herald (Dublin)

Evening Press (Dublin)

Irish Independent (Dublin)

Irish Press (Dublin)

Irish Times (Dublin)

Sunday Independent (Dublin)

Sunday Mirror (Dublin)

Sunday Press (Dublin)

Sunday Review (Dublin)

Clare Champion (Ennis)

Enniscorthy Guardian

Connacht Tribune (Galway)

Limerick Leader

Midland Tribune (Birr)

New Ross Standard

Roscommon Herald

Kerryman (Tralee)

Munster Express (Waterford)

The People (Wexford)

Wexford Free Press

History Ireland

Irish Digest

Newspapers in Great Britain

Financial Times
London Daily Telegraph
London Sunday Times
Times (London)

Films, Documentaries, and Television Coverage

"The President's Journey," NBC News, 1963.

"Welcome, Mr. President: Highlights of President Kennedy's Visit to Ireland June 26th to 29th, 1963," Radio Telefis Eireann (RTE), 1963.

"Kennedy Tour. Irish Acclaim Highlights Visit," Universal-International News, 1963.

"Kennedy Trip. Irish Roar Welcome After German Visit," Universal-International News, 1963.

Unedited White House footage of President Kennedy in Ireland.

Speeches

Remarks by President Clinton and President Robinson of Ireland in Exchange of Toasts, the White House, Washington, D.C., June 13, 1996.

Remarks of Senator Maurice Manning, "The Kennedy Visit," New Ross, Ireland, July 21, 2001.

Government Documents and Publications

Dublin, Corporation of the City of Dublin, *Dublin: Official Guide to the City of Dublin* (no publication date).

Eire / Ireland, Department of External Affairs. *Facts about Ireland* (1963).

Eire / Ireland. *Tithe An Oireachtais. The Irish Parliament — Democracy at Work* (no publication date).

Eire / Ireland, Department of Foreign Affairs (formerly Department of External Affairs). Protocol Files, 434/682, files 1-26.

Eire / Ireland. Cuairt Ar Eirinn D'Uachtaran Stait Aontaithe Mheiricea John Fitzgerald Kennedy, 26 go 29 Meitheamh, 1963. Visit to Ireland of the President of the United States of America John Fitzgerald Kennedy, 26 to 29 June, 1963.

Eire / Ireland. *Joint Sitting of Dail Eireann and Seanad Eireann on the Occasion of the Visit of John Fitzgerald Kennedy, President of the United States of America, Friday, June 28th, 1963.*

Eire / Ireland. *Weekly Bulletin of the Department of External Affairs.* No. 625, July 1, 1963; No. 637, Oct. 28, 1963; No. 639, Nov. 18, 1963; No. 640, Dec. 2, 1963.

United States, Department of State. Preface by William M. Franklin. *American Foreign Policy: Current Documents — 1963.*

United States, American Embassy, Dublin. *President John F. Kennedy's Visit to Ireland, June 26-29, 1963.*

United States, American Embassy, Dublin. *President Kennedy's Visit to Ireland, June 26-29, 1963. Directory.*

United States. *Public Papers of the Presidents of the United States: John F. Kennedy. Containing the Public Messages, Speeches, and Statements of the President. January 1 to December 31, 1962.*

United States. *Public Papers of the Presidents of the United States: John F. Kennedy. Containing the Public Messages, Speeches, and Statements of the President. January 1 to November 22, 1963.*

United States, Office of the White House Press Secretary. *Schedule of the trip of the President to Cologne, Bonn, Hanau, Frankfurt, Wiesbaden, and Berlin, Germany; Dublin, New Ross, Dunganstown, Wexford, Cork, Galway and Shannon, Ireland; Birch Grove, England; and Italy* (1963).

Books

Ayearst, Morley. *The Republic of Ireland: Its Government and Politics.* New York: New York University Press / London: University of London Press, 1970.

Barnet, Sylvan; Berman, Morton; and Burto, William, eds. *The Genius of the Irish Theater.* New York: New American Library, 1960.

Bence-Jones, Mark. *The Remarkable Irish: Chronicle of a Land, a Culture, a Mystique.* New York: David McKay Co., 1966.

Blair, Joan and Clay, Jr. *The Search for J.F.K.* New York: Berkley Publishing Corp. / G.P. Putnam's Sons, 1976.

Bottigheimer, Karl S. *Ireland and The Irish: A Short History.* New York: Columbia University Press, 1982.

Bradlee, Benjamin C. *Conversations with Kennedy.* New York: W.W. Norton & Co., 1975.

Brennan, John F. *The Evolution of Everyman: Ancestral Heritage of John F. Kennedy.* Dundalk, Ireland: Dundalgan Press (W. Tempest), 1968.

Brinkley, Douglas, and Richard T. Griffiths, eds. *John F. Kennedy and Europe*. Baton Rouge, La., and London: Louisiana State University Press, 1999.

Bryan, Walter. *The Improbable Irish*. New York: Taplinger Publishing Co., 1969.

Burns, James MacGregor. *John Kennedy: A Political Profile*. New York: Harcourt, Brace & Co., 1960.

Carroll, Joseph Robert. *A History of the Carrolls of Eile, Tipperary, Limerick and Lawrence, Mass.* Unpublished manuscript, 1979.

Carson, William A. (Introduction by David Gray). *Ulster and the Irish Republic*. Belfast: William W. Cleland, 1956.

Chubb, Basil (Introduction by David Thornley). *The Government and Politics of Ireland*. Stanford, Calif.: Stanford University Press / London: Oxford University Press, 1970.

Cohane, John Philip. *The Indestructible Irish*. New York: Meredith Press, 1969.

Connery, Donald S. *The Irish*. New York: Simon and Schuster, 1968.

Coogan, Tim Pat. *Eamon de Valera: The Man Who Was Ireland*. New York: Harper-Collins Publishers, 1993.

———— *Ireland Since the Rising*. London: Pall Mall Press, 1966.

———— *The Troubles: Ireland's Ordeal 1966-1996 and the Search for Peace*. Boulder, Colo.: Roberts Rinehart, 1996.

———— *Wherever Green is Worn: The Story of the Irish Diaspora*. New York: Palgrave, 2000.

Cronin, Sean. *Washington's Irish Policy 1916-1986: Independence — Partition — Neutrality*. Dublin and St. Paul, Minn.: Anvil Books, 1987.

Curtayne, Alice. *The Irish Story: A Survey of Irish History and Culture*. New York: P.J. Kenedy & Sons, 1960.

Curtis, Edmund. *A History of Ireland*. 4th ed. rev. London: Methuen & Co., 1942.

Davis, John H. *The Kennedys: Dynasty and Disaster, 1848-1983*. New York: McGraw-Hill Book Co., 1984.

Delaney, Mary Murray. *Of Irish Ways*. Minneapolis: Dillon Press, 1973.

Dumbrell, John. *A Special Relationship: Anglo-American Relations in the Cold War and After*. London: Macmillan Press / New York: St. Martin's Press, 2001.

Fanning, Ronan. *Independent Ireland*. Dublin: Helicon, 1983.

Fay, Paul B., Jr. *The Pleasure of His Company*. New York, Evanston, and London: Harper & Row, 1966.

Ferguson, James. *W. & A.K. Johnston's Clan Histories: The Kennedys, "Twixt Wigton and the Town of Ayr"*. Edinburgh and London: W. & A.K. Johnston & G.W. Bacon, 1958.

FitzGerald, Garret. *Towards a New Ireland*. London: Charles Knight & Co., 1972.

Foster, R.F., ed. *The Oxford Illustrated History of Ireland.* Oxford and New York: Oxford University Press, 1989.

From Here to the White House. Belfast: Northern Ireland Tourist Board / McCaw, Stevenson & Orr (printers), 1983.

Fuchs, Lawrence H. *John F. Kennedy and American Catholicism.* New York: Meredith Press, 1967.

Gibbon, Colin. *Land of Kennedy's Ancestors.* New York: Vantage Press, 1969.

Giglio, James N. *The Presidency of John F. Kennedy.* Lawrence, Kan.: University Press of Kansas, 1991.

Gleeson, John. *History of the Ely O'Carroll Territory or Ancient Ormond.* Kilkenny, Ireland: Roberts' Books, 1982.

Goodwin, Doris Kearns. *The Fitzgeralds and the Kennedys: An American Saga.* New York: Simon & Schuster, 1987.

Gray, Tony. *The Irish Answer.* Boston and Toronto: Little, Brown & Co., 1966.

Greeley, Andrew M. *The Irish Americans: The Rise to Money and Power.* New York: Harper & Row, 1981.

Hahn, Emily. *Fractured Emerald: Ireland.* New York: Weathervane Books, 1971.

Hamilton, Nigel. *JFK: Reckless Youth.* New York: Random House, 1992.

Hennessy, Maurice N. *I'll Come Back in the Springtime: John F. Kennedy and the Irish.* New York: Ives Washburn, 1966.

Hoagland, Kathleen, ed. *1000 Years of Irish Poetry: The Gaelic and Anglo-Irish Poets from Pagan Times to the Present.* New York: Grosset & Dunlap / The Universal Library, 1962.

Irish Tourist Directory, Comprising Hotels, Boarding Houses, Restaurants, Garages and Other Businesses in the Irish Free State. Dublin: Irish Tourist Association, (no publication date). Courtesy of Robert L. White.

Irish Visit: Complete Text of President Kennedy's Speeches with Illustrations. Dublin: Grafton Advertising, 1963.

JFK Memorial Book. Editors of *Look.* New York: Cowles Magazines & Broadcasting, 1964.

Kee, Robert. *The Green Flag: The Turbulent History of the Irish National Movement.* New York: Delacorte Press, 1972.

Kennedy, John F. *A Nation of Immigrants.* New York: Anti-Defamation League of B'nai B'rith, 1961.

———— *A Nation of Immigrants.* New York: Harper & Row, 1964.

———— *Prelude to Leadership: The European Diary of John F. Kennedy, Summer 1945.* Washington, D.C.: Regnery Publishing. 1995.

Kennedy, Rose Fitzgerald. *Times to Remember.* Garden City, N.Y.: Doubleday & Co., 1974.

Keogh, Dermot. *Twentieth-Century Ireland: Nation and State.* Dublin: Gill & Macmillan, 1994.

Lieberson, Goddard, ed. *John Fitzgerald Kennedy . . . As We Remember Him.* New York: Atheneum, 1965.

Lincoln, Evelyn. *My Twelve Years with John F. Kennedy.* New York: David McKay Co., 1965.

Longford, Lord (Frank Pakenham). *Kennedy.* London: Weidenfeld & Nicolson, 1976.

Lucey, Charles. *Ireland and the Irish: Cathleen Ni Houlihan Is Alive and Well.* Garden City, N.Y.: Doubleday & Co., 1970.

Lyons, F.S.L. *Ireland Since the Famine.* London: Fontana Press, 1985.

MacDonagh, Oliver. *Ireland.* Englewood Cliffs, N.J.: Prentice-Hall, 1968.

MacLysaght, Edward. *Irish Families: Their Names, Arms and Origins.* New York: Crown, 1972. (Originally published Dublin: Hodges Figgis & Co., 1957.)

Manchester, William. *One Brief Shining Moment.* Boston and Toronto: Little, Brown & Co., 1983.

Martin, Ralph G. *A Hero for Our Time: An Intimate Story of the Kennedy Years.* New York: Macmillan Co., 1983.

McHugh, Roger, ed. *Dublin 1916: An Illustrated Anthology.* London: Arlington Books, 1976.

McMahon, Sean. *A Short History of Ireland.* Dublin: Mercier Press, 1996.

A Memory of John Fitzgerald Kennedy. Visit to Ireland, 26th-29th June, 1963. Dublin: Wood Printing Works, 1964.

Mills, John FitzMaurice. *The Noble Dwellings of Ireland.* New York: Thames & Hudson, 1987.

Mitchell, Arthur. *JFK and His Irish Heritage.* Dublin: Moytura Press, 1993.

Murphy, John A. *Ireland in the Twentieth Century.* Dublin: Gill & Macmillan, 1975.

Nunnerly, David. *President Kennedy and Britain.* New York: St. Martin's Press, 1972.

O'Brien, Lawrence F. *No Final Victories: A Life in Politics from John F. Kennedy to Watergate.* Garden City, N.Y.: Doubleday & Co., 1974.

O'Brien, Maire, and O'Brien, Conor Cruise. *A Concise History of Ireland.* New York: Viking Press, 1972.

O'Brien, Mark. *De Valera, Fianna Fail and the Irish Press: The Truth in the News?* Dublin and Portland, Ore.: Irish Academic Press, 2001.

O'Clery, Conor. *Daring Diplomacy: Clinton's Secret Search for Peace in Ireland.* Boulder, Colo.: Roberts Rinehart, 1997.

O'Connor, Frank, ed. *A Book of Ireland.* London and Glasgow: Collins, 1959.

O'Donnell, Kenneth P., and Powers, David F., with Joe McCarthy. *"Johnny, We Hardly Knew Ye": Memories of John Fitzgerald Kennedy.* Boston and Toronto: Little, Brown & Co., 1972.

O'Faolain, Sean. *The Story of the Irish People.* New York: Avenel Books, 1982.

O'Hanlon, Thomas J. *The Irish: Sinners, Saints, Gamblers, Gentry, Priests, Maoists, Rebels, Tories, Orangemen, Dippers, Heroes, Villains and Other Proud Natives of the Fabled Isle.* New York: Harper & Row, 1975.

Oram, Hugh. *The Newspaper Book: A History of Newspapers in Ireland, 1649-1983.* Dublin: MO Books, 1983.

O'Toole, Fintan. *The Irish Times Book of the Century.* Dublin: Gill & Macmillan, 1999.

Pakenham, Thomas. *The Year of Liberty: The Great Irish Rebellion of 1798.* Englewood Cliffs, N.J.: Prentice-Hall, 1970.

Rorabaugh, W.J. *Kennedy and the Promise of the Sixties.* Cambridge and New York: Cambridge University Press, 2002.

Salinger, Pierre. *With Kennedy.* Garden City, N.Y.: Doubleday & Co., 1966.

Schlesinger, Arthur M., Jr. *A Thousand Days: John F. Kennedy in the White House.* Boston: Houghton Mifflin Co., 1965.

Shannon, William V. *The American Irish: A Political and Social Portrait.* New York and London: Macmillan Co., 1963.

Shell Guide to Ireland. Lord Killanin and Michael V. Duignan. New York: W.W. Norton & Co., 1962.

Smith, Amanda, ed. *Hostage to Fortune: The Letters of Joseph P. Kennedy.* New York: Viking, 2001.

Sorensen, Theodore C. *Kennedy.* New York: Harper & Row, 1965.

Strober, Gerald S. and Deborah H. *"Let Us Begin Anew": An Oral History of the Kennedy Presidency.* New York: HarperCollins Publishers, 1993.

Tobin, Fergal. *The Best of Decades: Ireland in the 1960s.* Dublin: Gill & Macmillan, 1984.

Whealan, Ronald E. *Historical Materials in the John Fitzgerald Kennedy Library.* Boston: John Fitzgerald Kennedy Library, 2000.

Wibberley, Leonard Patrick O'Connor. *The Trouble with the Irish (or the English, Depending on Your Point of View).* New York: Henry Holt & Co., 1956.

YdenneK, R.M.J. *The Irish People and the Presidency of John F. Kennedy.* Dunganstown, County Wexford, Ireland: The Kennedy Homestead, 2000.

Sources of Illustrations

Index

By the same Author

The Real Woodrow Wilson:
An Interview with Arthur S. Link,
Editor of the Wilson Papers.

About the Author

James Robert Carroll has been a reporter for three decades, covering Washington since 1983. A graduate of Boston University, he started his career as a correspondent for *The Boston Globe*, then worked for *The Daily Transcript* in Dedham and the now-defunct *Beverly Times*, both in Massachusetts. He covered California government and politics in Sacramento for The *Orange County Register* for more than five years before moving to Washington for the *Long Beach* (California) *Press-Telegram* and Knight-Ridder Newspapers. Since 1997 he has been Washington Bureau Chief for *The Louisville Courier-Journal.* Among other honors, Carroll has won the National Press Club's award for best regional reporter in Washington and the National Press Foundation's award for energy and environmental reporting. He is also the author of *The Real Woodrow Wilson: An Interview with Arthur S. Link, Editor of the Wilson Papers.*

Carroll has had a long interest in presidents, dating from his days as a teenaged volunteer in presidential campaigns in the 1960s. As a reporter in Washington, he has covered the administrations of the last four presidents. Ireland likewise has been an abiding passion. He has visited the nation a half dozen times and written news and travel stories from Ireland for American newspapers, as well as reported from Washington on Irish affairs. He and his wife, Carol Vernon, and their daughters Fiona and Brenna, live in Alexandria, Virginia.